PRAISE FOR
Chronicles of an Olympic Defector

I met Andy Törő in 1968. We were both on our way to the Olympic Games in Mexico City. He shared how it was impossible to achieve his dream of becoming a naval engineer and to continue competing in the sport of canoeing if he remained in Hungary. He shared how he defected to the USA. His words were fascinating, powerful, sad, and inspiring. They took me on a sacred journey to the center of my soul. As I listened, his words challenged me to never let go of my dreams, or more importantly, to never allow myself to be trapped in a poverty of dreams. He made me a better person. When he became a US citizen, he made America better! His book will take you on a fascinating journey and you will be better because of it. An inspiring read.

Billy Mills
1964 Olympic Track and Field Gold Medalist

Chronicles of an Olympic Defector is a fascinating read and a truly inspiring story of Andy Törő's journey through life with struggle, disappointment, and success. Andy and I have been friends and fellow athletes since October of 1964, when my family was able to help him defect from the Tokyo Olympic Games. Over the years, I have heard many of these entertaining and colorful stories about his life and I am thrilled that he has finally compiled them in this book. Our lives share a common thread of Olympic spirit and the desire to excel in sport. The reader is sure to experience a unique journey and an inspirational ride.

Marcia (Jones) Smoke
1964 Olympic Kayak Bronze Medalist

As a young farm boy, I first met Andy Törő on the Michigan canoe racing circuit, and later as my coach rising up through the junior and senior national team ranks. Andy's defection from the eastern block during the Cold War is a fascinating and gripping story. I'm thrilled that he is finally telling it for all to hear in his chronicle. An inspiring read!

Greg Barton
Two-time Olympic Kayak Gold Medalist

It is my honor to have known Andy for over four decades—as a coach and as a top Olympic administrator in the US and I can attest to the fact that he is widely admired and deeply respected throughout the Olympic and canoeing world. His book is a remarkable true-life story of his passion for canoeing that led him to his freedom. He brought with him to the United States a wealth of knowledge and experience. Andy had a remarkable impact helping to guide the Olympic movement in his top leadership position in the USOC. These are some of the highlights of a fascinating and colorful figure and the path he's taken is reflected in his chronicle. An enjoyable read.

Norman Bellingham
1988 Olympic Kayak Gold Medalist and Former Chief Operating Officer of the United States Olympic Committee

This book is dedicated to my family: my wife Jane, daughter Katalin, and son Tamás. I hope that they will benefit from looking into the kaleidoscope of my life and realize and appreciate their heritage.

I also dedicate this book to my many friends who have encouraged me to document my life story and share my Olympic experiences, as well as my lifelong love of canoeing, with them. The sport that ultimately gave me my freedom was, and still is, a major part of my life. I am grateful for their persistent encouragement and never-ending curiosity, which led me to write this chronicle.

www.mascotbooks.com

Chronicles of an Olympic Defector

©2020 András Törő OLY. All Rights Reserved. No part of this publication may be reproduced, stored in a retrieval system or transmitted in any form by any means electronic, mechanical, or photocopying, recording or otherwise without the permission of the author.

The views and opinions expressed in this book are solely those of the author. These views and opinions do not necessarily represent those of the publisher or staff.

For more information, please contact:
Mascot Books
620 Herndon Parkway, Suite 320
Herndon, VA 20170
info@mascotbooks.com

Library of Congress Control Number: 2018904818

CPSIA Code: PRV1219A
ISBN: 978-1-68401-549-8

Printed in the United States

A true story of struggle, courage, and freedom

CHRONICLES OF AN
OLYMPIC DEFECTOR

ANDRÁS TÖRŐ
1960 Olympic Medalist

PARTICIPATION MEDALS

*"Our Olympic journey will never end.
The struggles and triumphs will continue forever."*
— Author

1960 Summer Olympic Games, Rome

1964 Summer Olympic Games, Tokyo

1972 Summer Olympic Games, Munich

1976 Summer Olympic Games, Montreal

TABLE OF CONTENTS

PREFACE	1
CHAPTER 1: *The Early Years*	5
CHAPTER 2: *The School Years*	25
CHAPTER 3: *Introduction to the World of Sports*	37
CHAPTER 4: *My First Olympics: Rome*	59
CHAPTER 5: *Between Olympic Games*	87
CHAPTER 6: *Olympic Defector, Tokyo Olympic Games 1964*	111
CHAPTER 7: *First Steps in America, the New World*	131
CHAPTER 8: *My Years at the University of Michigan*	149
CHAPTER 9: *Making the US Olympic Team, 1972 and 1976*	185
CHAPTER 10: *My Years in the Olympic Movement*	211
CHAPTER 11: *Memories of my Olympic Tenure*	237
AFTERWORD	259
A NOTE FROM THE AUTHOR	265
APPENDIX: *Chronological Summary of Personal, Professional, and Sport Achievements of András "Andy" István Toro (Törő) OLY*	269
ACKNOWLEDGMENTS	279
ABOUT THE AUTHOR	281

PREFACE

Every living thing on this planet has something in common to share about their journey on this place that we call Earth. The story of their journey is filled with many unique and interesting anecdotes to tell. I am no different, and this is my story that I want to share with you.

The European edition of the *New York Herald Tribune* reported on October 24, 1964:

> *Japanese police had identified a Hungarian athlete, from the first Communist nation to defect during the current Olympic Games, as András Törő. He had placed (fourth) in the Canadian canoeing men's single event.*

The following news item originated from Anchorage, Alaska, by AP and hit the news service all over in the world. The *Japan Times* reported on Monday, October 26, 1964:

> *Hungarian Defector Gets Temporary Asylum—A young Hungarian Olympic Games sportsman who defected in Tokyo was given at least temporary asylum in the United States here Saturday in a sudden change of plans.*

A Colorado paper got the news via the *Tokyo* (AP) and reported:

> *The Olympian, András Törő, 24, a good-looking youth who finished fourth in the Canadian canoe singles, was the first Iron Curtain sportsman to defect during the Tokyo Olympic Games which wind up Sunday...flew to the United States to ask asylum, Japanese police reported.*

CHRONICLES OF AN OLYMPIC DEFECTOR

On the October 24, 1964, the *Seattle Times* newspaper reporter Marshall Wilson wrote:

> *András Törő, 24, the Hungarian athlete who finished fourth in the Olympics canoe singles, brings a refreshing honesty to the United States, a country he chose after defecting in Tokyo Thursday... Törő, speaks a smattering of English. But found a warm welcome here.*

After all these years, it is hard to assess how many people read those articles or how many countries carried the news about a communist-country athlete who defected from his Olympic team to choose freedom and a better world to live in. At least, that was my hope in leaving the Hungarian Olympic Team during the 1964 Tokyo Olympic Games in which I finished in a disappointing fourth place. It was certainly a news item since it happened during the Olympic Games, which were well covered by the worldwide media. Any controversial news during the Olympic Games would make the headlines for sure. I was not looking for publicity—only a place of freedom in which to live.

Interestingly, my recent research of the Hungarian newspapers from that time did not reveal any mention of my defection. Many years later, in speaking with my brothers and old teammates, they told me that the news traveled by mouth. The newspapers (controlled by the government at that time) tried to suppress this defiant and unpatriotic event.

Defecting during the Olympic Games or any major international sporting event was not uncommon during the years of the Cold War. Even today, in countries where the form of governance is not democracy, citizens will disagree with the political system and choose to seek something new and different, however dangerous. Personal freedom and the hope for a better future are strong incentives for making such decisions. Defection is a hard personal decision often motivated by deep resentment of the political system or a major personal disappointment. In any case, the belief of a brighter future was my greatest motivation. Leaving everything behind and hoping for a new, better future in the unknown seems primal to me. The great migration of the human species is proof of that. It is in human nature to try to change the outcome.

PREFACE

After WWII, my native country, Hungary, was under Soviet occupation and was oppressed, particularly after the uprising of 1956. Traveling abroad was only for the privileged class, which included Communist party functionaries, scientists, and international sportsmen. Needless to say, these individuals were envied by the general public for obvious reasons. They always had something new to show off from the West—a pair of shoes, a fashionable sweater, or a wristwatch. On the crowded streetcars or in the movie theater, the public noticed such things. It stood out as unusual and as a sample of the free world that few could conceive of or hope to see.

One might think that my sport, canoeing, is an odd sport for Hungarians to practice. For reasons unknown, Hungarian youth were (and still are) attracted to this sport. Perhaps the Boy Scout movement before WWII left a legacy of this outdoor activity. In my case, it was reading translated excerpts from the Fenimore Cooper novel, *The Last of the Mohicans*. I was very much impressed by the way the North American natives lived off the land in harmony with nature, respecting their heritage and culture. I was particularly fascinated by how they used canoes for transportation, scouting, and hunting. Almost every facet of their lifestyle required knowledge of these boats, including how to build and propel them.

I began to read more about the North American indigenous people and their way of life, philosophies, and spiritual thinking before the continent was discovered by white men. I empathized with the way they respected and worshipped every living thing and how their nomadic life was subsumed by nature. They are the only indigenous people who did not leave any permanent structure on the surface of the planet except their burial sites. Individual ownership of land never occurred to them. It is a concept that I still struggle with, even though I own a minute part of California. I cannot reconcile the idea of the first man who decided that the piece of the land he stood on was his. Where did the right to do that come from? I believe in what Chief Crazy Horse (Oglala, Lakota, 1868) once said: "One does not sell the earth upon which the people walk." This is a very powerful philosophical statement.

I could not find any historical evidence that these indigenous people of North America were using their canoes for racing. In my imagination, some

Native American youths would have certainly challenged each other for competition. I always believe that there's a natural urge to challenge, compete, and try to be the fastest and strongest. The North American native way of living made a canoeist out of me for life, and I attribute my education and profession as a naval architect to my early fascination with the lives of the North American indigenous people.

My destiny was shaped by following my brother Lajos' footsteps, when he joined the Honvéd Sport Egyesület (Army Sports Club) in 1952. He was recruited by Elbert Andor (Tonya), a high school friend. Little did he know then that he would play a major role in Lajos' little brother's destiny. This happened in the spring of 1953. Seven of us (I was the youngest) from our little town of Pestszentlőrinc were canoeing in the same club. You could have called us the "Magnificent Seven" because, over the years, we won more junior and senior national championships than any other group I'm aware of. Only my brother Lajos still lives in Hungary. The other members of the "Magnificent Seven" are scattered all over the world. Most of them left during the 1956 Revolution. Others, like me, defected at an opportune time, and a few of us are still alive to tell the story.

CHAPTER 1
The Early Years

My family lived on the outskirts of Budapest, the capital city of Hungary (Magyarország), in the XVIIIth district, Pestszentlőrinc. Budapest is actually two different cities, Buda and Pest. Buda, on the west side of the Danube (Duna) River, is the old city, established before 1,000 AD. It is the hilly side with a magnificent castle and old fort that offer panoramic views. Pest, on the east side of the Danube, is newer and on flat land, spreading more to the east and south. Pest is industrialized and the outskirts are spread with family housing in the so-called "garden district." Budapest is a beautiful city. Pictures of the Parliament building along the Danube, of Margaret Island dividing the river just upstream, and of the old castle on the Buda side appear in many travel catalogs and travel advertisements. It has become a destination city with newly renovated buildings downtown and a vibrant social life.

My town, Pestszentlőrinc, was part of this garden district, close to the airport and a major highway (not in the western sense, only two lanes then) from the east. In those days, there was not much air traffic either. On the road, there were only commercial vehicles, trucks, and buses; private cars were nearly non-existent. Just outside of our small town near Vecsés, the Russian tanks stopped on this highway during the 1956 Revolution to negotiate peace with the Hungarian revolutionary leaders before they retook the city. They agreed to meet the Russian Commander at a WWII monument on the highway, only several kilometers from my family's home. After this historical meeting, the Hungarian Revolutionary negotiators were captured and later executed. Just a small, sad piece of history of the town where I grew up.

Pestszentlőrinc is about one hour and twenty minutes from the center of Budapest by streetcar, which was the only form of public transportation in the early fifties. Our house was a 10-minute walk from the last stop of the streetcar line. For many years, Streetcar No. 50 was my mode of transportation from one end of the line to the other. I rode it to school, to canoe practice, and to see friends. Any time of the year, it was a long trip to take. The streetcars were always crowded, with people hanging out the sides. In the summertime, it was pleasant to stay on the back platform, cooling off in the breeze. But in the bitter winters of sub-zero temperatures, when I did not have gloves, the brass handles were awfully cold. A ride did not cost much, as I remember, and students had monthly passes with their picture which was good for any public transportation.

My extended family—my godfather (Pista), Uncle (Kis András), godmother (Juliska) holding me, my mother and father and my uncle (Kis Sándor). In the front, my brother Imre and brother János (holding a goat).

THE EARLY YEARS

We were a family of six, including my parents and three older brothers, and struggled to make ends meet. My older brother, János (*Jancsi* was his nickname), was almost ten years older than me. My next brother, Imre (*Imrus*), was eight years older, and Lajos (*Lajcsi*) was two years older. We lived in a two-room house with no inside plumbing or electricity. This house was purchased by my family just after the war and was originally a single room with a small porch. My father added the second room, which served as a kitchen and pantry. In later years, the two structures began to shift apart due to foundation weakness, and a wide crack appeared. Needless to say, heating the room in winter was a challenge, and we could see snowflakes in our bedroom during the stormy winter days. We had a potbelly stove in our bedroom with a

Standing by the old well in our garden
(used until we were connected to city water).

long pipe to the chimney that helped keep us warm, and I often helped mother to chop kindling and light the fire. I wanted to help her as much as I could, knowing how hard she worked to provide for our family. Many times, the stove and pipe became red hot, which was both frightening and dangerous, but the heat felt good—at least until the bitter cold outside ultimately sucked it from our home.

The reason my parents liked the place was because it had a big parcel of land with over twenty fruit trees, including sweet cherry, sour cherry (my favorite), apricot, plum, apple, and peach, and at the perimeter of the lot were many grape vines, which provided the family not only fresh fruit in the summer but jam and preserves in the winter. The large garden my mother tended grew a wide variety of vegetables and flowers. My father did not appreciate growing flowers until my mother started selling them at the market. Understandably, he appreciated anything that could be turned into money!

In the early spring, when the weather got warmer, we began the family ritual of tilling the garden soil. My father lined up the boys, gave us each a spade, and marched us across the whole property, turning the soil. It was hard work keeping up with my father's long gait. Once in a while, he checked on us to make sure that we were digging deeply enough. I actually liked doing this work, gaining great satisfaction by helping my family and smelling the freshness of the earth. I felt like the earth was coming alive again after a long winter's frozen slumber.

My mother would follow our labors by raking the ground smooth, parsing out beds for different vegetables. Planting the seeds was always a major event. My parents would argue about what went where, but mother always prevailed. By the end of the day, the whole garden was transformed. We all admired our creation that would provide food for the family for the rest of the year.

We had a well, which provided us with drinking and washing water, as well as water for the garden. It was always a chore to get water, since we had no pump, and the only way to get the water was by rope, crank, and bucket. I remember the first time I was allowed to turn the big cast iron wheel, and I could hardly reach the handle at the top. The well was about fifteen meters deep with round concrete cylindrical rings, each about a meter tall, stacked

THE EARLY YEARS

My father with the harvesting crew standing next to the threshing machine. He is the engineer, first on the right.

atop each other. These rings created a long vertical shaft down to the water table. One summer we had a drought, and the garden needed a lot of water, but the well was running low. My father decided to add a couple more rings to make the well deeper so as to reach more water. He purchased the additional concrete rings and my brothers lowered him down, sitting on the bucket. He started digging, and we cranked the dirt up to the surface where we spread it on top of the garden. The existing rings slowly began to sink as the well got deeper. We added the new rings to the top. At one point, my father started yelling as the water began to rush in and swallow him up. He did not know how to swim or tread water. We quickly lowered the bucket down to him and pulled him up in the nick of time.

My father, Törő János, was born in 1905, in the eastern part of Hungary called the *Hajdúság* in a small town of Hajdúböszörmény. This region of the country was settled by one of the original seven tribes of the Huns (Magyars) who traveled into and settled the Danube Valley. The oldest origins of the Huns can still be traced to this region. This region was not occupied by the

Turks during the 400 years of occupation, so there was very little genetic mixing.

My father had only four or five years of elementary education. When he was old enough, he had to work on his father's farm. They were basically peasants, and he apprenticed to learn how to operate big agricultural steam machinery. He had a good sense of how all the mechanical parts fit together and worked, and this apprenticeship gave him a lifetime occupation.

My mother, Kis Julianna, was born in 1908 in the same town as my father. She had only four years of elementary educa-

My mother at age 20, 1928.

tion, just enough to read and write. She had to work when she was ten years old, taking care of her younger step-siblings. Her mother had died when she was only three years old. My grandfather, Kis András, remarried and her stepmother did not like her at all. At an early age, Julianna learned to sew, and that helped her throughout her life as a way to support her own family. She was barely five foot two, but she had the strongest determination and will you can ever imagine. She lived to be almost 90 years old.

Speaking of her sewing, there is an interesting story I learned after she passed away when I was looking through her papers. In about 1944, during the war, she applied for a home working permit for doing sewing and alterations at home. On the questionnaire was an item she had to fill in about her religious affiliation. We were Protestant and her birth certificate documents this. However, if she had been Jewish, she would have never gotten a permit. At that time, Hungary was beginning to persecute the Jews, sending them to the working and concentration camps.

My parents were married in 1930 in their hometown. There is only one picture of the wedding and reception, and a small certificate issued by the township. They moved in with my father's parents until they got their own place. By that time, my father had his license to operate steam machinery. He was hired by the local harvesting team to run the steam threshing machine. It was a good job for him, as he was always technically oriented and enjoyed working with his hands.

My father was a chain smoker, sometimes rolling his own cigarettes in newspaper. His fingers were yellow where he held the cigarette. His small, Hitler-like mustache was also yellow from the smoke. His breath always reminded me of bad tobacco, and his teeth were yellow and crusty (he never brushed them). Cleaning teeth and going to the dentist were unheard of in our family. I have never smoked, although I tried once when I was young. I thought that it was a grown-up thing to do, and I wanted to grow up quick. Once, when we were out in the country tending the goats, we rolled up some dry leaves in a piece of newspaper and smoked it. After several puffs, I got sick and threw up. That was the last time I smoked.

My father was a nervous man with a very short temper, and we were terrified of him. All Mother had to do was threaten to tell him if we did something wrong or misbehaved. Thinking back on it, I really did not know my father. We had very little interaction and certainly no real father/son bonding. He never played with me that I can remember, though I craved his affection. I told myself that I was the youngest and he had just run out of energy. I think he loved all of us in his own way, but he never showed any affection or kindness. I would have given anything just to have a pat on my head or an encouraging word from him, but it never came. He projected a tough presence, and there was definitely no talking back or disputing his decisions. Only rarely did I see him just sitting down to read an old discarded newspaper that he picked up on the streetcar. He always found something to do around the house, some project to make something useful for the family. There were only a few books in the house to read, since buying books cost money. Occasionally, when he made some good deals at the market, he took us to the local movie theater. That was a very special treat, but getting there was a painful experience. He walked fast with a long gait, and it was hard to keep up; my mother was short, and her gait was much shorter that my father's, so I used to stick with her. She always trailed behind the family when walking to the theater. But I did not mind walking with her and holding her hand.

For a couple of years right after the war, you could still see western movies. The communist system was slow to catch up with cultural oppression, and the movie theaters still had some Western reels in their storage. I saw Walt Disney's *Pinocchio* many times, and it's still my favorite animated film. I really envied that little wooden boy whose father loved him so much, and I wanted to be Pinocchio. Then, during the Soviet occupation, the movie theater programming changed dramatically. Soviet realism films appeared with subtitles, glorifying the communist system and workers' (the proletariat) achievements. That was the only entertainment in town, so we went to see them anyway. A film is a film, even when it is bad and pure propaganda. For real entertainment, we collected June bugs in the springtime and snuck them into the theater in a paper bag, releasing them during the show. The bugs flew into the projection lights and appeared on the screen. It was comical and more entertaining than the Soviet movies!

The cigarette smoking that caused my father's lung disease kept him out of military service. During the war, he was eligible age-wise, but they did not take him because his lungs often collapsed. He carried a medical exemption paper. He still worked during the war, and the jobs were plentiful because very few men were left at home. The Germans took every able-bodied Hungarian to the Russian front. Over a half million Hungarians served with the Germans at Stalingrad. Many did not return. They became Russian prisoners of war and were sent to the notorious Siberian camps or killed in the conflict.

I was born during the war on July 10, 1940, in Budapest, Xth district, Kőbánya. The direct translation of this town is "Rock Quarry" and accurately so because of the rock mining operation in that region. My mother, after three boys, wanted a little girl, but here I was—another boy, a disappointment. My mother cried at first, but she grew to love me just the same, as all mothers do. According to family lore, my father's comment was, "That's okay; he won't need any ribbons in his hair."

My family had moved to Budapest the year before I was born, the first house my father bought. It was not the one I grew up in, but it was nearby. When the Germans were retreating, the situation got very rough in Budapest—many

My birth certificate, July 10, 1940.

people were afraid that the Germans would hold the city to stop the Russian advancement, and so they fled. We followed suit and moved back to my grandparents' place. I was only four years old, but I remember spending many days in my grandfather's root cellar, which doubled as a bomb shelter. It would not have protected us much in the case of a direct hit or even a near hit. It was, essentially, a hole in the ground with a mound of dirt on it. It was nice and cozy though, with a kerosene lantern providing some heat and illumination. The family felt safe in this makeshift shelter, and that was all that mattered.

There is a story about my first steps according to my oldest brother, János. We were still at my grandparents' place in the summer of 1941, a relatively calm period of the war in Hungary. I was about one when a small traveling circus came to town. They set up their tents and performed their acts. It was a very small group, with only a couple of wild animals (mainly bears) and trained horses, jugglers, and clowns. János took me and sat in the first row on the ground with me between his legs. The show was going on, and the clowns came in to entertain. One of them had a long sausage wrapped around his neck and was happily chewing on it while juggling. I pointed to the clown, stood up and took a couple of steps on my own toward to him. I had never walked before, so it really surprised my brother. He picked me up and rushed home, wanting to show my mother my first steps. He loudly declared, "*Bandi* (my nickname) is walking." He set me standing on the ground and encouraged me to go, but I didn't take another step until a few months later. However, sausage became my favorite food. Even now, if I see a piece of sausage or even a picture of one, I salivate and start walking!

Me at the age of 2½ in our backyard.

Another story often told about me by my mother happened at a family gathering when I was about the same age. We had a mulberry tree in our garden, and in the early summer, the sweet, ripe, juicy mulberries would drop to the ground. There are two kinds of mulberries; one is yellowish-green and the other deep purple. Our tree was the yellowish-green type, which is sweeter than the dark kind. These yellowish-green mulberries covered the ground and, before I could walk, I loved to crawl under the tree, pick up the mulberries, and stuff them into my mouth. The chickens liked mulberries as well, and we didn't have to compete because there were many ripe ones to choose from. However, the chickens, as they do, left their droppings on the ground among the mulberries. I could not distinguish between the ripe yellowish-green mulberries and the chicken droppings. The expression on my face reflected the difference, to my family's great amusement. I was introduced to microbes at an early age; perhaps they will contribute to my longevity!

In Hungary in those days, there was a tradition that the Christian name be given to a child by his or her godparents. My name András was given to me by my godfather, Uncle András (or *Bandi Bácsi*) on my mother's side. Every common name has a "name day" on the calendar and is celebrated on that day by the family. András Day, a larger celebration than my birthday, is on November 30th every year. That day, we got together at my uncle's house to celebrate my, his, and one of his son's name day. My father was in charge of the wine, which he got on the black market, filling a 5-liter glass bottle covered with woven twigs. As long as I can remember, we always had a big party with lots of food, baked goods, and red wine. After dinner, the adults played cards on the big table and quietly talked about politics while the youngsters played under the table. The party lasted until the last scheduled streetcar departure for home. Even now, I often ask my American family to observe November 30 as my name day but, unfortunately, it hasn't caught on.

During WWII, in the spring of 1944, the Russian Army was moving east and was just outside of my grandparents' town. Conflicting rumors spread—they were coming to liberate us or they were barbarians and would rape all the women and pillage. We were afraid of what might happen to our mother. Fortunately, nothing tragic happened.

However, one interesting story of the liberation is worth mentioning. One day, a Russian soldier came to our house with several horse blankets on his shoulder. He saw my mother's sewing machine and, after a lengthy attempt at cross-cultural communication filled with frantic gestures, got my mother to understand he wanted her to make pants out of those horse blankets. There was also some urgency, as he was shipping out to Berlin the next day. She had little choice but to oblige. The soldier was about the same size as my father, so my mother did not need to take any measurements. Unfortunately, her sewing machine, an old Singer treadle type, was barely strong enough for the heavy horse blankets. I had to get under the table to help push the treadle up and down to make the needle punch through the fabric. My mother worked all night and we made the deadline, and we wondered what kind of payment, if any, we would get. The soldier showed up later that day with an enormous block of rock salt on his shoulder. It could not have been a better payment for my mother's work.

During the war, inflation was so high that money effectively had no value.

My grandfather, Kis András, in his WWI uniform.

The government kept printing money as fast as they could, but it lost value as soon as it got on the street. On the other hand, bartering was good as ever, and salt was more valuable than gold. My mother broke up the rock salt and traded it for eggs, bacon, roasted chicory (used as coffee), and other staple items. I learned to appreciate salt as one of life's most precious commodities.

At the end of the war, when the Russians pushed the Germans back toward Berlin, my family moved back to Budapest. Budapest had been badly hit but not destroyed like some of the German towns. I saw many burned-out buildings, but it was safe, and the city slowly returned to life. The railroad and streetcar lines were repaired first, and transportation was restored. My family purchased the house that I call home. It was "my Hungarian home, my homeland, the Fatherland, my Motherland," where I lived and grew up from 1946 until I defected.

The first year in the new home was very hard on the family, as we did not have the grandparents' farm support. On my grandfather's farm out in the country, we always had something to eat or barter. Chickens always scratched around the garden, and the local mill always made some flour, even if it was corn. But in the city, we lost that support. There's one incident in particular that stays with me. One day, I was hungry and asked my mother for some food. She cut up the last piece of stale bread and gave me a piece. There was nothing on it, just a piece of stale bread, so I asked my mother to put a little lard on it. Lard or bacon grease on a piece of bread with red paprika sprinkled on it was the most delicious treat for any Hungarian, particularly during the war (I am salivating just writing about it). Just like peanut butter and jelly in America or vegemite in Australia, the *zsiros kenyér* was a main staple for Hungarian households. For a more affluent family, goose fat was used instead of pig fat. Even now when I go back to visit, I have a slice. Well, my mother looked at me and began to cry, heartbroken that she had no lard to give. She felt she was failing to provide for her family. Now, as a parent myself, I know how she felt—every parent's responsibility is to provide for their children, and failing is not acceptable.

With only two rooms for the six of us, the word privacy did not enter my mind or my vocabulary until I came to the United States. The four boys slept on one pull-out sofa converted into a bed where I, the smallest and the youngest, was always in the middle. It was good because I had the warmth of my brothers' body heat, particularly in the winter, but they always rolled on top of me. As we got older and bigger, the bed seemed to get smaller. When my older brother was drafted into the Army, one silver lining was that we had more room on the sofa bed. Every morning, the last person to get out of the bed had to fold it up and restore it to a couch so it did not take up too much space. I usually ended up with this chore when I was old enough.

My mother and father each had a separate bed. It's a European custom for the parents to sleep separately, and they often have separate bedrooms. I was surprised to see that in the US, parents sleep in the same bed. On especially cold nights when I was little, my mother asked me to sleep in her bed with her, head to toe, to keep her feet warm.

Right after the war, all food was rationed. My family had a small coupon book for different goods like potatoes, flour, sugar, eggs, and milk. Everything was rationed on a per-person basis; however, staples were often not available. Sometimes, for instance, it took weeks to get our flour ration. There were scouts from the neighborhood who went to see what came into the market and rushed back to the community with their report. Many times there were false rumors, so we would line up at four in the morning for potatoes that never arrived. On bitter cold winter mornings, it was particularly hard, since I always had hand-me-down shoes and clothes from my brothers. My mother stuffed newspaper or a piece of cardboard into my shoes to cover up holes in the soles. It did not help much in the rain and slush, but that was all I had. When the clothes got handed down to me after going through my three brothers, they did not look too good. It never entered my mind to complain however, and in fact, I actually liked wearing my brothers' clothing. It made me feel big and grown-up. Of course, my mother would sew clothes for me as well, which she did when I started school.

Getting enough coal in the wintertime to heat the house and cook was always a challenge. We had the kitchen stove and a potbelly stove in the bedroom, which required kindling and coal. Coal was also rationed, and the local coal yard had a tall fence and a couple of ferocious guard dogs, making it very hard to steal coal. When the horse-driven delivery cart came by, we followed it for a long time because a few lumps would fall off the cart onto the bumpy roads. Also, out in the country about five kilometers from our house, there was a dump where the power-generating plant threw out its burned coal. We sorted through the heap, some coals still hot, to find useable chunks. It was hard work because the competition was fierce. Everyone who knew about this place came to scrounge. Thankfully, a kind train engineer would sometimes throw a shovel-full or two of unburned coal overboard for us, which we raced to collect as the train rumbled on. Scavenging was a significant part of my childhood. I grew up with it, so being resourceful in this manner became an instinct. I am not ashamed to admit that I still not only practice it, but enjoy it. It is rewarding to provide something for the family or the pets or the fireplace at no cost. But in post-war Hungary, this minimalist existence was a necessity. I often helped mother to chop kindling and light the fire. I wanted to help her as much as I could, since I knew how hard she worked to provide for our family.

My childhood before school was filled with many of these adventures. I was always one step behind my brothers, trying to help the family. We knew all the places in the neighborhood where we could find "free" things. In Hungary, the streets are lined with fruit and nut trees—cherry, apricot, almond, and walnut. I always considered these trees community property, but still ended up having many close calls with the "owners." As a result, fruits from the street trees always tasted sweeter!

As long as I can remember, my family had at least one goat, one pig, and, of course, a couple of chickens. My mother always called the goat *Mici*. We had many Micis over the years that provided milk for our family. Mother milked her every morning, although I would take on that chore sometimes. We drank the goat milk, which was very nourishing, and my mother also made cheese from it, saving the whey for baking. These very intelligent goats were my playmates as well. You can butt heads with them and twist their horns, rub their heads between the horns, and run with them. In the butting game, you have to be careful because they take it seriously and always play to win. Mici was always tied to an apple tree in our garden, which had tasty, wonderful fruit that ripened in the early part of the

With my mother and the ever-present goats at our backyard, 1944.

summer. It was always a challenge to beat the goat to the fallen apple. Many times, I ran out when I heard the thud of the fallen apple to find our Mici already munching on it and seeming to smile at me. I loved our goats!

Our house was only one block from the edge of town, so we were near the agricultural fields where corn and sunflowers grew. Acacia forests were nearby as well, and goats loved fresh cuttings from these trees. You could never give them enough; they would eat every bit of the tree—thorns and all. In the summertime or after school, my chore was to walk with the goat to the fields or go alone to collect some greens that she liked. I knew which ones she preferred, so I always carried a sickle for cutting, a sack to carry the greens, and a sling shot. The slingshot was my favorite toy, and I learned from my brothers how to make it. Selecting the handle was the most important task. I was always looking for a "Y" tree branch with equal, symmetrical sides. Cutting the branch and drying it was also a science; you have to do it just right so it maintains its shape and strength. For rubber, we used old bicycle inner tubes and cut them up into centimeter-wide strips. Assembling the sling shot also takes knowledge and practice, and my brother and I became experts. With many hours of practice, I became a pretty good shot, too. I have not practiced the skill in years, but I made sure that I made one for each of my children when they were young.

As I mentioned earlier, we also had a pig that required family attention. My father got one piglet in March or April, and we kept it until December. Talk about intelligent animals! They are very cute as well, and I've always liked the way they talk. They express different feelings with different grunts. My mother used to talk to them all the time. By fall, they got really big, which was the point. We slaughtered them the day after Christmas, on my father's name day. It was an exciting time. The whole extended family got together, and everyone had chores to do. The relatives came the night before and slept in our bed. We, the children, slept on the floor or on the kitchen bench. The whole house was turned upside down. No one got much sleep that night, but we still had to get up before dawn.

Slaughtering a pig in your back yard is a gruesome business, as you can imagine, and my mother cried every time. She had to entice the pig with a bucket of corn to come out of his sty. My father used to say, "I have four sons because the pig has four legs." We each grabbed a leg and my father did the final act. He had a military bayonet which, the day before, he and I would spend a couple of hours sharpening. I turned the grinding wheel, one of my father's homemade tools, which he repurposed from a large water stone wheel. I didn't like this job because it took a long time in the cold. The speed of the wheel was as important as the lubrication. My father was very impatient so when I turned the wheel too slowly or too quickly, or forgot to lubricate the wheel, he was quick to smack me. I was just a kid and I could not concentrate that long, especially under father's intense pressure.

The pig provided meat for my family and other relatives for a year. We processed every part of that animal—no piece was wasted. My father had a homemade flame thrower, which he used to burn the hair off the pig after it was slaughtered. Then the dismembering and processing would take place. My aunts, Juliska Néni and Zsuzsa Néni, had the chore of preparing the casings for the sausage—a very tedious and unpleasant job, but one they did better than anyone. That involved turning the pig's intestines inside out and scraping off the lining until only the transparent casing remained. Father cut the ham and the slabs of bacon to smoke and boil, and we had a small smokehouse in the back of our garden. Home-made smoked sausage with a lot of red paprika and other spices is, to me, the tastiest thing in the world. Mother even collected the pig's blood for blood sausage, a unique delicacy for Hungarians.

At the end of the day, we had a big meal—fresh meat from our beloved pig. My mother was sad over losing her dear pet and would not have an appetite that evening, but she prepared a delicious, tasty meal anyway. The family continued this practice until I was 14 or 15. Many years later, Lajos and I contemplated reenacting the pig slaughter in memory of our father. Unfortunately (or fortunately), it has not happened yet, but we occasionally think about it, mainly as a family joke. I'm afraid those skills will be lost forever, and I don't have four children to hold onto the pig's legs; plus, recreating my father's flame thrower would be a challenge.

In the summer of 1946, the local church officials told my parents that my brother Lajos and I were eligible to be part of a church-sponsored family relief program. My family came from a long line of Protestants. In the part of Hungary where my grandparents lived, the Protestant religion was quite widespread. Sometimes, my mother attended local church services and we joined her. She always donated some money to the church despite being very poor. After the war, religion was discouraged by the communist system, and as a result, the church suffered greatly. By the end of the '50s, all religious services were canceled by the state and most of the churches closed due to financial troubles.

There was, however, a relief program run by an international religious organization to help families with four or more children. The selected children were taken to Sweden or Denmark for the three summer months. My mother cried. She did not want us to go, but my father convinced her it would be good help for the family financially. There would be fewer mouths to feed, he said, and we could save money, which was needed to pay off the new house. So, at the end of the school year, in June of 1946, Lajos and I left Budapest on a train for Denmark. We traveled across Europe in a northerly direction to the port town of Travemünde, Germany, then a train ferry to Gedser, Denmark, and finally to Copenhagen. Spending two days on the train, traveling through the middle of war-torn Europe, was a memorable and thrilling experience for a wide-eyed, six-year-old Hungarian kid who'd never left his mother's apron.

Everywhere we looked from the train's windows, we saw the war's handprint—burned-out towns seemingly still smoldering, scorched forests, bomb craters, and abandoned military equipment. However, the bleak landscape did not dampen our excitement for this adventure. My brother's presence gave me security and confidence. In Travemünde, we stayed overnight waiting for the ferry boat to arrive. We slept in some military barracks where I had an embarrassing accident. During the night, I had to go to the bathroom that was down the hallway, but I was afraid of the dark. At home, since we did not have indoor plumbing, we had to go to the outhouse in the far corner of our lot, and my mother always accompanied me. I liked to go with her because she did not tease me or leave me alone in the dark like my brothers did. She understood and was very compassionate about my phobia, which stayed with me for a long time. So, during that night in Travemünde, I soiled my pants and I could not sleep the rest of the night. In the morning, everyone around me commented on the terrible smell. I tried to ignore them, afraid of being discovered as the source and sent back home for being immature. As soon as we got back on the train, I cleaned up by going into the train's lavatory and throwing away my underpants. My brother did not say anything, but he knew.

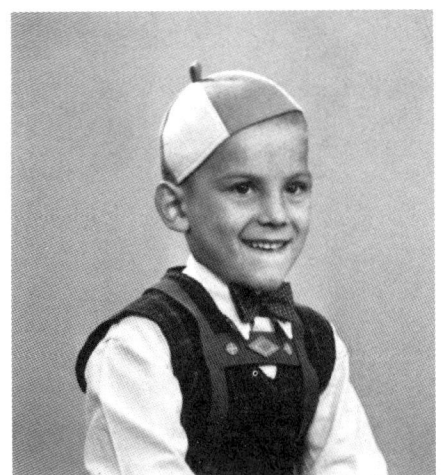 

My pictures in Denmark, nicely dressed up in the summer of 1946.

Denmark was like a dream. For the first time in my life, I was on foreign soil, hearing a different language, seeing different styles of clothing. Denmark did not suffer any war damage, since they'd surrendered to the German Army and submitted to occupation. In the summer of 1946, everything was green and flowers were abundant. However, my brother and I were separated at the distribution center. He was given to a rich landowner who had six children of his own, and I went to an elderly farm couple whose adult children had married and moved away. Although my brother and I were geographically close, we did not see each other often. Homesickness hit me after a couple of days and I cried, missing my family and, in particular, my mother. My new Danish family did everything they could to make me feel at home. They had a small farm, so it was nice to have fresh milk and dairy products every day. To my great surprise, they set a can of milk next to the road with a ladle and a small tin can for the money. It was an honor system for the locals to buy milk from them. This would have never worked in Hungary, except maybe in some very small rural community.

My Danish summer went by very quickly. Once a week, I rode a bicycle to town sitting behind my new Danish mother. Bicycles were everywhere—people rode them to the railroad station and took the train to the city. No one bothered to lock the bicycles, and I was very impressed by the honesty and kindness of the Danish people. Just before I left, my host family took me to Tivoli, which made an everlasting impression! Many years later, when I returned to Tivoli as an adult, I still had a wonderful time. It will always be a magical place in my mind after seeing it through the eyes of a young child.

When the summer ended and we arrived home, my brother and I were speaking Danish to each other. My mother cried because she did not understand what we were saying. Later on, I learned that my Danish family had wanted to adopt me but my mother had firmly declined their offer. We kept in touch with them by letter over the years. One of our neighbors was fluent in German, and she helped us read and write the letters.

CHAPTER 2
The School Years

In the fall of 1946, when I arrived back in Hungary from Denmark, first grade had already started. I was behind from day one. The main task in first grade was learning the alphabet to write and to read. The Hungarian language is very different from any other language in the world. According to linguists, it is distantly related to Finnish. Historians say that there were seven Hun tribes that traveled together from Asia Minor and settled down in the Danube Valley. One of the tribes split and a faction moved to northern Europe in what later became Finland. Many archeological findings support this historical fact. However, over time the two languages evolved so differently that now there's very little resemblance.

The Hungarian alphabet has 42 characters, and each letter has one sound that's always associated with it. Some sounds are made by two letters but they still have only one consistent sound. If you learn how to pronounce the letter sounds, you should be able to read any Hungarian text. You may not know what you are reading, but you sound Hungarian. The grammar, however, is very much like Latin. So, in the first grade, a child learns the alphabet—42 letters, 42 sounds (and, of course, the multiplication table, which was on the back page of every workbook—mathematics was an important subject in the Hungarian education system from an early age). By knowing the alphabet and the sounds for each letter or letter combination, you would be ready for a lifetime of reading and learning in Hungarian.

During my first two years, I went to a one-room school, within walking distance from my house, where the first two grades were taught together. Our teacher was a beautiful but tough young lady, and we all had crushes on her. Still, when we were not listening or paying attention (which was often the case each day), she made us hold out our hand, palm up, with our finger tips together. Then she hit our fingers with a short, flat ruler. If you pulled away, she doubled the punishment, so we learned to behave quickly. If you were very naughty, she made you kneel in the corner on corn kernels until you were ready to behave. There were always a couple of kids in the corner, and I put in my time there as well.

My second grade class picture, I am in the second row, second from right.

One day, my father brought home an old world atlas, which he got at the flea market (*Ócska Piac*), his favorite place. Budapest has a huge flea market where you can buy almost anything, old or new, for a reduced price. This atlas became my favorite of all books, and geography became my favorite subject. I spent hours looking at the different places in the world and, in particular, was impressed with the large body of water called the Pacific Ocean with its small islands. I dreamed and wondered about the Hawaiian Islands on the Northern Hemisphere and the Tahitian Islands on the Southern Hemisphere. Would I ever see those beautiful places? The image of warm endless beaches with crashing waves, the smell of tropical flora, and exotic food fueled my imagination. My dream was that someday I would visit these islands and many other places in this book. Many years later when I did visit the Hawaiian Islands and Tahiti's Bora-Bora, I remembered my longing and felt great pleasure in the fulfillment of my dreams. The atlas and my Danish experience planted the bug in me to be a traveler for life.

Around 1952, our district stepped into the 20th century, and we got electricity. City water took a bit longer to reach our house. Electricity was something new and an oddity, and my father did not like it at first because it cost money to use. The first electric appliance he got was a radio. Even before we had electricity, we had a crystal radio. If you are not familiar with the crystal radio, you should check out an old *Popular Mechanics*. It takes a quartz crystal and an earphone. You wire the earphone to the crystal, and magically, it works. Hungary had two radio stations, both blasting communist propaganda, but you could also find good music, mainly Hungarian gypsy music and light operettas as well as international news. Our crystal radio had enough range to listen to the Radio Free Europe broadcast. My father always listened to it after dinner, although it was illegal, and if you got caught you could be sent to jail. The local Communist Party informers walked the streets and listened to the houses; it was their duty to report any infractions. My father always turned the sound down so low that we could hardly hear it. My mother was afraid that we would get reported and they'd take Father away and the whole family would be black listed.

In the late '40s and early '50s, Hungary underwent many changes. A new constitution was adopted with the influence of the Soviet Communist Party. The Hungarian Communist Party gained majority status without any opposition and formed a new government. Shortly afterward, the newly formed government nationalized all private commerce and industry. The State became the owner of all factories, mines, steel mills, land, and soon after, all private real estate and homes. The communist idea was that there would be no more exploitation by the capitalist system. The *people* had taken over all assets and every aspect of life. "Everything belongs to the people," the communist slogan said. Initially, there was a lot of sentiment in favor of this, particularly among the poorer segment of the population. On paper, this new concept of governance sounded like a promising life for the masses. However, it did not take too much time to realize that the future would, in reality, be very bleak. Free speech was suppressed, and any opposition was not tolerated. The media became the Party's propaganda machine—all written text was censored, and all artistic creation had to meet communist standards and Party themes.

Communist ideology dictated all facets of life. The judicial system and due process changed dramatically, and people began disappearing without any notice. Traveling abroad was permitted only for a few well-known scientists and artists who agreed with Party guidelines and carried the little *red book*. For the youth, the *Communist Pioneer* movement replaced the traditional Boy Scouts and was mandatory for all students. The group leaders strictly enforced participation where they taught communist ideology and its alleged benefits. The Pioneers had to wear red bandanas around their necks to be identified. In schools, starting with 4th grade, Russian language become a mandatory second language, and all foreign language teachers had to switch to Russian. I hated studying Russian and learned just enough to pass the exams. However, later on in my life, I realized that it would have come in handy to know Russian better. Even now, I still have some of the phrases, songs, and poems stuck in my memory.

Perhaps the most significant change with the new government was the creation of the AVO, a political police force modeled after the infamous Soviet KGB. It became very clear that the new government, controlled by the Soviet Union, was going to rule by fear and terror to carry out their communist ideology. AVO's success was based on recruiting civilian informants, whose responsibility was to report any anti-communist or anti-government activities. The offenders were removed from society by armed police, and in many cases, they were taken away and never heard from again. The fear they created was so strong and paralyzing that the population was stunned. It took almost a decade for it boil to the surface, manifesting in the 1956 revolution.

Our family, according to one of our relatives who researched our genealogy, is related to Törő Pál, the leader of a peasant revolt in the year of 1755. The Hapsburg rulers crushed the revolt and hanged my great-great-great grandfather. It was a public hanging to discourage any more civil disobedience. There has always been a streak of anti-authoritarianism in my family, an instinct to challenge the establishment's orders. Many years later, in Berkeley, California, I saw a bumper sticker on an old beat-up, colorfully painted VW van that said *ALWAYS QUESTION AUTHORITY*. I like that

THE SCHOOL YEARS

bumper sticker and the philosophy it represents.

My early years in school were uneventful. I was a good student, managing to get good grades with little effort. When not in school, I helped the family by faithfully executing all my chores. Many episodes flash in my mind as I think back to those years. Once, my father brought home a large sack of rusty, bent nails. I never found out where he got them, but I knew *why* he got them. We needed to mend our wooden fence, and one morning he asked me to help. We sat down and straightened out all those rusty, bent nails. I wondered if it wouldn't be easier to just buy new ones but, of course, that cost money. He had a piece of railroad rail about twelve inches long, which was his most precious tool besides his hammer. It was basically his anvil and he used it for everything—a solid piece of metal on which he could bend and form metal plates and sheet metal, punch holes, and use for just about anything that needed to be made or modified. He could repair and make everything for the household. He inspected every nail that I straightened, rejecting the ones he did not like. I learned from him not do a lousy job, do everything right the first time, and reuse things that are still good. Interestingly, one of my first tools in America was a piece of rail just like my father's, and I still have it.

My mother always asked him to do things around the house. He did not like to be told, but he always obliged. He was very handy and creative with his hands, and he could fix anything with the limited tools he had. He had his own way of teaching us to be self-sufficient and frugal. In those years, I did not appreciate it, but later I was grateful that I had a father who was a minimalist. It was not by choice, I might add, but he made the best of the hand that life dealt him. I often wonder what my father would have had done with all the tools we have available now.

I did not like to work with my father. I had to do everything the way he wanted or I would get punished. I was the youngest and the smallest in the family, so he did not have any patience left for me. I believe he used it up on my three brothers before me. But I think he liked me in his own way, though he certainly did not show it at all. I had great respect for him and longed for his affection, and a kind word would have been wonderfully encouraging. It never came, I believe, because he was just too drained emotionally and physically. His responsibility to provide for the six of us wore on him every day. I would have given anything to know what he was thinking when he walked to the streetcar station every morning at five o'clock, six times a week all year around. I knew that the political and social situation bothered him a lot. Occasionally, he expressed it quietly to us just to make sure we knew he disliked the communist system.

I do not know too much about my father's childhood, since he never talked about it. I do, however, have one vivid memory of my father's grandparents, which illustrates the traditions he grew up with and were passed along. It was the Christmas we spent at their house in Hajdúböszörmény during the war. Theirs was a typical peasant farmhouse with a hard-packed earthen floor and two rooms. A big, white beehive oven filled one the corner of the large room that was the living room, kitchen, and dining room all combined. In another corner of this room stood a big heavy wood table with wooden chairs. Another side of the oven protruded into the other room which was the bedroom. It heated the little house in the winter time as well as providing the hearth for cooking and baking. At the top, there were two ledges where the kids could sleep. The beehive stove corner was my sleeping place along with two of my brothers, and it was cozy and warm during the cold winter nights. Some of the neighbors who did not have a beehive oven brought over items for my grandmother to bake, particularly at Christmas time. They always bartered in exchange for this favor, and my grandparents did not mind, since it worked both ways.

The Christmas tradition is that the father of the family takes the younger kids out for a walk or goes to the theater. Mother and the older siblings will bring in the tree and decorate it, so when the young ones arrive home, they have a beautiful surprise. That year when I was three, my older brother took me out for a Christmas Eve walk, and when we returned there was a decorated Christmas tree on the middle of the dining table. I said (so the story goes), "Jesus was here!" I can't remember that I got any presents, but I was dazzled by the appearance of the Christmas tree.

In the Hungarian tradition, Christmas is to celebrate Jesus' arrival on Earth as a savior. Santa Claus is celebrated on December 5th, Saint Nickolas Day, when children receive presents depending upon their behavior during the year.

THE SCHOOL YEARS

Getting ready for the Santa Claus celebration, 1947. I am in the middle.

On December 4th in the evening, you polish your shoes and put them in the window for Santa Claus (*Mikulás* in Hungarian) to stop by and reward you. According to tradition, if you were good, he leaves you candies, but if you were bad, you get coals. When you got up on the morning of December 5th, you would see what was in your shoes. When I got to be old enough, I would always joke that I would be bad all year in order to get coal for heating in the winter.

Easter is another big religious celebration in Hungary, just like anywhere in the Christian world. The folk custom we learned was to sprinkle perfumed water (rose water) on girls and receive a colorfully painted hardboiled egg or a kiss in return. These beautiful painted Easter eggs are decorated with traditional Hungarian motifs and are still sold year-round as a favorite tourist souvenir for visitors to take home. Easter was always my favorite time. I lined up with my brothers, always trailing behind them, to visit the girls in the neighborhood. We sprinkled rose water on the giggling, squealing girls and collected our reward of decorated eggs. At the more affluent homes, we were invited in for refreshments of ham and pastries. At the end of the day, I had a small basket of pretty eggs. At home, we proudly showed mother our loot. I found it hard to break the lovely painted hard boiled eggs, but they were a welcome addition to our family larder. This tradition almost disappeared during the Russian occupation due to its religious connection. After I arrived in the US, I was surprised to see that Easter is celebrated, albeit without rose water and chasing girls.

We grew up without any presents at birthdays, name days, or even at Christmas. I can't recall receiving any personal presents on any of these occasions, but secretly I always hoped for some, of course. If there was anything, it was always something for the whole family. For instance, one Christmas, my father made a wheelbarrow (*talicska* in Hungarian). It wasn't really a wheelbarrow as it's known in the West; it was more like a long, low, and flat cart with one wheel and long handles. My father used it to haul sacks of coal or food for our pig from the streetcar stop to our house on a daily basis. It was not really a toy, but my brothers and I often used it as such. We rode that thing all over the place, and I usually sat on it while my brothers pushed. Many times, they sent me flying off the wheelbarrow, which was the fun part.

Another family Christmas present I vividly remember came during a particularly meager Christmas dinner. My mother presented us with tropical fruit—mandarins. She got two of them from a religious relief group at the market. My father's first reaction was, "How much did they cost?" but my mother did not answer. She beamed as we tasted tropical fruit for the first time.

To make ends meet as we got older, my mother took in sewing projects. Not far from our home was the Used Goods Market (*Ócsaka telep*), where all sorts of things could be bartered or purchased. My father would stop by after work and buy some large, used overcoats, military jackets, and blankets still in good condition. He brought them home and we proceeded to take them apart. Many times, I helped Mother remove the stitches and pull a garment apart. She ironed the pieces out and recut them to her own pattern to make a smaller size short jacket. They all looked very good, almost like new, when she finished. Her old Singer sewing machine sometimes needed help to punch through thick fabric, so I helped her to push on the treadle under the machine. I liked to do that as she was always complimenting me on my good help. When she made three or four new jackets, my father took them to a different market in the country on Saturday or Sunday, a trip that required train transportation. Usually very early in the morning, around 4, my father and one of the boys took the bundle of jackets on the family wheelbarrow (*talicska*) to the railroad station about five kilometers from our house. I always envied my brothers who got to go along with him to the railroad station and bring the wheelbarrow back. I could not wait to be old enough to do that chore. I did always accompany my brother in the evening to meet Father on his return trip. It was always very exciting to see how much he had sold. It determined his mood for the rest of the week, and sometimes, depending on his success, he managed to bring home some treats from the market. It was always something edible, like pastry or cheese.

During dinner that evening, he would recap his day's adventure, telling us how he sold every item and what kind of deal he made. He never gave much credit to my mother for making the goods; according to him, it was all his skill as a salesman. But the most exciting part was when he took the wad of money out of his pocket and started counting. It was all hard cash, and I have never seen anyone have such joy in touching and feeling money. I also have vivid memories of him returning with the whole bundle, having sold nothing. Those were sad evenings, and everyone in the family suffered. Not a word was spoken at the dinner table. He'd just smoke one cigarette after another. What he regretted most was losing the price of the train trip. When I was older, I did accompany him to the railroad station. Sometimes, between cigarettes, he tried to explain to me, in simple words, the art of salesmanship. At that time, I did not comprehend the importance of his tactics; only after coming to the USA did I eventually realize the power of selling and salesmanship. My father used to say, *"Life is all about selling; everything revolves around selling and buying."* How right he was.

One day, my father showed up with a bicycle. We were all very excited about having a vehicle that we could use. The problem was that it was a track bicycle with a continuous drive and no brakes. My brothers all knew how to ride and how to brake with their feet, rubbing the sole of their shoes against the tire, but I did not know how and it was too big for me anyway. However, I was dying to try it and begged my brothers to teach me. So, one day my brother, Lajos, decided it was time for me to learn. I could not get on the seat so I had to go under the frame. It was awkward, but I did not mind as long as I could try. He was holding on to the back. We practiced several days, and I was doing pretty well. So, he let go.

Going straight was no problem but at the end of the street, I had to turn. I was going pretty fast and I hadn't learned how to slow down without brakes, so I crashed into the neighbor's fence. Luckily, I did not get hurt but the bicycle was damaged. I was terrified that my father was going to ring my neck for damaging his bicycle. My mother came to my defense when my father came home. He was mad at me, but I did not get spanked. The worst part was that I had to help him to mend the neighbor's fence.

Another time I vividly remember was when my father made a sled. We needed the sled to replace the wheelbarrow in the winter time to carry the heavy bags of food he collected for the animals over the ice and snow. We would meet him at the last streetcar stop and haul the bags home on the sled.

One winter day after a big snowfall, my brothers decided to go sledding at the local dump where there was a small hill. We bundled up and three of us headed out with the sled, me sitting on it as my brothers pulled it. The snow was too deep for me to walk. At the hill, there were other kids with the same idea, all sledding and having fun. My brothers took a couple of single runs before we decided to try all three of us at one time. Lajos and I were sitting in the front and my brother, Imre, was pushing the sled hard to get going down the slope. As we got moving downhill, we started to go faster and faster. It was time for Imre to hop on. When he did, the sled flattened out as the runners collapsed. The joints were not reinforced enough. Needless to say, we were in big trouble again.

It was a sad trip home. We all walked very quietly until I had a brilliant idea. I said, "Why don't we fix it?" My older brother liked that idea much better than getting a beating. At home, we showed it to our mother and explained how we wanted to fix it. She gave us some money to buy hardware and screws. We worked on it all day, and when we met my father at the streetcar stop, we were happily pulling the sled. As he threw the bag on the sled, we all held our breath in anticipation, and the sled held. Later on, we told him what we did. He inspected our repair, and I could see a small smile on his face. It was the only smile I remember that he ever showed. While I wished I could read his thoughts, I think he was proud he'd taught us how to fix things and that his boys were just like him.

Fall was a special time of the year because of the harvest. All the fruits were ripe and needed canning, and my mother made all the jams, preserves and pickled vegetables for our family. We had an outdoor kettle that my father built for making all the different fruit jams. Mashing up the fruit with sugar and reducing it with heat to jam consistency was my mother's specialty. We tended the fire with wood I gathered in the nearby forest and occasionally tasted the boiling brew. After my mother approved the consistency, we transferred the boiling jam to jars and sealed them with parchment paper and string. After the jam cooled, it created a vacuum, sucking the parchment paper into a hollow shape—proof of air tightness and preservation. By the end of the fall, our pantry shelves were lined with different colorful jars. It looked very pretty, but most importantly, it tasted even better. My mother used big jars, the smallest being about a liter size.

My favorite process was making sauerkraut in our big barrel. Mother bought all the spices and the cabbage at the market. As usual, father had constructed the cabbage shredder. It was a long board with two sharp blades inserted, and at the top was a small box in which the cabbage fit. Pressing down on the box and the cabbage, moving it back and forth across the blades, the cabbage was shredded. The board was laid over the barrel so that the cut cabbage fell into it. My mother added salt and bay leaves. Then it was time for my performance. My mother scrubbed my feet until they were clean enough to pass her inspection, and I hopped into the barrel and started stomping. I danced in that barrel until the juice covered the cabbage. The salt and acidic juice of the cabbage really worked. When I got out, my feet were pinkish white and cleaner than when I was born. Occasionally, my mother cut up a quince and threw it into the barrel for extra flavoring. When we finished, she put a cloth, a wooden lid, and some bricks on the top for weight so while it was fermenting it would not spill over. This sauerkraut provided us with abundant vitamin C during the winter months. Even now, sauerkraut dishes are a favorite and bring back good memories.

My father never really got into jam making. Instead, he made moonshine. Actually, I did not know the expression "moonshine" until I came to this country. He called it *pálinka* or *shligovic* which is a Slavic word for "plum brandy," I guess. We had two Italian plum trees and they were the tastiest plums I've ever had. (They are not common in California; at least I can't find them at the market).

He collected all the fallen ripe plums in a small barrel. When it was almost full, he added a bit of sugar to accelerate the fermentation, and when it started to smell of alcohol, he got out his homemade distiller. This was a medium size kettle with a hole in the lid where he attached the copper coil. This copper coil was submerged in a bucket of cold water. Near the bottom of the bucket, the end of the coil protruded out the side where he collected the distilled alcohol to make *pálinka*. He placed the fermented fruit into the kettle and heated it to boiling, at which point the alcohol would begin to evaporate. As the steam passed through the coil, it cooled and became liquid alcohol again. He usually went through the process twice to purify it, and at the end, he could light the liquid. It was very strong, at least 90 proof, and tasted just like the plums themselves.

He made about three or four gallons for the winter, and every morning he had a small shot glass before he got on the road to the streetcar station. That's all he had for breakfast. I never saw him drinking anything else except maybe some red wine at his name day celebration. I still have a fascination with this process and I keep telling myself I should make an apparatus just like my father's and distill some of our local California fruit. My mother always added some flavoring to her share of the *pálinka*. Peach, vanilla, and cherry essence were her favorites. This gave a different taste to the alcohol and also diluted it somewhat.

She made these liquors, not only for drinking, but for cooking. She was an exceptional baker, and her pastries, with a touch of liquor, were out of this world. She never used any recipe books. At least, I never saw her using one. She discouraged alcohol consumption in her home and it was forbidden for us to even taste her *pálinka*. But sometimes, I'd sneak into the pantry to try some. It was good with a kick, and I am still partial to sweet, fruity liquors.

We did not officially open any jars until the first snow or if a jar became unsealed and began to spoil. My brother, Lajos, who loved all the preserves, especially apricot and plum jam (barack and szilva lekvár), discovered that if he poked a small hole with a needle through the parchment paper, some green fungus would begin to grow on the top of the jam. In other words, it began to spoil, and we would have to eat it. My mother got wise to this trick, but she never mentioned it. She was pleased that we appreciated her jams so much.

CHAPTER 3
Introduction to the World of Sports

The year 1953, when I was introduced to organized sport, was life-changing for me. The sports club system in Hungary at that time was very unique, with each club offering many sports, concentrating on the Olympic ones. Of course, soccer was the most popular and got the most funding. There was a performance incentive system administered by the Minister of Sports. Each sport's national championship had a point system, and the more points a club collected, the more funding they received from the Minister of Sports. International competitions, World Championships and Olympic Games were also heavily weighted in the system. Clubs were rewarded for developing top caliber athletes.

When I was in my last year of elementary school, one of my teachers recommended to my parents that I participate in a Nationwide Sport Identification program. The government announced that there would be several facilities in Budapest on a certain day in the spring where students from 14 to 16 years of age could sign up for aptitude testing. We could leave our classes to participate, which was good incentive to do it! My mother let me participate in this program, and I was tested on the Margaret Island sports field. We had to run 400 and 1,500 meters, throw the javelin and a small hard ball, high jump, long jump, and kick a soccer ball. All of these tests occurred on one day, and our results were recorded for evaluation. Considering my size and weight (I was very small, light, and skinny), I did very well in all those events, particularly in running. I always liked running. I was fast with a good kick at the end. Looking back on my sporting career, I would have been a good 800- or 1,500-meter runner. I liked strategy, and I always daydreamed about running a great middle distance race. My mother received a letter, weeks later, suggesting that I consider pursuing some sport, perhaps athletics or soccer. But fate steered me in another direction.

My brother, Lajos, in the Olympic single canoe, 1955.

My brother, Lajos, had been a member of the *Honvéd* (Army) Sports Club for a year and a half and liked it. When the letter came and he heard my parents talking about it, he suggested that I come down to his club to try canoeing instead. My parents did not like the idea at first. "You are too young," my mother said. My father was concerned about the cost of the ticket for the streetcar to Margaret Island for practices, an unnecessary expense. Also, summertime was coming and my main chore was tending the goat. I promised that I would get enough food for her early in the morning and in the evening. "I will be safe, traveling with my brother," I argued. When my parents finally agreed, I was the happiest kid in town. My destiny began.

So that summer of 1953, upon the suggestion of Lajos, I joined the *Honvéd* Sports Club, too. I was 13 years old. One slight problem was that swimming was a requirement for everyone in the club. Prospective members had to swim 200 meters without touching the wall in the swimming pool. I was not a good swimmer and just barely passed the test.

At first, I was mainly tasked with washing the club boats as they came back from workouts. Occasionally, the coaches had me join a juvenile-aged group in the war canoe. The war canoe is a long boat for 10 paddlers and a steersman. The boat had no seats. Each paddler had a canvas bag filled with shredded cork to kneel on. It was a very primitive but versatile cushion for the knee, which supported all of your weight. The bag molded to the boat and did not slip while we were paddling, but after half an hour, the cork compacted and it felt like kneeling on rocks. Five of the crew paddled on the right and five on the left. Our club had two of these war canoes, one for racing and one for learning and practicing. By the end of the summer, I was selected for the honor of stroking the boat on the left side. Stroking the boat was a position of responsibility and leadership, and I was proud to be picked. The steersman at the stern of the canoe was always a senior paddler or assistant coach, and we definitely needed supervision. The Danube is a swift river with currents, eddies, and whirlpools, not to mention commercial shipping and barge traffic. Navigating on that kind of water takes skill and practice. At an early age, I got the sense of boat handling.

Practicing in the war canoe, 1955.

I loved paddling in the war canoe. My fellow young canoeists were the same age, and we formed a very close bond both in and outside the boat. The next year, we began racing in the first age group, or *the Juveniles*. At 15, when we became juniors, we won all but one race in both the 1,500- and 500-meter events at the Hungarian National Championships. We had a lot of fun, even during the daily summer practices. Our favorite activity on the Danube was to catch the wake of a side-wheeler tour boat. With an experienced steersman, we could surf on the wake. Sometimes, we would paddle up behind the stern of the boat and hold on to the rudder for a tow. That was my trick as a stroke. The rudder had a big hole above the water, and I could put my hand through it. The people on the boat all gathered at the stern to watch us. We were pulled along for a while until I let it go. It was certainly illegal, but we never got caught by the river patrol.

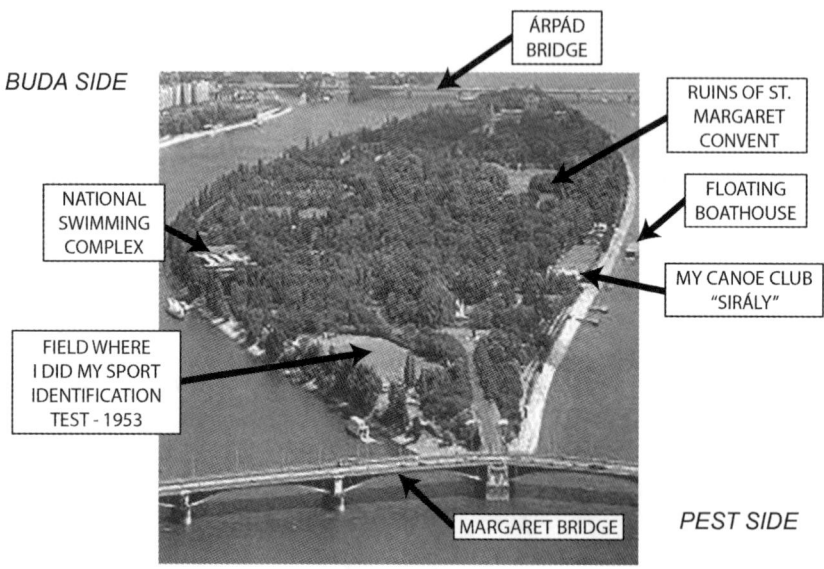

Arial view of Margaret Island on the Danube river.

My club, *Honvéd*, was located on Margaret Island (*Margit Sziget*), a beautiful, small island in the middle of the Danube, dividing it into the east and west branches. There were bridges at both ends of the island, but only buses were allowed on the island. The island has a great history. King Bela IV built a Dominican convent there for his daughter, Margaret (later Saint Margaret), hence the name Margaret Island. The ruins of this convent and church are still standing as a historical sight. This island became my second home for many years, and I have many fond memories of spending countless hours training on the waters around this lovely island.

INTRODUCTION TO THE WORLD OF SPORTS

There still are many impressive sport facilities on the island. The famous architect Hajós Alfréd won a silver medal at the 1924 Paris Games for his design of the national swimming stadium. Hajos Alfred was also the first Hungarian Olympic Champion, winning two swimming gold medals in the 100- and the 1,200-meter events at the first Olympic Games in 1896, Athens, Greece. In these Games, swimming events were not held in a pool but in a bay.

On Margaret Island, there's still a public swimming pool with a wave maker, a small soccer and track field, many tennis courts, and several floating boat houses for rowing. At the north end of the island is the Grand Hotel, a very exclusive resort. In those days, it was only for top officials of the communist party and foreign visitors. Many times, we passed by on our training runs and wondered about the people sitting on the terrace enjoying the scenery. Our boat house, *Sirály* (meaning *seagull* in translation), was built on land at the West side of the island and had a big terrace with wonderful scenery that was free for us every day. On the very northern tip of the island, there was a clay pigeon shooting gallery. Many times, as we were rounding the end of the island, the broken pieces fell into our canoes. It felt like they were shooting at us, which added to the excitement particularly in high water when the current was strong enough to stop the boat after every stroke and we were close to the gallery.

With the Honved Canoe Club floating boathouse in the background, I am racing the season-opener race around Margaret Island.

Our boathouse, *Sirály,* was shared with another canoe club, *Épitök*—our arch rivals. We each had our own floating dock from where our boats launched. Both clubs had many National, World, and Olympic medalists over the years. Next to our boathouse were many tennis courts where Army officials played. We would use one of the tennis courts for a small soccer practice field. In a building next to our club, we had a paddling tank. It was a winter exercise facility and a great coaching tool for paddling technique. In it, the water moves and the simulated boat is stationary. We spent many hours in the winter practicing in this tank. Next to the boat storage was the boathouse's locker room with showers. The hot water for the showers came from the local thermal spring is that still along the Danube. Thousands of years ago, the Romans built several thermal baths along the river that are in use today. The phosphorous smell of the water is still imbedded into my memory. It was a gang shower, and there was a pecking order as to who could use which showerheads. I remember being chased out one time when I was still a juvenile by some senior paddler because I did not have any pubic hair. It hurt my feelings but not to the point of quitting. Nature will take care of it, I reminded myself.

Next to the *Sirály* clubhouse was a small two-story resort complex for the Hungarian Army senior officers. This resort had several rooms for sleeping and a large dining hall with a terrace upstairs. On the ground level, there was a small boat repair and building shop. On the water, they had a floating clubhouse that stored many rowing wherries on the lower level and cabins on the second deck. After 1957, our club changed its name to the *Honvéd Kayak Kenu Szakosztály* (Club) and moved into the elite environment of this floating clubhouse.

Back to 1953 and my first summer of paddling. I had proven myself to be a good paddler and playful teammate. The coach saw some potential in me and asked my parents to allow me to continue training with the club in the fall and winter. I was just starting high school, which was an hour streetcar ride from the club. My parents agreed under the condition that my school work take priority. I was very happy! I liked the club and my Magnificent Seven teammates. They were older than I was, so I felt safe in their company. They always bought fruit to share among us as we traveled home on the streetcar.

INTRODUCTION TO THE WORLD OF SPORTS

In the fall, as long as the weather cooperated, we continued to paddle on the water in the war canoe with the coach's supervision. One cold day, the coach called off all on-water activity and we went into the boat maintenance phase of the year. All the boats were wooden or canvas-covered wooden boats, and we had to clean and sand them down for the boat builder to varnish during the winter months. It was hard and tedious work, and the old boat builder was very fussy about their condition. Uncle András *(Chochol András, 1892-1980)*, as he wanted to be called, was a short little man but an excellent craftsman, and his varnish finish on the boats was exceptional. In later years, when I was on the national team, he made me a canoe paddle that was remarkably light yet strong. You had to be special to get a paddle from him, and he showed me planks of wood that were his precious prizes. They were North American Western Redwood—a very light, low density wood with parallel grains running lengthwise on the plank. He cut this wood only for special projects, mainly for paddles, and mine was made of this wood. He told me that the trees yielding this wood were the tallest in the world, and only found in North America. He said if I ever traveled to that part of the world to make sure I saw them, and I promised to do so. I was only hoping, but now, whenever I travel in Yosemite or the Muir Woods and see those giants, I always think of Uncle András and his story about this particular wood. He never asked for any compensation for my paddle, and I used it for several years until it wore out. Later on, when I was on the national team and on my second trip abroad to West Germany, I bought him a pouch of good smelling tobacco for his pipe, and he appreciated my gesture. He made me another paddle when I was the top single paddler in the country.

The summer of 1954 was very memorable and made an everlasting impression on me. The club leaders decided to take many of the paddlers on a two week camping tour called the "Big Loop." The Big Loop starts and ends in Budapest. The route is down the Danube River, up the Sió River to Lake Balaton, across Lake Balaton to the river Sáva, a portage to the river Zala, then to the city of Győr at the Danube and Zala River confluence, finally returning on the Danube to Budapest. What more can you ask for as a fourteen-year-old kid? At first, I was not scheduled to go because they thought I was too young

Lining up for lunch during the Big Loop Tour. I am at the left with the big hat and in my first hand-me-down uniform, two sizes too big and well worn.

and would not be able to paddle day after day, but the Magnificent Seven successfully lobbied for me to be included. I was the youngest on the trip and the smallest by weight (only 42 kilograms or about 92 pounds) and extremely happy. It was a great voyage with many unforgettable experiences, such as seeing my country from the rivers and lakes and paddling many kilometers a day to stay on schedule. It was pleasurable on the hot summer days and even in the rain.

A support group followed us with a military cooking trailer and most of our gear, but we had to help prepare the food—peeling potatoes, chopping up carrots, and collecting fire wood. We pitched tents every evening and took them down in the morning. Every evening we had a camp fire where we sang, told jokes, and recounted races late into the night until the coaches told us to go to our tents. After breakfast, the coaches briefed us on the day's schedule, and then we paddled away. The weather was mostly sunny and warm for the first week, and by the end of the trip, I was significantly darker.

The second week it rained and we got the news that the Danube was flooding. To be safe, the group leaders made the decision to cancel our return on the Danube to Budapest. Despite the warning, some senior paddlers still completed the loop. The rest of us took the train back to Budapest and the boats were trailered back to the club. That was disappointing, but the experience lived with us forever, and we forged unbreakable bonds on that trip that lasted the rest of our lives. Many years later, we still talk of the Big Loop and the adventures we shared through the countryside and on the waterways. This trip injected canoeing fever into my veins forever. I made a decision during that summer to spend the rest of my life connected to canoeing and the outdoors. I grew to love it so much that nothing could come between me and canoeing.

In the fall of 1954, I was admitted to a technical high school specializing in steel structures and metal work. We all wore a special hat, which represented the school uniform. The school was about a one-hour streetcar ride from my house, so every day at 6:30, I was on my way with my books and two slices of bread spread with lard and wrapped in newspaper in my lunch bag. That's all I had all day until I got home for dinner. (I always tell my children that if I had enough food (especially peanut butter), and proper nutrition during my childhood I would have been over six feet tall and much stronger.) The studies were easy for me, and I particularly liked the shop and the phys. ed. classes. I was the only one in phys. ed. who could climb the five-meter rope without holding onto it with my feet. I was very proud of that and I always manufactured opportunities to show off that skill. In the shop class, I already knew how to work with all the tools, having learned from my father. This came in handy as I always finished the assignments first and got good grades.

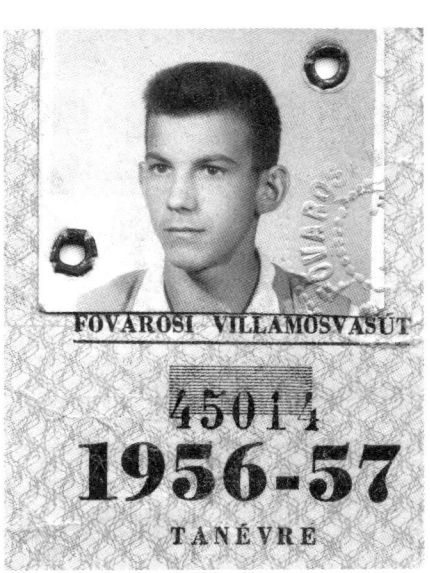

My school year streetcar pass.

My high school class graduation picture, 1958.

During my high school years, I spent a lot of time at my club. Right after school, about 3 o'clock, I took another one-hour ride on the streetcar from my high school to the club. I usually played a half hour of soccer on the small field next to the club until enough of us were there to take the war canoe out. Most of the time, we paddled around Margaret Island (a six-kilometer paddle) or made a longer trip upstream on the Danube. We always paddled upstream first! After the workout, we took care of the boat, had a shower, and went home on another one-hour streetcar ride. I usually got home about 7 in the evening, ate dinner, did my homework, and went to sleep. That was my daily routine. The competition season began in May. Every weekend, there was a race somewhere in the country. Honvéd was one of the biggest clubs in the country and participated in every race.

The junior competition distances were 500- and 1,500-meters for single, double, and the war canoe. The first year, I was stroking the war canoe on the left side and we won all the races we entered. We were national champions in the junior war canoe class. In the fall, the coach decided I was good enough to

First strokes in the high-kneeling position (left side) using a touring kayak at the young age of 14, 1954.

venture out in the single. I switched sides and became a right-handed paddler. The reason for this was that my brother paddled on the left side and I was hoping that someday we would double together. By that time, he was the top junior canoer in the country and my idol. I wanted to be like him so much. Another reason to switch sides was that the long-distance race of 10,000 meters (an Olympic event until 1956), was run with a counterclockwise turn, so it was easier for the right-handed paddler to come around the turn.

Every fall, there was a general meeting of the club members. At this meeting, the club leader handed out the club's racing certificates to each member. This was my first official sport document and identification. We used it for entering races and taking the medical examinations that were mandatory twice a year. On this certificate, my body weight was recorded as 44 kilograms (96 pounds) and I still have it. During this meeting, the coaches and leaders handed out the club sweat clothes and shoes. The elite senior paddlers were first and they received all the new gear. The juniors were next, receiving all the better hand-me-down gear, and finally, the juveniles got anything leftover. Each item given to me had my identification number stamped on. I believe that my first number was 89. I got a worn out sweatsuit that was at least two sizes too large and a pair of tennis shoes that were both worn and too big. Nevertheless, I was elated with my "new" uniform, like a kid in a candy store. I was part of the *team*! I loved that used uniform and promised myself that whatever it took, I would someday get a brand new one. Showing off any sports uniform always made me feel that I had elevated status, that I was part of an elite group. My brother fared even better, and I was proud of him. He had some good junior racing results, which rated some of the better hand-me-downs. When I took home that first hand-me-down uniform to show to my parents, they were proud that I'd become a full member of the club. My mother said, "I can alter and mend them if you like." My father said something like, "Don't they have any new ones?"

During my Olympic years, the uniform was an important part of participation. Many times during the Games, I traded parts of my uniform with other nations' athletes for parts of theirs. These traded uniforms became my prized possessions. Returning home from the Games, these traded items were even more precious than the Hungarian issue, but I have never sold them or given them away. Even now, I have suitcases full of Olympic uniforms, and every time I look at them they bring back good memories of Olympic Games.

Another privilege given to a racing member was that I got a small locker (about two cubic feet) to put my gear in so I didn't have to carry it with me all the time. It barely held my shoes and clothing, particularly in the winter, but as you advanced and placed higher in the competitions, these lockers got bigger. The foundation of the clubhouse hierarchy system was built on results. Your locker was small, medium, or large depending on your results. After my first Olympics, I had one of the biggest, most luxurious lockers in the club.

Practicing in the single gave me the freedom I loved. Without supervision, I could go anywhere on the water! At the same time, there was a lot of responsibility, too. The river was dangerous. Small boats had to deal with a lot of barge traffic and the current. The single canoes were very fragile boats in those days made out of a single layer of two-millimeter wood veneer with wooden transverse ribs, a larger regulation canvas deck in the front, and a smaller regulation canvas back deck. All of them were carefully crafted masterpieces, with the veneer planks stitched together with brass rivets, then sealed and varnished.

INTRODUCTION TO THE WORLD OF SPORTS

In the Olympic style single canoe at the young age of 16, 1956.

They were so fragile that just a small hit on the hull would crack the planking. Needless to say, the club's boat builder was busy all the time.

The single boat I took out the first time was a learning canoe, much wider and heavier than the racing boat I used later on. On windy days, I had a hard time carrying the boat from the boathouse to the dock. A hand-me-down canoe paddle with a stamp burned into it was given to me. At every international competition, the boats had to go through strict boat control. Upon weight and measurement control, the officials would burn a stamp onto the boat to show that it was legal to use for racing. Many athletes asked the officials to stamp the paddle as well. This used paddle had one of those stamps, and while I can't remember for sure, I think it was one of the World Championship stamps. Being too old for the top paddlers to use, it was handed down to the juniors. The shaft was in pretty rough condition, worn at the place where the paddle touches the boat during steering. A lot of miles were in that paddle—the blade was cracked and the varnish was almost gone. I sanded it down, carefully preserving the stamp, and my older brother, Imre, showed me how to repair it. I then asked the boat builder to varnish it for me, and when it was finished, I had a handsome almost-new paddle. It was new to me anyway and I was proud of it. The coach commented on my handiwork, and a couple of years later, I passed my first paddle on to the next generation.

Perhaps the most memorable times during my war canoe years were the tour trips we did during the summer. Almost every weekend when there were no races, we took off upstream in war canoes for a couple of days. The reason we started out going upstream was because on Sunday, for the return trip, we would not have to paddle much. We could just drift along with the Danube's current having a lazy day all the way back to the boathouse. Someone always had to

Taking a rest in the war canoe, drifting downstream on the Danube.

attend to steering in the stern, but the rest of us could jump overboard, play in the water, or rest in the boat sunbathing. Many times, we slept on the river bank in tents or under a turned-over canoe or in a canoe tied up to the shore.

For food, we foraged in the orchards and fields and provided for ourselves for two days. Along the Danube, there's a rich agricultural landscape with fruit orchards and vegetable fields on both sides of the river. We knew when the strawberries were ripening and the fruits were ready to pick. We always paddled over to the opposite side of the river to forage for our food so we did not have to worry about being surprised by an angry farmer later. There were no bridges for over 30 to 40 kilometers, so we didn't have to worry too much. There were some close calls but we were never caught. We believed we were just applying the socialist principal that was pounded into our brains at school. "Everyone gets an equal share." Life was good.

We always had a campfire in the evening, and the older paddlers cooked for us in a kettle over the fire. The younger ones collected fire wood, and after dinner, the older ones told stories about racing and shared some of their experiences. Then we'd sing some songs around the campfire before going to sleep. The peacefulness of sleeping along the river bank is indescribable. I really missed it when I made the national team and paddling became a very serious business.

After I became a national team member with all the training camps and competitions, I didn't have time to do these weekend voyages anymore. My priorities changed, and I sorely missed the camaraderie of paddling together, the camp fires, the storytelling, singing, and joking that bonded us. I'll never forget those times and I still love to go camping in northern California. I cannot, however, apply the socialist principals that I got accustomed to and practiced in the Hungary of my youth. The capitalist system frowns on the "take an equal share" idea. While "everyone is created equal" is the founding principal of this country, individual wealth makes everyone different in practice.

For my first two years, 1954 and 1955, I raced in the war canoe, stroking it in the juvenile age category. In that age group, there were no single or double canoe events. You were expected to learn proper stroke technique in the team boats. Olympic-style canoeing, also called *Canadian style* or single blade canoeing, is a very difficult sport. Single Olympic canoeing (C1) is perhaps the most difficult of all sport motions and techniques. First of all, you have a 5.2-meter long boat which is very narrow and unstable. Even by itself on the water, it flops over to one side. Its width and weight are set by the racing rules (In recent years, the width restriction has been eliminated, making the canoe even more unstable). The paddler kneels in the canoe on one knee in an upright position and paddles only on one side, never changing sides. Hence, there are right-handed and left-handed paddlers. In the double canoe, there is one paddler on each side of the boat. In recent years, there has been a trend of having both paddlers on the same side. Some of these boats have raced very successfully, even at the international level. In the single canoe, due to this asymmetric body position, paddling is difficult and going straight is challenging. It takes at least two years of regular practice to master the control of the boat so you can go where you desire. In this unstable environment, and with the difficulty of boat control, execution of a consistent canoeing stroke is almost impossible. There are slight changes from one stroke to another, so coaches try to teach a basic technique that the individual paddler can adjust to become his own style. Strength and body structure will affect this individualized technique.

I was fortunate in my early years that I had the best coaches in the country at my club. Tálos Zoltán, coach of the junior canoers, and Blahó Kalmán, coach of the senior paddlers, were both university-educated coaches and trainers, and conducted all training activities in the club. They were very dedicated and experienced, knowing the techniques and the physiology of the sport. I learned much from them that I could apply in my later years as a coach.

Then came 1956, my first junior year when I could compete in the single canoe against my brother, who was the best in the country. I was also stroking the junior war canoe team. At the national championships, my brother and I won all the events we entered, except when I finished second behind him in the single events. Our club got all the trophies because of our success, and after the race, the coach filled one of the trophy cups with Triple Sec, a sweet liquor that I had never tasted before. We emptied the cup and I do not know how I got home; my brother said I was very limp on the streetcar and he had to carry me home. The taste of Triple Sec (which I am partial to even now) still reminds me of that victory banquet.

The year 1956 also brought many changes to Hungary, as there was widespread dissatisfaction with the government. Resentment toward the occupying Russians reached the boiling point on October 23, 1956, when university students took to the street to demonstrate against the communist system, demanding change and challenging the establishment's order. As I recall, October was cold and rainy that year and we were not training on the water by then. I was down at the club sanding boats for winter repair. My brother did not come down that day and neither did many of the older paddlers. Going home on the streetcar, I learned about the protest and saw people gathering on the street. There was a unique energy in the air that you could feel—everyone was excited and loud voices could be heard. Arriving home, my mother asked where my brother was and I had to tell the truth that

I didn't know. She was very concerned all evening. He arrived later with my father and they told us of an uprising in the center of the city. The Hungarian radio stations stopped broadcasting, so we did not know what was happening. Radio Free Europe reported that there was widespread revolt in Budapest against the government and the Russians. The Hungarian Army had fired on protesters at the radio station, resulting in casualties, and my father's pessimistic opinion was that a lot of blood would be shed for nothing. As it turned out, he was right.

Later on, we learned that during the night the radio station was taken over by the revolutionaries who began broadcasting "the truth." Many units of the Army sided with the revolution and put down their weapons. The Communist Party leaders fled the city and a new government began to form. Budapest was free! It was a spontaneous, genuine uprising, a true revolt. The next day, we all wanted to go into the city, but all public transportation was grounded and the major roads were barricaded at the city's perimeter. We saw trucks loaded with young people shouting anti-communist slogans and waving flags with a burned-out socialist emblem in the middle. The burned-out flag became the symbol of the revolution. They were encouraging the population to join and take up arms.

Famous picture of the Hungarian revolution, October 23, 1956.

That afternoon, Soviet tanks, which were stationed around the city, rolled into town. They were quickly taken out by Molotov cocktails. After the third day, there was no major fighting going on in Budapest. In some isolated areas, AVO members (the Hungarian Secret Service who had guns) tried to defend themselves. The AVO was a hated group. They had unilateral power to take anyone at any time if they felt that the individual was against the communist system and the government. On the fourth day, my brother and I had a chance to go to the city with one of the trucks. We wanted to see what was happening at our club, the Army Club. My mother cried and insisted we not go, but we did anyway. We got as far as the center of the city, where we saw a lynching that I will never forget. The crowd had recognized an AVO member dressed in civilian clothes, captured him, and hung him from a tree by his feet. They stuffed money in his mouth, beat, spit, and urinated on him until he was dead. It was a very powerful scene that still haunts me on occasion. We saw several burned-out Russian tanks and scorched bodies around them. Several buildings were damaged and power lines were on the pavement.

We walked to the club where all the older paddlers were gathered, discussing the possibility of defecting. Some of them were serving in the Army and had learned that the border patrols were not guarding anymore. Budapest was free, but other parts of the country were still under the Soviet control. Some of the top paddlers were on the Olympic team and would be leaving soon to go to Melbourne. They had only a couple of days to make a decision before they would ship out with the Olympic team for Czechoslovakia, where they would fly on to the XVI Olympic Games held in Melbourne, Australia. There was no air traffic in or out of Budapest due to the unrest. Later on, I learned that it was a difficult trip because the team leadership was all Communist Party members, and some of the team members resented their presence and actually petitioned to have them removed.

The Magnificent Seven discussed the possibility of leaving the country together. We were all brothers and would take care of each other. I was the youngest and I wanted to go if my brother would. We discussed it at home, but my parents did not want to hear about it. Lajos was about to graduate from high school and they didn't want him to interrupt his education. They definitely thought I was too young to be without parental supervision, and also had legitimate fears for our safety, so they convinced us to stay. (Much later, I learned from one of the paddlers who left during that time that he was detained in a youth detention camp because he was only 17 until the authorities found him an adult sponsor. This would have happened to me if I had defected at that time).

The other five Magnificent Seven teammates all decided to defect, and the next day, they were on a train to the border, crossing into Austria with what they could carry in their small bags. Eventually, they ended up in Canada and New Zealand, bringing an end to that special brotherhood.

Several years earlier, in 1954, the government built a military compound for a small Soviet Army unit in the countryside near our house. I hated to see "my" open fields disappear and I had to walk much farther out in the country to get food for the goats. As the 1956 revolution gained momentum, the soldiers in that compound fled, and it was occupied by the revolutionaries. The despised compound was then looted by the locals, myself included. I snuck in and got an old rifle and several hand grenades. My mother almost fainted when I brought them home and insisted I take them back, which I reluctantly did.

Budapest was free for almost two weeks. The Hungarians asked the West for help but only empty promises came. Unfortunately, there was another international conflict at the same time—the Suez Canal incident. This was strategically much more important for the whole world than the Hungarian revolution. The Suez Canal crisis overshadowed everything and the Hungarians were left to manage their own affairs alone against the big Russian bear.

Needless to say, the revolution was defeated by overpowering Russian forces during the second week on November 5th, and Budapest was reoccupied. The revolutionary leaders were executed and people began to flee the country. The western border to Austria remained open until mid-December and nearly 200,000 Hungarians left the country.

Much ill-will surfaced between Russian sympathizers and freedom-loving Hungarians. I got a taste of it, too. Coming home from the club one afternoon on the streetcar, I was wearing a lapel pin with the Hungarian flag and a canoe paddler in the middle. The pin was given to me by my coach before he defected, and I treasured it as a reminder of him. A person standing next to me on the streetcar looked at my pin and asked me to get off the streetcar and follow him. I refused, and he pushed me off the car at the next stop where the police station was. He took me in and told the police that I was one of the instigators wearing a revolutionary pin. He showed the police his Communist Party little red book. He was one of the hated informers. I tried to explain that the pin was really sports memorabilia, and that I was one of the top junior paddlers in the country. After a long discussion, they believed my story and let me go. However, this incident left a bad taste in my mouth.

After graduating from high school in 1958, I got a job in a factory that manufactured locomotives and passenger train cars. This company exported these trains to Asian countries like Burma and Vietnam. I was assigned to a group assembling reduction gears and train axels. We worked on one of two shifts—either six in the morning to two in the afternoon or two in the afternoon to ten at night—six days a week with only Sunday off. I was happy to get a job (my father was too), but it was hard to accommodate my training schedule and, at that time, I was the top junior canoer in the country. I petitioned my coach and the club's leadership to help me get time off from work for training, just like the top senior athletes in the country. After the winter training camp (when I was excused from work), a letter came from the Sport Minister of Hungary granting me four hours of leave with pay each day for training, and Saturdays off during the racing season until further notice. On the top of that, I got paid time off for every training camp (which was three to four months out of the year). It made me incredibly happy to be considered worthy of such allowances because of my sports performance. I was almost sold on the system and wanted to repay the leaders with my results.

At work, my group leader and all my group members were jealous. I would punch the time clock at ten after my morning practice every morning instead of six. The local Communist Party leaders approached me about joining them, but I declined with the excuse that I was too busy with my training and travel to be a contributing member. They frowned upon my decision, and I noticed later on that I did not advance in the workplace, although I had more of an educational and technical background than some of the Party members.

My wages were low, but I figured what the hell, I work only four hours and get payed for eight. I lived at home, had an occasional meal ticket at the club, and my expenses were low. Returning from the winter training camp in 1959, the coach submitted my name for a stipend called "calorie money." That was a sport system subsidy/incentive that provided financial help for living expenses, food, and incidentals for the elite athletes. It was a monthly payment almost as much as my salary at work, and with more results, it would increase. I got approval for calorie money too. Suddenly, I was rich! At least, I thought I was, and my father liked it even more than I did.

My parents then talked to me about helping the household, and at first, I couldn't believe what I was hearing. *They don't love me anymore!* I thought, until I realized that life was catching up with me. This was reality—I was earning lots of money and I should help to support my family. After all, I was taking advantage of the food and shelter the family provided. Having an apartment and being on my own was impossible, plus, there were no apartments available anywhere. When adult children married in that time, they had to live with one of the parents. My oldest brother, Janos, had married, and he and his new wife lived with us. They moved into the pantry for several months until they found an apartment. So, I began to pay monthly rent to my family. It wasn't much, and I could afford it. Not having a bank account, it was all cash. As a matter of fact, my family did not have a bank account either, as Father did not believe in banks. He remembered the worldwide Depression in the late 1920's. I kept all my money in the family dresser under my shirts and underwear. It was all piling up there, at least one hundred *forints* (Hungarian currency) at the time. My father's favorite pastime on Sunday morning was to count my money, and he knew better than I did how much there was. After I defected, he took my money, left my mother, and moved to the next town where he bought a lot and built a small house on it. This was the worst consequence my defection brought to my family, all thanks to my calorie money.

By the national racing rules, you have three years to be in the junior category at 16, 17, and 18 years old. The first year, I overlapped with my brother who was two years older. He won everything, and I was a close second. In 1956 at the Junior National Championships, the Törő brothers won more gold medals than all the other clubs combined. In 1957 and 1958, I continued to add to the Törő's gold medal collection. After winning every event I entered at the 1958 Junior Championships, two weeks later the national coach invited me to the Senior National Championships. It was a great honor to be invited and it meant that the coaches had an eye on me for the future. The excitement was high in the family; both *Törő* boys were being considered for the national team.

At the 1958 Senior National Championships, my brother won the 500-meter single-canoe event. I made the final and was fifth, not a bad result for a junior. In the 10,000-meter distance event, I was leading the pack at 2,000 meters when the more experienced senior paddlers started to reel me in. I ended up fifth, again not a bad result. After the championships, the national coach invited me to join the national senior team to go to the winter conditioning training camp in Tata. It was a six-week-long camp in January and part of February in 1959. Some of my club friends did not recognize me when I came back from this camp, as I was bigger and stronger all around. Hard training, good food, and a lot of rest helped me build up my physique. My confidence grew as well. I was ready to have a good racing year in 1959 and 1960, an Olympic year.

CHAPTER 4
My First Olympics: Rome

Before the National Championships in 1959, Farkas Imre approached me. He had recently split from his partner in the two-man canoe. The year before, they were 5th in the 1,000-meter Olympic distance at the World Championships and were badly beaten by a younger Hungarian team. His partner thought it was time to change. Farkas had a bronze medal from the 1956 Olympic Games in Melbourne with this partner at the 10,000-meter distance. He was a left-handed paddler and one of the best steersmen in the country and I was honored that he asked me to try out with him. He did not like to paddle in the single, preferring the double. Not having much experience in the double, I had to get used to this boat and the rhythm of another paddler. In the front, at the stroke position, I set the pace and the cadence. The double requires a special feel for balance because of the offset position of the two paddlers. This balance is very delicate, especially when you try to go fast. Luckily, my partner had many years of experience and helped me to quickly adjust to the boat.

During our first outing, all the coaches came along in the motorboat to see how we were doing. My adrenaline was up, and I wanted to look good so the coaches would approve of this partnership. After a long paddling session, we came back to the dock and the head coach said it was up to us. My new partner said, "Let's give it a try." The news spread very quickly on the river. A new double canoe would enter the competition featuring Farkas, the best steersman, paired with me, the best junior single paddler (As you will see later, we lived up to their fears).

The 1959 National Championships were the last selection races for the team that would compete at Duisburg (West Germany) in the European Championships. With great anticipation, we entered and won the 500-meter event. However, this distance was not on the European Championship program.

The 1,000-meter was and that was won by my brother and his partner. We came in third, so we were left at home, my brother and his partner making the team. Unfortunately, at the training camps after the nationals, my brother got a summer cold, which worsened and affected his heart lining. They did not race at the European Championships; they were relegated to the alternate position and the number two team got to race. It took Lajos several years to recover from this illness and he never came back to paddling again. My dream to paddle with him in the double evaporated. One good thing resulted from his illness—he did not get drafted into the Army.

My brother, Lajos, with his partner, winning the C2 1000m at the Nationals, 1959.

At the European Championships, Farkas' old partner paired with a new partner and won the 1,000-meter double event at the Olympic distance, making them the favorites for the 1960 Rome Games. To edge out a proven team for a spot on the Olympic team is very hard. Farkas and I discussed this situation. He thought that winning the 500 at the National Championships indicated that we had speed and, being young, I would only get better and adjust to the longer distance. He encouraged me to stay with him. The winter conditioning training camp came and I emerged very strong and perhaps a bit overconfident.

That winter was harsh. In early March, when we usually began to paddle on the water, it wasn't possible because there were still ice sheets floating by. The team coach decided to train in Italy with a selected team on the Olympic course for two weeks until the situation at home improved, but Farkas and I were not invited, which made us pretty mad. As soon as the team left for Italy, we hit the water twice a day. It was hard, cold, and brutal! We had to dodge ice floes on the Danube and feared for the safety of our fragile boat more than our own safety.

Many times, there was ice on our paddles and frost on our hands, and we did not wear gloves. After two weeks, we had accumulated a lot of quality mileage, and our motivation was high. We knew what we had to do and who we had to beat. When the team returned from Rome, we learned that the weather there had not been cooperative and they hadn't paddled as much as they intended. However, it had been a good shopping trip and of that, we were jealous.

The regular four-week on-water training camp was in April, just north of Budapest on the Danube. There, every week at least once, we had time trials on a 2,000-meter course with one turn. Farkas and I never lost a time trial and won all the selection races. The coach had no choice but to enter us in the international races, where we had to prove over and over that we could handle the pressure to be considered for the Olympic Team selection. I was confident in my partner, knowing he had gone through all this before, and I enjoyed being on the winning team. Farkas enjoyed showing his ex-partner that he had made a mistake in dumping him.

The spring training camp's daily routine was quite simple. We woke up at 7 am and, after we assembled, recorded our weight and pulse rate on a big chart posted on the wall. The girls hated to do that because we always teased them about their weight. The coach often stood at the scale so that we could not cheat. Then we went for a short jog of a couple kilometers along the river, which often turned into an all-out sprint at the end. After the jog, we had breakfast and a short rest before going out to morning practice on the water, which lasted about an hour and a half. Afterwards, we took a quick shower and had lunch in the cafeteria. In the afternoon, we had free time until about three thirty. Usually we read, played card games, or even took a nap, while the young, very energetic ones played soccer; I was among them.

The afternoon training session was very hard. It consisted of a warm-up with heavy weight lifting and other exercises that the coach dreamed up, then we were on to the water for at least two hours with the coaches supervising from a motorboat. Exhausted, we came off the water, had a quick shower, then dinner in the cafeteria followed by free time. In the evening, watching TV was the favorite activity. Television broadcasting was just beginning in Hungary, so there were only two stations to choose from: the news or Soviet movies. It was boring, but that's how we killed time until it was time to sleep. Only the married team members were allowed to leave the camp, and even then, only on weekends.

At this training camp, my life changed—I fell in love. I was almost twenty and had never had a serious relationship with a girl. Occasionally, I went to the movies with a coed group of the club members, but we were always in a group. Dating never occurred to me; it took too much time from paddling, where my focus was. Emotional involvement would have been too much of a distraction from canoeing, and I couldn't allow that to happen. But in this training camp, I really got the love bug. One evening, we organized a fun performance by hanging a sheet and creating shadow skits that mocked our coaches. Needless to say, I was one of the lead actors. We needed some diversion! These training camps could be very boring, and we had to create our own entertainment. After the performance, as we were walking back to our room, one of the kayak girls that I liked and often teased kissed me good night on the mouth. I could not sleep that night or many nights following.

Farkas noticed the change and confronted me on this issue. I lied to him that there was nothing happening and nothing to be concerned about. A couple of days later, I had a chance to talk to the girl about that kiss, and she said it was sincere. That was the last thing I wanted to hear, since any commitment besides my paddling was out of question. We were only a month away from the first selection trials and the boat was moving fast. Our potential to make the Olympic team looked promising. My partner was eager to get revenge on his old partner, and I was the new kid on the block and wanted very much to be an Olympian. Adding to the turmoil, my coach pulled me over after one workout and cautioned me about having sex with a teammate during the training camp. I suppose someone had tipped him off, but I told him paddling was more important to me than anything else in the world and

MY FIRST OLYMPICS: ROME

I wouldn't jeopardize my chances. At the earliest opportunity, I told that girl that we should go slow and not be obvious. She agreed that love should not be mixed together with paddling. However, this was easier said than done, as we were together in that training camp 24/7, and our sexual desire was strong. *"Use your sexual energy to pull harder,"* my partner said, and I did. I was glad when that training camp was over and we went back to our respective clubs. *Not seeing her every minute would change my emotions*, I thought. However, I was wrong, and it did not. Suppressing all my emotions about her was harder than the training, but I had to do it. Everyone was telling me it would affect my performance.

Winning the first selection race for the Hungarian Olympic team, 1960. Photo credit: Hemző Károly.

Farkas and I won our first two selection races with decisive margins over the previous year's world champions, and our Olympic berth looked promising. I wanted to show the whole world that I was not in love and nothing could affect me. But at the same time, I did it for her. I wanted her to be proud of me, and she was. My hope was to get on the traveling team so we would spend the summer apart, but my luck did not hold up. She also did very well in the double kayak event and made the traveling team with her partner. Things were getting complicated, but I was proud of her for making the team.

Winning the domestic selection races did not assure us an Olympic berth. The final selection was based on two more international races and one more domestic selection race. I pretty much kissed my work place goodbye. The Sport Minister issued a "leave with pay" document for all potential Olympic team members, so I didn't have to punch in and out on the hated time clock anymore. My fellow workers were proud of me, but envious as well.

If I recall correctly, my first ever international race was in Romania. It was a dual meet. Based on the previous year's results, their team was very strong, particularly in the Olympic canoeing events. I was looking forward to some strong international competition to test our preparation, but at the same time I was scared of potential failure. We needed to prove that we could hold up under pressure. I was sure that Farkas could handle it; he was an Olympic medalist. On the other hand, I was just a "green" paddler without any international experience.

Getting on the "traveling team" was exciting. It was the first time for me to represent my country at an international canoeing competition. This was the race that I had dreamed about since I joined the canoe club. The traveling team position did not assure an Olympic berth, but it was definitely the first step, and the coaches kept emphasizing this to keep us on our toes. This consistent reminder did not help me; it added to the already mounting pressure.

The race in Romania turned out to be as we hoped for. Farkas and I won the double canoe (C2) 1,000-meter event, not by much but enough to come in ahead of the other Hungarian team. Farkas felt that he was back in his "old" Olympic shape, which really helped my confidence. After the race, the coaches were satisfied with our result, again emphasizing the importance of each race

With my partner, Farkas, winning the C2 1000m in Grunau, East Germany, 1960.

for the Olympic selection. Returning home, the press picked up our result and it was satisfying to read our names and racing analysis in the newspaper as potential Olympic entries.

The coaches announced that there would be two more international races in our preparation schedule, and based on their results, they would announce the Olympic team for the 1960 Rome Summer Olympic Games. There wasn't much time to train because of the tight traveling days, which actually helped me to recover.

The next two international races produced the same results with some improvements in our time, which was very encouraging. We consistently beat the other Hungarian team, assuring us the number one spot on the list for consideration on the Olympic team. The coaches paid more attention to us, and we appreciated their attention, hoping for more time improvements before the Olympic Games. By mid-July, the team was done with all the pre-Olympic races and the coach announced the Olympic Training Camp squad. When I heard my name, I was very excited. After all the first-place finishes, it was not a surprise, but I was one step closer to being an Olympian.

On July 26th, 1960, I received an official letter from the Secretary of the Hungarian Olympic Committee inviting me to be on the Hungarian Olympic delegation for the XVIIth Summer Olympic Games in Rome, Italy, held between August 25th and September 11th, 1960. This letter of invitation assured me of being an Olympian forever. The canoeing team was moved to the official Olympic training camp in the town of Ráckeve, a small town on the little Danube (*Kis Duna*). The team took over the local school with classrooms set up to serve as our accommodations. It was not the Hilton by any means, but it was adequate. The main thing was that the river water was clean and calm, and this part of the country was a favorite spot for the canoeing community. Many national championships were held here, so we knew the water very well. We did time trials twice a week on a 1,000-meter buoyed course.

In early August, we learned that we were scheduled to depart on August 24th for Rome. Three weeks of hard training remained, and the weather was great, as I recall. We paddled twice a day with an additional strength training workout. The married team members could go home on Sunday, but they had to report back Monday morning. There was not much entertainment in town and no TV, so we entertained ourselves by posing for muscle man pictures, some fishing, and card games. We occasionally went to town to the theater or to have a pint of beer at the local pub. The coaches did not like us doing that, though they frequented the pubs themselves. One of the older team members had a tape player with all the latest Italian songs (*schlagers*) that we listened to over and over as part of our preparation for the upcoming trip to Rome. We got fairly good at singing them phonetically!

Fooling around in the training camp.

In our boredom, we also started practicing how to get on the podium and accept our anticipated medals. We constructed a makeshift podium and played the Olympic hymn as we stood up on the highest platform. For Farkas and me, only the gold medal was on our mind. We had beaten all the teams we had raced against that summer: the Romanians (our arch enemies), the Czechs, the Poles, the Germans, and the Scandinavians. It was clear to us that we would get a medal, and likely, the gold one.

One day, the support team came

from Budapest, bringing us some books about Rome, including the historical sights we might want to see, and a language book to learn some phrases. Also, they took our measurements for the official tailored uniform. The Olympic team was always outfitted with tailored suits and shoes. It is known that the Hungarian Olympic team is traditionally one of the best dressed teams at the Opening Ceremony.

The boat builder came and brought us a brand new two-man canoe. We had not expected a new boat, so this was a great surprise and an emotional lift. We set up the kneeling platform and foot braces and anxiously launched the boat. We were pumped up to try it out! The coaches followed us in the motorboat. We were moving really fast when suddenly the boat lurched to a stop, accompanied by the terrible sound of ripping wood, as I was thrown onto the front deck. We had struck a submerged pole and torn up the boat, just like what happened to the Titanic. Needless to say, the coaches were not too happy. My partner said it was a bad omen to sink a boat before the Olympic Games, but I shrugged it off. The boat builder, a master craftsman, took it back and four days later showed up with the boat repaired so well that you could not tell that it had been damaged. We launched again, and this time we were more careful. Anytime you get a new boat, you feel faster and we felt sure this boat would help us make our Olympic dreams come true.

In my 1960 Olympic parade uniform.

On the tarmac at the Budapest airport ready to depart for the 1960 Rome Olympic Games.

Departure day was getting close. We got our uniforms and proudly tried them on. We packed the boats on a trailer to be driven to Rome. The day before leaving, we went home to show off our uniforms and the other things we got as members of the Hungarian Olympic team. There was a reception at Parliament where we took the Olympic Oath, promising to do our best and represent our country honorably. The next day, we gathered in the city and were bussed to the airport where a big crowd of supporters came to send off the team. My mother and my brother, Lajos, came. I was sad knowing that my brother's dream had shattered with his illness and our dream to race together would always be only a dream, but he said he was very proud of me and wished me good luck in Rome. He was getting married in the fall, and I promised to bring back his wedding rings. My mother had tears of joy in her eyes—her little boy who should have been a girl was now an Olympian.

We boarded one of the Hungarian Airline's Russian-made (Ilyushin Il-14) airplanes and were off to the XVIIth Olympic Games, my first Olympiad! The plane ride was exciting—looking out the windows seeing the blue Adriatic Sea and the Italian peninsula and the famous architectural wonders of Rome as we approached the city. Those images are imbedded in my memory forever.

As I recall, Rome's Leonardo DaVinci airport was very busy. It was newly built for the Olympic Games. Our Iljushin Il-14 airplane stood out like a sore

MY FIRST OLYMPICS: ROME

1960 Olympic canoeing venue, Lake Albano's grandstand.

thumb among the many modern Boeing airplanes carrying other Olympians from all over the world. We were issued our credentials, and the organizers rushed us to the Olympic Village, a newly built housing project. Farkas and I settled into a very comfortable apartment with two bedrooms, our home for the next two weeks.

The coach told us that after lunch we would go out to the racing course for the first time. Lake Albano (*Lago Albano*) is a beautiful oval-shaped volcanic crater lake. The town, Castel Gondalfo, is the locale of the Pope's summer residence and is on the crater's rim—a truly magnificent setting for the canoeing and rowing venue. As our bus rolled through the gated boathouse area, our amazement was even greater—a brand-new facility with a wonderful view waited for us. We found our section in the boathouse and saw that our boats had arrived and were already on the racks. I was very excited and anxious to get on the water. Our preliminaries started in just two days and the coach had decided we would not march in the Opening Ceremony. Disappointing, as I was at my first Olympic Games and wouldn't be able to participate in the biggest celebration of the Games which I had heard so much about from my older teammates. The Opening Ceremony is a melting pot of all the best athletes in the world. It is a celebration of unity and hope that the next two weeks of fair competition would bring them even closer together. However, I

At the Rome Olympic Village entrance.

figured it was a small price to pay for getting a medal and we could still watch it on TV. Rome was the first commercially live televised Summer Olympic Games in history. It was a new and exciting opportunity to be able to watch the Olympic Games in real time.

The tarmac in the front of the boathouse was very hot (over 40 degrees celsius) as we carried the boat to the launching dock, nearly burning our feet. But the first couple of strokes felt magical on that deep, pristine water. The last day before the preliminaries, we had a light workout with a couple of sprints, and felt good, ready for tomorrow. After returning to the Olympic Village, we ate at the Hungarian cafeteria. The Hungarian team always brings a good chef to cook for the athletes as part of the official delegation. In the Olympic Village, he has a small place to prepare good Hungarian cuisine for the athletes and for the delegation officials. We even had some good Hungarian wine once in a while. We could have had other choices in the international cafeteria but we did not want to risk digestive problems before the race.

In the middle of the Olympic Village, just across from the Hungarian cafeteria, was the Orange Club, a dancing and music entertainment hall where the male and female athletes could meet. It was truly an international gathering for the world's young athletes. In those days, the male and female athletes lived separately in the Village, with the female quarters surrounded by high fence and a security gate. At the Orange Club, the latest rock-and-roll records were playing loudly with familiar Italian melodies mixed in. After dinner, this place was jammed with athletes, their hormones on fire. A few girls preened for attention, mostly Americans. One night, a black American girl was dancing with a white guy in their USA shirts. Their dance was X-rated, even by today's standards. They crawled all over each other to the rhythm of the rock-and-roll music. She looked like a Nubian Queen, and the whole Hungarian team was in love with her. I learned that her name was Willye White, a sprinter on the USA relay team from Chicago, and she was only sixteen years old. Some twenty years later, I was fortunate enough to meet Willye at a US Olympic Committee meeting and told her the story of how much we loved and admired her during the Rome Games. She replied, "Keep talking, baby. Keep talking." The more I got to know her, the more I learned of her many fine qualities as an outstanding human being as well as athlete. I was glad that I had the chance to remember her in her youth.

The Opening Ceremony was on TV so we went to the Orange Club to see it. The Village was deserted except for a few stragglers like us who had elected not to participate. We recognized some of the kayak and canoe athletes from other countries. Watching the Opening Ceremony made me sad. Would I have another opportunity to be part of such pageantry? The Olympic Opening Ceremony creates a spiritual bond between Olympians, and can only be experienced every four years. It is a global celebration of elite athletes who have sacrificed so much to rise to the highest level of their sport and to be the best in the world. Each participating nation proudly displays their athletes marching behind their national flag. During this long ceremony, the energy builds to the point of explosion, symbolized by the lighting of the caldron. Days later, this peace and harmony will turn into fierce competition in the spirit of the Olympic creed.

Long after the Opening Ceremony was over, the teams slowly made their way back to the Village cafeteria for dinner. The athletes were exhausted, but as they straggled back into the Orange Bar, we could see the glowing smiles on their faces. The Games had now begun. Our coach was right about the Opening Ceremony being very exhausting, but they are emotionally uplifting as well.

We returned to our apartment and tried to sleep. The team doctor came to give us a vitamin B-12 shot to boost our energy for tomorrow, he said. I have never liked needles, so I got lightheaded and almost fainted—not a good thing to do before your race. Needless to say, I slept fitfully that night with many things rolling around in my head, many unanswered questions. The next two days would bring the answers.

On Friday, August 26, 1960, the racing started with preliminary heats. We arrived early at Lake Albano. The weather was perfect, with a slight breeze from the side, not strong enough to be a concern. Canoeing, being an outdoor sport, is always affected by weather and on racing day, it's the first thing we check. As someone light of weight, I always liked a tail wind.

In the boathouse, the team spirit was very high. We all knew that this was show time! The coaches gave us a pep talk and then everyone went off to get their equipment ready. As teams started coming back from their events, they had big smiles on their faces. Everyone was advancing to the semi-finals or finals. Then it was our time.

Farkas and I were in the second heat of the 1000m double canoe, and this heat appeared to be the weaker of the two. The coaches helped carry our equipment to the dock and wished us good luck as we stepped into our canoe and pushed off. As I

In the front of the boathouse, Lake Albano, 1960 Rome Olympic Games.

recall, we didn't talk much as we approached the starting line, but Farkas tried to calm my nerves by saying we'd been performing at Olympic levels all summer and this should be no problem. "The most important thing is to make the finals directly." I was thinking that I had to show him that he'd made the right choice in teaming up with me. As we backed into the starting platform, my heart rate was very high. I looked down the course over the clear, glassy water and could barely see the finish line at the horizon. The weather was warm and calm, and I knew that we couldn't ask for better conditions. On top of all my other thoughts and emotions, I was just plain thrilled to finally be here and realizing my dream of competing at an Olympic Games. I knew my friends and family were right there with me, particularly my brother, Lajos. He should have been on the team, too. Then the starting gun went off.

After a good start, I concentrated on a good cadence and I felt strong. After a while, I took a glance around to assess our position. We were ahead at 500 meters and I felt like we were in control. The rest of the race was spent maintaining our position. We won with a time of 4:29.42, just 0.2 seconds in front of the French team. Even though that was close at the end, it put us directly into the finals. Farkas thought that we had had a good race with the right cadence. However, our time was only the third fastest overall. In the first heat, the Russian and the Italian teams posted faster times. A meeting was called after the preliminaries where the coach congratulated us for our performance but warned us that our time was not the fastest and that we must do better in the finals. We took his comment seriously, knowing there would be a hard race ahead of us to get a medal. Farkas said, "That was only the preliminaries, we can do better. Most importantly, we are in the finals. In the final, anything can happen. It is another race." I was very exhausted after the race and I knew I could not have done much better. We went back to the Village to rest and contemplate, and I had very little sleep again that night. The next day was for the repechages and semi-finals for those boats that did not advanced directly. Farkas and I went down to the lake for a light paddle and to cheer on the team members who were racing in their semi-finals. The Hungarian team did very well in the preliminaries, and all of our boats advanced to the finals.

Monday, August 29, 1960, the day of the canoeing finals arrived. This was

Finish line sequence of the C2 1,000-meter race, 1960 Olympic Games.
Photo source: YouTube screenshots.

the day we had trained for and sacrificed everything for, the day I will never forget no matter what else happens to me. There was a TV in the boathouse so we could watch our fellow team members' performances. The first final was the men's single-kayak 1,000-meter event. The Hungarian, Szőllősi Imre, was favored to win and we had no doubts, as he had won all his races during the year. The starting gun fired and the race was on, but the Danish paddler, Erik Hansen, was ahead by 500 meters. Szőllősi began his final sprint but he could not reel Hansen in; the damage had been done and he came in second. Our team, watching the TV in the boathouse, was devastated—a sure gold medal had slipped away. Many of us cried. If Szőllősi got beat, what was in it for us? Luckily, in the next event, the single-canoe 1,000-meter, our Parti János won. We cheered in the boathouse and became more optimistic.

Finally, it was time for our race. The coaches carried the boat down for us again, and Farkas and I got on the water. It was customary to go out twenty minutes before the start to warm up and head to the start line. We did not talk much during the warm up. Then Farkas stated simply, "I would like to get another medal." I could not have agreed more and I hoped that all the practice of getting up on our makeshift podium during training camp was not wasted. I hoped that I would be adding my name to his in the Olympic history books. By the luck of the draw, we were assigned to the outside lane 8. It was a good lane from which to keep track of the competition (which was only to our left), but it had more wind and some disturbed water. We backed into the starting pontoon, and an Italian Navy cadet held on to the stern of our boat, which was the customary starting procedure. My pulse was up. Here I was, living my dream at the starting line of the Olympic Games. This was my chance to put my name in the record books forever; my chance to do my best for my country, my family, my brother, my girlfriend, and myself.

The starting gun went off. After the initial strokes and sprint, which we had practiced many times, I set a pace that I thought would be fast enough to carry us to a victory. At the 500-meter buoy line, I glanced to the left. We were crossing the line in a close 5th place! I panicked and I heard my partner's scared voice, "Let's go, we are behind!" I picked up the pace. I cannot remember too much about the next 500 meters, it hurt too much. I could faintly hear the cheering of the crowd and knew the finish line was close.

As we crossed the finish line, the Italian team next to us tipped over right at the line. According to the racing rules, if the team is attached to the boat in any way as the bow of the boat crosses the finish line, it is not a disqualification. They beat us by 0.12 of a second (4:20.77), for the silver medal! But on the far side, the Russian team was over 3 seconds ahead of us (4:17.04) for the gold medal. The officials called us to the podium, which meant we medaled with a time of 4:20.89 but as we paddled over, we were disappointed. No words were spoken, as we had expected a better result. We approached the grandstand where the podium was set up on the dock. An attendant came to hold our boat while we walked somberly over to the podium and lined up in our position behind third place. We were called up first and presented with our bronze medals. When the president of the International Canoe Federation put the medal around my neck, I felt a confusing mixture of emotions. While I was disappointed that this was not the color medal I had hoped for, it was an Olympic medal nevertheless and that was pretty thrilling. I also felt relief the racing was over and that we had placed in the top three. The picture of us on the podium reflects our feelings. (See photo insert page V.)

The Italians were exuberant with their silver, and the crowd was very appreciative for the only medal Italy won in canoeing. After hearing the despised Russian national anthem for the victors, we all congratulated each other, as is customary. As we paddled back to the boat house, I finally congratulated Farkas. He expressed his disappointment at having two bronze medals and said that this had been his last chance.

I wondered if I would I have another chance at Olympic Gold, but the answer to that had to wait four more long years. It was over for us in Rome. "Weeks to train, a day to compete, and a lifetime to remember," as the famous track coach, Ducky Drake, once said.

During the entire 1960 racing season, we had never seen this Russian nor the Italian team. We had beaten everyone else who came to the international races; however, this was little consolation for us.

The silver medal Italian team had an interesting story. They were coached by my former Hungarian club coach, Blahó Kálmán, who left Hungary during the 1956 revolution. The Italian Federation hired him to form a canoeing team (the Italians had only rowing until that time). Their Canoeing Federation was established two years before the Olympic Games. Blahó approached the Italian Navy and recruited thirty sailors (Farkas always suspected that the boat holder held onto our boat just a second too long). In three years, he put together a very strong canoe and kayak team, and his two-man canoe team had beaten us. Before the race, Blahó had said he expected the team to do well, but we hadn't taken him seriously.

After the race, we had a team meeting and the Hungarian Delegation leaders came to the boathouse to congratulate us. The team overall had exceptional results—everyone medaled and we won the total point trophy as well, which was very much appreciated by the team leaders. They told the team that the medalists could stay until the end of the Games and as a reward, we'd go sightseeing in Napoli, Pompeii, and Capri with the Modern Pentathlon Team who'd won their event. It was great news—two more weeks in Italy, more per diem money, and free entrance to all Olympic events! What else could you ask for?

Fooling around in Naples.

My girlfriend was on the team as an alternate for the women's double kayak event. After the race, she congratulated me and said that she was very proud of me. She gave me a kiss that reignited my feelings for her but, sadly, she had to go home. Since our event was over, no one cared that we were open about our relationship, and I was hoping to rekindle it.

Needless to say, the Napoli, Pompeii, and Capri tours were magnificent, with lots of good memories. But more memorable to me was the time I spent watching the other sports: track and field with Wilma Rudolph and Rafer Johnson

My niece Marika, sister-in-law Marika, myself, brother Lajos, Mother, brother Imre, and my aunt Julianna.

and Abebe Bikila, the barefooted Ethiopian Marathon runner, boxing with Cassius Clay (Muhammed Ali) and many others. It was also important to cheer for the Hungarian athletes. The camaraderie among the Hungarian athletes was outstanding.

Living in the Olympic Village after our event was unimaginable, with free room and board and unlimited travel in the city with our accreditation! This city of ancient civilization and culture made a great impression on me. At the entrance was a statue, *Lupa Capitolina,* depicting the twin brothers Romulus and Ramus suckling on the she-wolf who raised them. They were the founders of ancient Rome according to myth, and this statue was the symbol of the Rome Olympics.

Admittance to the Village required only wearing your uniform and the occasional accreditation check. Security was very relaxed compared to today's protocols, which made the whole Olympic experience much more pleasurable. I am glad that I was a part of the 1960 Games, perhaps the only "pure" Olympic experience I ever had.

MY FIRST OLYMPICS: ROME

Receiving my Rome Diploma from the Hungarian Canoe Federation president.

It was very hard to leave Rome and the Games after we participated in the Closing Ceremony on September 11th, 1960. That was a magical event. We marched onto the field with boundless enthusiasm, friendship, harmony and peace—everything that the Olympic spirit stands for. Yet there was a somber undertone, knowing that this special time was over. And for many, this would be the last time they saw their friends and arch rivals. They had traded hats, uniforms, and souvenirs which they would cherish forever, reminders of the spiritual bond created during the competition (I have many memorabilia that I collected during these Games still in my possession). Many proudly wore their medals, not to show off but as symbols of their accomplishment. After the cauldron was extinguished, the athletes milled around almost aimlessly, in a daze, trying to prolong the magic. Some were already dreaming of coming back in another four years to find it again.

Arriving back at the Budapest airport, the Hungarian Olympic team had a wonderful reception. All the Communist Party officials were there to congratulate the team for their patriotic performance and for all the medals they brought home. My family was there to meet me along with hundreds of other families and well-wishers. Lajos was very emotional about my success, and I wanted him to know that this medal was partly his and that I was pursuing the dream for both of us. My mother was crying with joy and gave her little boy a big hug.

However, over the next days I felt a huge vacuum in my life and soul. There was nothing more to do for a while except to go back to normal life (work). I was at the peak of my physical being. What was I going to do with my energy and pent-up testosterone? There were no more serious competitions to train for until the winter training camp. My partner went back to his club and I returned to mine. I had to resume my work in the factory (which I thought I had left for good) from 6 am to 2 pm every day. It was a discouraging mental change. My coworkers were proud to work with an Olympian and appreciated my gifts (usually a box of Gilette razor blades). I was hoping for a promotion, but it never came. My supervisor jealously remarked, "You wrote your name into the Olympic history book, but that does not translate into the work place." He tried to talk me into joining the Communist party, pointing out that it was the only way to advance in the work place. He thought I would be a career factory worker. I declined.

The daily work became a big drag, and I felt demoralized. My social life wasn't any better. I still lived with my parents and had a long commute to work. Some of my teammates talked about having apartments and buying cars, which were slowly becoming available for private use. I did not have the financial means, so I could only dream about it. The peer pressure continued to mount, but I felt my future was bleak. Reality had reared its ugly head. My girlfriend returned to her club and back to work as well. We started to live different lives—she involved in her club's social life and I in mine. Occasionally, we met on the weekends. Canoeing was still my priority in life, and against all odds, I was totally committed to improve upon my international results and my calorie money to prove that I was still an Olympian.

A couple of weeks after our arrival home, we were invited to the Parliament to be honored for our participation and performance. All the Olympic medalists received the *Szocialista Munkáért Érdemérem kitüntetés*, a distinguished medal for the work we did for the Socialist system. It was a big deal for the Communist Party and its members, but I was not too excited about it. When I showed to my father, he said, "Next thing I know, you will join the Party." I assured him that would never happen.

After the 1960 Olympic Games, my partner's club organized an award trip to Potsdam, East Germany, for the club members who had done exceptionally well that year. It was also an end-of-the-season race. Although I was not a member of the club, thanks to my canoeing partner, the club leaders invited me to go along and compete. It was a fall competition and not too serious, but was nevertheless a foreign trip, which we all craved. It was certainly a lot better than working in the factory. The city of Potsdam is a short distance from Berlin and famous for the signing of the treaty after WWII. A trip just to East Germany would not have been so great, but Berlin was another story. The city was divided into four sectors according to the Potsdam Treaty. One was the famous American Sector. Some of the older athletes had visited the American Sector and said that it is something to see. As a matter of fact, you could take the S-Bon train from Berlin's Soviet Sector across the border to the American Sector, they claimed. Now that sounded exiting!

We took an overnight train from Budapest to Berlin, and then on to Potsdam. By the time we had reached the Czechoslovakian border, the train had almost emptied out because most Hungarians could not cross. We just read, played cards, and otherwise passed the time until we arrived. Potsdam is a very pretty place on the outskirts of Berlin, with lots of waterways and forests. We stayed in one of the boat clubs, and didn't mind sleeping on cots and having a communal bathroom. We did very well in the competition, winning the two events we entered and receiving trophies and medals.

However, the biggest excitement was that a group of us decided to go to the American Sector one evening. The anticipation was great; could we do it?

What if we were detained for illegally crossing the border? There were many other questions on our minds, but the potential experience was worth the risk, we rationalized. So, we went to the S-Bon station. One of the athletes spoke reasonably good German and he asked all the questions. The station manager sold us tickets and told us where to get off the train—after the Zoological Garten station, there would be the Kurfürstendamm Strauss in the shopping district of Charlottenburg. Just what we wanted! But the station attendant warned us to be punctual and not board earlier trains. The German railroad is very famous for being on time. If the train is scheduled to be at the station at 12:34, it's going to be there at 12:34, not a minute earlier or a minute later. We were anxiously waiting for our train to arrive and sure enough, it was right on time. It was late afternoon and slowly getting dark. The Soviet Sector was gray and desolate, with no traffic on the streets and no pedestrians. It was almost a ghost town, and the scars of the war were everywhere. A few street lights barely illuminated the roadways.

Our excitement increased as we approached the border. The conductor came and looked at our passports and tickets and didn't say anything. We looked at each other. It looked like smooth sailing to West Berlin. As we crossed the border, the scenery changed dramatically. From the train, we could see the glowing panorama of the American Sector. I had never seen anything like it. Later on, when I was traveling west on US Highway 10 and approaching Las Vegas from the mountain pass, I had the same kind of vista with a glowing panorama of city lights.

Kurfurstendamm Strasse lived up to our expectations! Disembarking from the station, the glowing neon movie theater marquees, department stores, and all the advertising were almost too much to absorb. Also, the burned-out ruins of the famous cathedral, Keiser Wilhelm, which was preserved as a symbol of human suffering, was gorgeously illuminated. One of the athletes who had had several trips to the West led us down the avenue. The first order of business was to buy a glass of Coca Cola, and as I recall, it was about twenty-five cents. In those days, I could get talked into anything. I had never had Coca Cola before and was told that it was the favorite drink of the western world. I gave it a shot, but it tasted awful, just like the throat medication my mother used to give me in the winter time when I had strep throat. I did not like it then and I do not like it now. What really bothered me was that I had just wasted twenty-five cents. It may not seem like much, but in those days, when my per diem was about two dollars a day, it was a lot to me.

Foreign money was not easy to come by. Hungarian currency, the *forint*, was not convertible on the international market, so any foreign currency purchase had to be done illegally. The government was very strict about this and enforced the law. Many athletes and other travelers to foreign lands got caught and punished severely. Despite of all that, the illegal market for foreign currency was well established. People always smuggled in American dollars, West German marks, and British pounds. Most of the connections were through Hungarians who left during the 1956 revolution or before and were living in the West. They came to Austria to meet their families and gave them money to bring into the country; old grandmothers were rich in those days, they said.

One of the athletes on the team had a connection and he supplied us with American dollars. I had actually seen my first American dollar many years before, when I was about ten years old. One day, my father came home from the market and proudly pulled a one-dollar bill from his pocket. We could not believe it, and we admired it like it would have been Christ's shroud. We were touching the Free World. "This is an evil product of the capitalist system," he said sarcastically. Mother was very concerned about him going to prison and told him to get rid of it before an informer found out. I wanted to keep it forever, but the next day he sold it. It seemed like he just wanted to show off that he was able to do illegal things.

Our friend on the team seemed to have a steady supply of American dollars and charged a great deal for them, but it was worth every penny. Buying the dollar in Hungary and then converting it to more profitable goods in the West was worth the investment. Wrist watches, women's nylon stockings, and razor blades were a few common items easily resold in Hungary for great profit. It was definitely illegal and one took much risk to smuggle these items in, but the financial reward was satisfying. We also got great satisfaction from defying the communist system. It was sort of a personal revolution.

Walking around Kurfurstendamm Strasse was an unbelievable experience—the street was a showcase and advertisement for the western capitalist system. The motion picture *West Side Story* was playing in one of the theaters with the marquee so bright it was almost blinding. We had heard of this movie and had listened to the soundtrack through the Free Europe radio station. We had to see this picture, but it was a big decision. Almost all of my per diem was spent for the ticket to *West Side Story*, but it was worth the price. One of the athletes with a bit more free cash also bought the soundtrack, which we listened to for many years in the training camps.

It occurred to me, while walking around West Berlin, that it might not be too bad to live in the West. I could see these types of things every day. However, another Olympic Games was coming in three years, and I wanted to improve on my results.

After the theater, we walked around and window shopped. I still had $40 in my pocket and my friend suggested we go into a department store to spend the money. It was amazing to see all the stores open until midnight. This was unheard of in Hungary, and the selection of merchandise was mind-boggling. On the top of all that, everything was on sale for half-price: buy one, get one free. (I wondered if we could get only the second one for free!) We split up in the department store and agreed to meet an hour later to catch the train back to our accommodations on the east side. I purchased five inexpensive wrist watches—they were gold-plated with flashy metal wrist bands, but a decently good resale item. In addition, I picked up a half-dozen women's stockings and a couple packages of razor blades for shaving, which was all I had money for.

On the train back to Budapest, we all bragged about our purchases and the potential profit we would make back home. This was the first time I had tried such a deal and was apprehensive about the border crossing. The older guys assured me that it was easy if we could get through customs (a big IF). Train border crossings were particularly notorious, and there were many stories circulating among the athletes of strip searches and jail time. Often, the border guard made the passengers switch trains at the border to make smuggling more difficult, and we were very worried about this possibility.

The usual question from the border guards was "What time is it?" and the automatic reflex reaction was to look at your new wrist watch or wrist watches, depending on how many you had on your arm. We practiced the response "I do not know" to prevent this mistake. My partner, who had five years of experience and a proven smuggling record, suggested we hide our goods behind the heating grill. It seemed like a good ploy, unless they made us change trains. We would just have to work quickly to retrieve the goods, he said. As soon as we closed the heating grill, I could not take my eyes off it. My whole life savings and business investment, as well as my future were hiding behind that grill.

At the border, my pulse rate was up and heavy sweat beaded my forehead. The official came and asked the question "What time is it?" One of the athletes, our decoy, looked at his Russian wrist watch and answered. The official looked at his watch and shook his head. He must have thought that we were amateurs and had come from East Germany. He never suspected that we had visited West Berlin's American Sector. So, he let us alone and went on to the next cabin, and the sigh of relief was loud in our compartment. My first foray into smuggling was successful. I made a threefold profit on my investment at home. It was beginner's luck, which continued to follow me throughout my life. But just a few months later, two modern pentathletes got busted with dozens of wrist watches and paid the price.

As the years went on, I got braver and had more money to invest. The market was hot for Western goods. I got portable radios, tape players, 8 mm movie cameras, and other fashionable goods not available in Hungary. All were sold for good profit, and my pile of money grew in the family cupboard under the well-washed towels. I considered myself rich, although I really didn't care about the money. Acquiring it was the challenge, and I liked to show off my latest goods at the club. Secretly, I was dreaming of having my own place somewhere in the city or even a car, but that would require a lot more smuggling.

After 1956, the government relaxed the laws about having private cars. Fiats and VW bugs started to appear on the streets. I remember the first private car I saw belonged to the rabbi of the downtown synagogue. The story was that he got it as a gift from a US Jewish organization. It was a canary-yellow Corvair parked in the front of the synagogue, and a very a popular attraction, with people lining up to admire it. Then, slowly, some of the top athletes—soccer players, fencers, and water polo players—bought used cars in Germany and Austria. Of course, we all were very jealous, particularly those of us who had to spend two hours each way on the streetcar.

As a young man and a top athlete, I felt it was essential to have the most fashionable clothing, basically to show-off. I bought fabric from Italy for a tailor-designed suit and shirt, as well as a fine pair of pointed leather shoes. The shoes were so uncomfortable to wear, I almost cried. They had very thin soles. They must have been no thicker than one sixteenth of an inch. Still, it was worth it to be fashionable. I would wear them to the club parties during the bitter cold Hungarian winters with very thin socks, and my feet were like ice. It took hours to warm them up in a tub of hot water at home. My mother used to scold me, but she obviously did not understand that it was a small price to pay.

At least I didn't fall for the famous Italian shoe scam. A group of athletes brought into Hungary several pairs of black, very fancy-looking, pointy-toed leather dress shoes and sold them to eager buyers. They were very inexpensive, which made them a fantastic deal. However, those fancy shoes turned out to have been made for the funeral trade and not meant to ever be danced in. They immediately began to fall apart, particularly in the rain, and sellers were just as surprised as the buyers. I'm not aware of any refunds being made.

CHAPTER 5
Between Olympic Games

1961 was a bad year for me. Earlier in the year at the winter training camp, I did not take things very seriously. I goofed off a bit too much and was too confident of my position on the team. The coaches and my Olympic partner warned me to change my attitude, but I was sure I could make it all up on the water in the spring. I still paddled double with Farkas, and we were planning on making the 1961 European Championship team in the double. Sometimes I went back to my club and paddled the single, just as a diversion. I liked to paddle in the single, however it required steering maneuvers that I did not have to do in the double. So, when I went back to the double, my rhythm was upset. Farkas noticed and I told him that when he retired, I would probably switch to the single.

The final selection race for the European Championship was at the 1961 Nationals. We concentrated on the 1,000-meter event because that was our specialty. We were ahead at 500 meters, but some young teams eventually reeled us in. We finished fifth, way behind, and we were very disappointed. Farkas suggested that we try the long-distance event and we did. It produced a similar result, a sixth-place finish. The national coach sat us down and talked to us about our future, and was particularly hard on me for not putting in enough intensive work. However, he still put us on the European Championship Team as alternates, not based on the year's results but due to our past Olympic experience. The championships were held in Poznan, Poland, not exactly a good place for my smuggling business. The Polish economy was in just as bad shape as the Hungarian economy. However, the team did very well, and some new faces emerged on the scene, some who might prove to be tough competition in the future. Since we did not race, my calorie money was reduced, and that really hurt my pocket. My father did not like it and neither

Waiting at the airport to depart for Poznan, 1961.

did I. He told me to do better or quit, but quitting was not an option, so I had to get better. I thought I might also try the single event.

During the championships, my girlfriend (who was also on the team) and I discussed our relationship and future together. I was too afraid to commit, but we discussed the possibility of leaving together. To where? My concern was how this would affect my future in the sport, since I was only 22 years old and figured I had many good competitive years ahead of me. I wanted to compete and make another Olympic team, so my girlfriend and I decided to go separate ways. I learned later that the coaching staff was very instrumental in encouraging her to break off the relationship. She actually decided to leave the team and to take a rest from kayaking. Left alone, I poured all my energy and sorrow in to my paddling strokes and hopes for a better future.

I was still relatively young and optimistic that in the single canoe I could do better. Competition in the single canoe was very strong, so I had to work on my technique—feeling the boat's response and steering—as well as getting into better condition.

After the 1961 European Championships, I had to go back to the factory. Since there was no training camp or competition, I had to work from six in the morning until two in the afternoon every day except Sunday. My coworkers had some sarcastic comments about my failing results, which I had to ignore. However, they also knew that when I did not travel, they didn't get the razor blades I gave to them after each trip. I continued to go to the club in the afternoon to work on my technique in the single. My partner decided that that was enough for him, and he retired, resigning from the team. We had a big party for him, and it was sad to see him go. That move left me in the single canoe. I did not mind at all, but I had no single results from the past two racing seasons as a senior, only from my junior years. I decided that I would concentrate on the single in 1962 for the World Championships, which were to be in Essen, West Germany, a strong incentive for me! I informed the coach, who agreed reluctantly to let me try. He still considered me to be a double paddler and told me I would have to prove to him (and the team, and myself) that I deserved that position. I knew I had to work hard to fight my way out of this box I had gotten in. I had a lot of work ahead of me.

A rule change also made my decision to go with the single easier. In 1962, the International Federation Racing Rule Committee changed the length dimension for the two-man canoe from 5.2 to 6.5 meters. The longer boat favored heavier paddlers. If I wanted to continue racing in the double, I had to find a big, strong paddler to steer the canoe. In my club, all the young paddlers had already paired up and other clubs did not want to release any of their competitors.

January 1962 came around, and the team went to winter training camp as usual, first to the mountains for skiing, and later to the National Training Center for conditioning. I was not a skier so that time wasn't very productive for me, but after three weeks at the conditioning camp I was one of the top three in the testing results. I felt good with my progress. At the end of February, we came back to Budapest, but it was still too early to get on the water. We practiced in the paddling tank and worked on conditioning twice a day until the Danube opened up.

I was the first on the water with my new single, which my club made for me, anticipating my upcoming results. As far as they were concerned, I was the best paddler in the club. On the World Championship program, there were two distances for single canoe, the 1,000-meter (the Olympic distance) and the 10,000-meter. I decided to try both, although the 10,000-meter was not an Olympic event, and neither the Hungarian federation nor the coaches put much emphasis on it. Winning the 10,000 required different training, but I figured that if I was good in one, it would carry over to the other.

Winning the Hungarian National Championships in the C1 1000m, 1962.

After the selection races, where I won both distances, the team went to a couple of international races in Denmark and Romania. The results were very good for me and I was selected by the coaches to race both distances at the World Championships. However, the Cold War was raging, and East

Germany decided to boycott the World Championships because it was in Essen, West Germany. They even demanded that the International Federation cancel the race. We knew that the real reason was that they were afraid too many athletes would defect. After long negotiations, the Board of Management of the International Canoe Federation ruled that the race would go on as an unofficial World Championships. The Hungarian team decided to participate, welcome news that changed the whole landscape. We would have a casual race with good shopping opportunities, and the coaches declared the results would count toward our calorie money.

Some of my Hungarian Championship medals.

The Canadian team showed up at the World Championships with two members from the old Magnificent Seven on their squad, and I was very glad to see them! My friends were surprised by my single results, since they knew all about my Olympic bronze medal. We talked a lot between races, about life in Canada, their canoe clubs, and canoeing in general. I mentioned to them secretly that I was still considering changing countries, and that if I defected, I did not want to stay in Europe. I wanted to join them in Canada. They said I should wait until the Olympic Games as that would be a better opportunity to make the move.

On the top of the podium at Essen Unofficial World Canoeing Championships, 1962, C1 10,000m.

I won the 10,000-meter event and I placed third in the 1,000-meter event. I was an unofficial World Champion but a race is a race, my first big international regatta in the single canoe. The coaches were happy, but they mentioned the importance of the Olympic distances, so I had more work to do. After returning from the World Championships, I sold all the goods I brought home at a good mark up. Perhaps because of the team's good results, we did not have any problem at the border.

After the racing season, I went back to work in the factory full time. But in late fall, preparation for the next year's European Championships started, and my work schedule went back to half-time. During fall conditioning, we played a lot of soccer matches at my club. During one of those games, I hurt my left knee, tearing the ligament. My left knee swelled and locked on me, and I was concerned it would affect my canoeing. I didn't tell anybody because I was afraid that my national coach would consider my injury a handicap and not trust me anymore. I could lose my position on the national team, and become a "has-been." My oldest brother's wife was a nurse, and she counseled me on how to take care of it. The injury slowed down my conditioning and for a long time, I favored that knee. Having an operation would have been very detrimental to my sport career, so I didn't have the operation until much later when I was in the US and reinjured my knee.

In the fall of 1962, my club offered me a job doing some maintenance and purchasing for the club. It was really a token job that allowed me to do more training and reduce the amount of time I spent each day traveling. I was given a cabin in the floating boathouse for daily use, and it even paid a little more than my previous factory job. I was very happy with this arrangement, although it was temporary and could be terminated at any time. I brought my brother, Imre, to the club to do boatbuilding, and he became one of the best paddle makers in the country, providing the national team with light, strong handcrafted paddles. After my defection, he continued in the boatbuilding profession but my club fired him, so he found work in another club outside of Budapest.

Before the World Championships, I befriended a beautiful girl kayaking in the neighboring club. She took the same streetcar home as I did, so it was very convenient to socialize with her. Then things got a bit more serious. I brought her fashionable sweaters, shoes, and stockings from the west. I wanted to make her a trophy girl. She very much appreciated my attention and reciprocated with a loving heart. She was petite, cute, and smart, just finishing her high school. She was a very likable companion and joined me for all the clubs' parties and frequently went to the movies with me. She appreciated my popularity and encouraged me to do better in the single. After my defection, I learned that she was heartbroken by my departure. I wanted to make it up for her but it was impossible.

1963 was another bad year for me, and looking back on my sports career, it appears that all the odd years were unlucky for me. The previous year's successes in the single made me overconfident and cocky. I questioned the coach, didn't follow the established system of training, missed workouts, and generally went against the grain. Even though I was the top young canoe paddler in the country, the coaching staff resented this attitude. My earlier knee injury bothered me all winter, and I could not do any cross training or skiing that winter or running that spring. The training camps were boring to me and I skipped many workouts. My base conditioning suffered greatly. When we hit the water in mid-March, I counted on making up my lost conditioning doing what I loved, paddling.

Paddling an Olympic-style single canoe, on either the left or right side, is one of the most challenging body positions in the whole spectrum of sports. The asymmetric orientation of the body in the canoe and kneeling on one knee while stroking is very challenging. It takes several years of good coaching and persistent training to be stable enough to steer a straight course with reasonable speed under any weather condition.

It was inconceivable to think that I could just stop canoeing. My whole existence and philosophy was wrapped around canoeing, and nothing else mattered anymore. Over the years, I had developed a sense of balance, good steering technique, and speed. When paddling in the single, you have to anticipate the response of the boat before the response actually happens. This becomes second nature, but must be continually fine-tuned with practice. This is the skill that takes you to a higher level. Every little ripple on the water, the wind direction and the body motion in the boat affects the speed you want to generate. With my new club coach, Kulcsár János, I studied technique by looking at pictures and home movies of top paddlers. We drew graphs and charts showing cadence against speed, and analyzed different techniques, spending hours figuring out what makes the canoe move efficiently and how to generate the most speed possible. I was lucky that my club coach was interested as a physical education teacher in those studies and I could learn from him. I educated myself to understand and apply the mechanics of canoeing, studying the physics involved both for the motion of the canoe (speed and resistance) and the propulsion.

A paddler must interpret the coach's advice and form a mental image of what to do. The image is transmitted to the boat via the body and paddle. This mental image interpretation and execution is an individual task. Some paddlers, although they hear and listen to the coach, cannot make the image transfer (uncoachable).

I was a relatively small-sized paddler. At 5'10" and 155 lbs., it was obvious from the beginning that I must be technically flawless in order to compete against the bigger and stronger canoers. With my coach's help, I made a conscious effort to analyze and execute the proper canoe stroke for my size and physical condition.

The other factor that contributes most to one's success in canoeing is stability. The canoe by itself is inherently unstable; if you put an Olympic-style canoe in the water, it will flip to the side. To make the boat stable and upright, the paddler (while kneeling on one knee) has to stabilize the boat. This is not an easy task, and the fear of tipping over has to be overcome and confidence developed to the level of having no doubt. Some paddlers never develop this level of balance, as the fear of tipping over is always in their mind. Needless to say, that fear adversely affects training progress and results. But in order to improve, you have to make mistakes, and without mistakes, there is no progress. In canoeing, the boat is the ultimate coach. The paddler must feel the boat's response through the paddle stroke. The canoe has no intelligence; it merely responds to your input. I was fortunate enough to start at an early age and overcome the fear of tipping even though I was not a good swimmer. I developed a feel for balance, and with confidence could apply a good technique.

In the spring training camp of 1963, the coach decided that I should do double again. I was better suited for double, he declared. I resisted, because

During an International long-distance race, 1963. I am on the far side.

paddling in the double again did not appeal to me. During the first selection races for the World Championship team that year, I got beat pretty badly in the single by couple of up-and-coming youngsters. After all, I was 23, not so young anymore. I decided to concentrate on the long-distance race based on my ability as a good technician. Drafting on the lead boat was legal and I was good at it. What bothered me, though, was that this race was not an Olympic event. I knew that if the coaches boxed me in to being a long-distance paddler only, it would be difficult to change their minds. The 1963 World Championships were in neighboring Yugoslavia, which was not much of an economic incentive for me. I ended up not qualifying for the team, but I was selected to be an alternate. When I heard the decision, I knew right away that the coach wanted to make a point. My prospects for the next year's Olympic Games were beginning to dim. Watching the World Championships from the shore made me crave even more to be on the starting team.

At the end of the summer, after a disastrous racing season, I was concerned my future as an athlete was also coming to an end. I also knew that my current job would not last forever. So, with the encouragement of my coaches, my mother, my new girlfriend, and some of the older paddlers, I applied to the Physical Education University in Budapest—a very prestigious, internationally known sports institution. With this diploma, many famous coaches all over the world successfully trained athletes in sport. The entry exam test included knowledge of all Olympic sports as well as being able to perform at the Class

3 level of proficiency in a given sport. Olympians always got preferential treatment during the examination. I did very well in the exam and got admitted to the university as a correspondence student, which meant I could leave for training camps and competitions and some examinations could be postponed or extended. The Physical Education University was a four-year institution, but some of the Olympic athletes took six to eight years to complete their degree because of their training and competitions. It sounded like a workable deal and promising future for me.

In those days in Hungary, it was mandatory to serve two years in the Army sometime between the ages of 18 and 24. They draft you unless you have a special deferment, such as being a top athlete or physically disabled as proven by a medical doctor. As a member of the Army Sport Club and one of the top athletes in the country, I had been deferred in previous years and didn't think I had to worry about military service. It never occurred to me that I might be drafted, although every year I had to go through the same routine. Eligible males had to go to the assembly hall at draft time, and if they called your name, you had to start your military service. Otherwise, you went home. Mid-October is the time when the Army draft takes place. So, in October 1963, I got the usual draft notice to appear in the assembly hall. It was my last year of eligibility, and the last time that I'd have to do this. I got to the hall first thing in the morning and sat in the last row with friends, playing cards. My non-paddling friends were very envious that I always got excused. We were having a good time, and I was winning all the hands. They had started to call the names in alphabetical order. If you were called, you walked out to say goodbye to your relatives and girlfriend if they came with you (they always did) and then got on the truck. When my oldest brother was drafted, I was there to see my mother cry.

Only a few of us were left in the room when my name, Törő, András, was called! At first, I thought it was a mistake and laughed. Then the sergeant called again. I could not believe it. I was not supposed to be drafted. They didn't know who I was! What was going on? The sergeant called again, and by that time his voice was angry. I stood up with a winning hand, totally stunned. "There has got to be a mistake!" I said to the sergeant. "My name is Törő András." I was sure he hadn't realized that I was *the* Törő András, famous canoeist. He looked at his list and said, "That's right, András, nice to meet you. Welcome to the Army." I pleaded with him to call the club president, who was a General. That afternoon I was expected at practice, and I had movie tickets with my new girlfriend. A French adventure movie, an Yves Montand's film, *Wages of Fear*, had premiered. And while it was impossible to get tickets, I obtained two. It had cost me a pack of American Gillette razor blades. *I cannot miss this movie*, I told myself. "You better get on the truck," the sergeant suggested.

As I did, the rest of the guys sitting there looked at me with big grins. I felt disgraced, not the decorated athlete anymore. I was one of them and it hurt my pride. But I consoled myself with the thought that it would only be a couple of days before they discovered their mistake. My club president would straighten everything out. But deep inside, I had an unpleasant feeling. I thought of the many episodes when I had disobeyed orders and opposed coaches' decisions in the training camps. It might be payback time.

Fortunately, the military compound where we were taken was in Buda. The first order of business was to have a haircut. Speaking of haircuts, my family had a hand operated shear. It was a pretty wicked tool, particularly in my father's hands. When he gave the haircut, it was a very unpleasant, painful experience. The way that tool worked was by squeezing the handle enough for the blades to pass over each other causing them to shear. If you don't do this correctly, it just pulls the hair. My father purposely, I believe, tore chucks of my hair out and if I pulled away he slapped my head. He enjoyed giving us haircuts.

My military photo ID, October 1963.

The military haircut was not much better than my father's. Here I was in the Army, bald, and nobody coming to my rescue. The telephone was unheard of, so one's only contact with the outside world was hopefully during the weekend visiting hours, three days away. We got our uniforms and went to the shower room where we had a short, cold shower and a DDT dusting after we dried. I craved the long, hot showers I had grown accustomed to at the club.

We then dressed in our new uniforms and were marched to our sleeping quarters—a huge room with about 50 to 60 bunk beds. I picked an upper berth. The mattress was stuffed with straw. I thought that some Hungarian farmers must have a lucrative straw contract with the military. Every morning for inspection, we had to make our beds so the sheets were tight and the edges were crisp. If the sergeant did not like it, he threw the mattress on the floor. To summarize my initial experience in the Hungarian Army, I would say that hell would be a resort vacation in Hawaii by comparison. I must admit I liked the physically demanding part of the Army, but mentally the experience was too degrading to take. I tried my best to find humor in it to survive until my release.

The first night, I could not sleep at all, with many scenarios about my sports future flashing through my mind. The following year would be the Olympic Games in Tokyo, so it was time to start preparations. The first training camp was three weeks away, and here I was, stuffing straw into my mattress. How about my calorie money? How long would I stay in this hole? So many unanswered questions filled my head while my newly acquired friends snored and farted away next to me on their straw-stuffed mattresses.

Finally, the weekend came and visitors arrived. I was anxiously waiting for my club's high ranking General to march in and take care of business, telling these peons that they made a serious mistake and should apologize. I waited and waited, but no General came. In fact, no one from the world of sport came; they had totally deserted me. Finally, my new girlfriend showed up, as pretty as ever in the red mohair sweater I bought for her in West Germany, no bra and black high heeled shoes (also from West Germany). At first, she did not recognize me—bald and in plain military khakis. She was so surprised that she cried and laughed at the same time. She told me that she waited for me at the movie theater that afternoon before she learned that I had been drafted. I told her that the first thing Monday morning she should go to my club and tell them what had happened to me and to also contact the national coach and ask him to do something. She felt my urgency and promised to help.

I also told her to see my mother because she would not know which military compound I was stationed in. Before I got on the truck, I had told one of my friends who had been excused to go see my mother, but we did not know where they were taking me. Later I learned that she was very concerned about my sport career and my father was concerned about the calorie money. After a couple of weeks, my mother came to visit and brought me some home cooking. My brothers and other relatives had a hard time believing I'd been drafted. They were all concerned with my sport career.

I have erased the following two weeks of boot camp from my memory forever. Two weeks went by and all I got was constant harassment from the squadron leader, a sadistic son of a bitch. He was jealous of my sports career and my Olympic results. He tried to mock me at every opportunity. I just blocked him out with a polite smile. However, being in much better condition than most of my mates, I excelled in all the tasks; I even had time to help and encourage them. There was a competition among the four squadrons, and the prize was a one day leave after the fourth week and the leader got one week leave—a great incentive to do well. However, it was also a great incentive for my squadron leader to get even tougher on us. I told my group that we were going to win this no matter what. We had a couple of weak links in the group so we split up the work load, and I surprised myself by how adaptable I became, almost liking the military. Perhaps what appealed to me was the tough regimentation and strict discipline. I also realized how easily one could be brainwashed and submit to the system. It was not like me to be obedient, but I wanted to survive. Many years later, I saw the movie *Papillion* and it reminded me of my service in the Hungarian military and how easy it is to give up and be submissive.

At the end of the third week, we had a 50-kilometer march in full gear and armory. For the last ten kilometers, I carried two sets of gear and guns to help one of our members who was failing. At the end of the march, I poured blood out of my boots. We had not been issued socks, only a piece of cloth (*kapca* in Hungarian) to wrap around our feet. This piece of cloth bunched up after the first kilometer and the rest was pure torture. But we made it, winning the contest to earn one day of leave. It was a small victory, but an important one.

As soon as I got out of the compound, I went straight to see my coach to discuss my situation. I found him at the training camp drinking double espresso coffee as usual. My teammates came and gathered around me, teasing me on my very uncustomary outfit as I was known to be a fancy dresser with Western-style tailored suits and shirts. The team enjoyed my situation and the fact that I was no longer competition to them. The coach did not promise anything but said sarcastically, "I cannot amend the Constitution; we all have to serve in the military." It was not a very encouraging visit with less than a year before the Olympic Games. I left the training camp with a heavy heart and fierce determination to do whatever it took to climb back to the top.

After visiting the coach, I went to see my girlfriend and got caught up on the latest club gossip. She wanted to know how long before I got out and I told her it could be two years. I slept at home that night in my own bed and had some of my mom's delicious home cooking. Needless to say, I was very somber going back to my unit and facing the next year without any hope and, on the top of all that, winter was coming. Just before Christmas, our eight weeks of basic training ended and we were to be assigned to a post where we would be stationed for the rest of our military career. I was trained to be a guard soldier, so there was a good chance that I might not be stationed in Budapest. That would certainly end my hopes of making the team again. With great apprehension, I received my assignment. It was to a military post inside of Budapest, actually not far away from my club! This small ray of hope gave me a new outlook on my future, and I was re-energized.

About a dozen of us were stationed as guards at this military compound, which was an equipment storage facility. Our duty was to patrol the perimeter of the compound, about a total of 200 meters. Our schedule was two hours of readiness, two hours of patrol, two hours of rest, four times a day round the clock. We would do this three days in a row, rest one day, and then do it again another three days in a row. It was a demanding schedule with not much sleep or rest, and frustrating for one who wanted to prepare for the Tokyo Olympic Games only ten months away. My renewed hopes faded very quickly once I realized there was no way I could train with this schedule. With this kind of calorie intake and sleep deprivation, I was physically devastated, and a deep depression set in. I could see no way out of this situation without outside help.

The winter came in with a vengeance, bringing plenty of heavy snow. I always hated the winter and cold, but under these circumstances it was even worse. Many times, I dreamed of those little islands in the middle of the Pacific Ocean in the *World Atlas* my father brought home. My lowest point was December 31st, 1963. I was on duty while all the older soldiers had a day off, and I had to pull double duty that day. New Year's Eve is a festive day in Hungary and my favorite day of the year. At my club, we always had a big party that began about six in the evening and went on until the last athlete was standing. I always had a great time, playing the latest western rock and roll tapes I'd brought from the west on my personal tape player. I was the life of the party and could not believe I would not be there this year. Here I was, in a barrack with a pot belly stove heating the small room where we prepared for our duty. Outside, the winter storm had dropped a foot of snow, and more was expected.

Earlier in the day, my girlfriend came to visit and to wish me a happy New Year. She looked beautiful, even in her winter wrap. It had been a long time since I'd felt her warm skin next to mine and I was longing for her, but had to suppress these feelings. I knew it would make my situation even more unbearable. After a long kiss, she said she had to go to the club to celebrate. I felt like someone had just punched me in the stomach, but what could I do? The last thing I wanted to do was go out in the cold and snow to walk the perimeter. Psychologically, I was really hurting. My future, as far as canoeing and making the Olympic team, was looking very dim. I did a lot of soul searching that night on my lone patrol.

From ten to midnight, I was on duty walking back and forth in my small, dark world. The snow was coming down heavily but did not deter the celebration in the city. My heavy boots and the cold, loaded Kalashnikov on my shoulder weighed me down. I heard music, cheering and fireworks on the other side of the eight-foot brick wall. Time was crawling at a snail's pace. The celebration was on and a new year was coming with renewed hopes for everyone else but me. Where would I be two years from now? No more sports, no more canoeing; I would be too old to compete. Perhaps I would be coaching.

Going back to my factory job certainly didn't appeal to me, and my newer job at the club had been a token gig because of my results. Joining the Communist Party was a way to get ahead, but not an option for me. My political philosophy was more democratic than socialist. My university education was also being delayed by this military service, and continuing after this long break could prove too difficult. My thoughts reinforced a belief that I had no future in my homeland. So, as I walked on that cold winter night with just an ember of hope in my heart in the middle of the celebrating city, I made the decision that at the soonest possible opportunity, I would join my Magnificent Seven friends in freedom, somewhere in the West. With luck, I might even see one of those small islands on the map that I had dreamed about since my childhood.

The military routine dragged on week after week with no improvement in my situation. I was getting more and more depressed, and my Olympic dream was slipping further away. The team was in training camp for winter conditioning at the national training center in Tata, 80 kilometers from Budapest. That was mandatory for everyone who was a candidate for future Olympic competition. After the four-week training camp, there was a team physical, which was a very demanding ten station test. The year before, my score had been among the top five for this test. *In my current condition, I would be dead last for sure,* I told myself. *Perhaps I should give up my Olympic dream and focus on something more realistic*, I wondered. I had my bronze medal, and that was more than most of my paddling friends had. I had my name in the Olympic history book, and that would be there forever. While that gave me a good feeling, I was 23 years old and still living with my parents with no possibility of having my own place. I had some money stashed away at home but not enough to start a married life, which I was thinking of with my girlfriend.

In the middle of February, I was summoned to the commander of the compound. I was afraid they wanted to relocate me and send me out of Budapest. Instead, he told me he had an order to let me go twice a week in the afternoon and on the weekends to join the team in training. I could not believe what I was hearing. Someone, somewhere, was looking out for me and did not forget me. While I never found out who it was, I thank him to this day. Leaving the commander's office, I was bursting inside with happiness. I felt like I was liberated! Setting my own schedule was not hard, but it took discipline. On the days away from the military, I joined the B-team in workouts. After each workout, I went back to the paddling tank and did an additional hour. My coaches could not stop me. On the weekends, I did my own training in the paddling tank at my club. I tried to be careful not to overdo it. My priorities were set and my motivation was high, but my calorie intake and the amount of rest I was getting were low, so my recovery rate suffered.

Practicing in the paddling tank, winter of 1963

The national A-team went to Italy for a two-week training camp at the end of March because a late, hard winter kept the Danube jammed with ice floes. However, that did not deter me from starting to paddle on the water. I had to put in quality water time; it worked four years ago, so it should work now. After all, canoe racing was the ultimate goal, not just great fitness. This early on-water training was brutal—cold, windy, and dangerous, and a capsizing could have been fatal. While the A-team was in Italy, I managed to do an average of 20 to 25 miles a day on the Danube. Later, I learned that they had a rainy, windy time in Italy and could not do much quality paddling, so I actually got ahead of them as far as on-water mileage went. However, they did have a good time and lots of shopping. I was not jealous, I was mad. My focus was to be the best again, back on the A-team and making the Olympic team. My goal was set and nothing, absolutely nothing, could derail me from my intention.

Later in the US, I read a quote from William "Bill" Bradley, the great US basketball player, 1964 Olympic Champion, professional player for the New York Knicks, and elected senator from New Jersey. He said, "When you are not practicing, somebody, somewhere, is and when you meet him, he will win!" I realized how true it was and still is.

The rest of March and April was more of the same, most of the time. I trained by myself, so no one really knew how fast I was. My speed was coming along, I told myself many times. Then the first official time trial was announced by the coach, and he invited me to participate. Of course, I accepted the invitation. The time trial was the usual two-kilometer distance, with one turn. We raced twice, with a half hour rest in between. It was on a course that we all knew, and instead of a gang start, we started in 30-second intervals, one boat after another. The coach announced that I would be the first to start since I was an invitee. There are good and bad things about starting first. I could set a pace that I could maintain. I was afraid that if I started behind someone, I would go out at too fast of a pace and burn out. However, going first I could not see who might be gaining on me. Luckily, after the turn, one could see the boats coming behind and judge the distance between the competitors. No matter where I started, I just wanted to compete and see where I stood regarding the pack.

After a quick start, I set a very strong, fast pace. That was my strategy, and at the turn, I had a good margin on the boat coming behind me. I realized that my pace was too fast to maintain, but the adrenaline was still pumping until the last quarter of the race, when I began to slow down. At the finish line, there was a big crowd—the coaches and onlookers all wanted to see the first time trial results. It was sheer guts that got me through the last 500 meters. I wanted to show everyone I was back. Crossing the finish line, I wanted to collapse. I was wasted, but my pride did not let me show it. My friends were signaling thumbs up, which was our sign for a record-breaking time. I paddled to the dock, and several of my friends came to tell me I broke the course record by ten seconds. As the other boats came in, I could see by their speed that no one had come close. For the second race, I set a slower pace and I was beaten by two boats, but I didn't care. I knew that I had sent a signal to the national A-team that I'd be a contender this season. The coach talked to me after the time trials about taking these races seriously and performing with maximum effort each time. He said he would recommend to the committee that I be reinstated to the A-team. That meant I would get calorie money again. However, I was still in the Army.

Some of the other club members, seeing my performance on the water, approached me about paddling double with them. I was very pleased that they noticed my determination and speed. But I didn't want to commit myself to anyone else because of my schedule and military obligation. It would have been unfair to the other paddler, I thought. But the word was out there that *Vanek* (my nickname) was trying to crawl back. That put me in a position of advantage.

I got my nickname from a Hungarian crime fiction novel written by Rejtő Jenő under the pen name P. Howard. He was a very popular writer and we all read his novels in the training camps. In one of his books, a character named *Vanek* was featured as a humorous gangster. I was always quoting *Vanek*, and his name stuck. I did not mind, since it was a persona I identified with.

The Hungarian Canoe Federation set the racing schedule for the year of 1964. The first selection race for the Olympic distance was set for the second weekend of May, with two more selection races to follow before finalizing the traveling team for the season. Usually, this traveling team remained the same for the year unless there was some injury, bad results or disciplinary problems. Doing my own thing, I trained to peak for the first race. I knew that I had to make a good impact right away to be considered.

I remember it as if it was yesterday. On May 3, 1964, two days after the Worker's Solidarity Celebration, I was called to the commander's office. He had a paper in his hand and with the customary salute, he began to read. "The High Commander's order is that after six months of exemplary service to the Peoples Republic of Hungary, Private Törő András István is to be honorably discharged effective at 20:00 hours of this day." My heart stopped, I felt dizzy and I almost fainted. I was free? I asked the commander to repeat it. He smiled and handed the paper over. Never in my life had I felt as relieved as I did in that moment. I saluted him and we shook hands, although I could have hugged him. That was the last time I saw him.

Going back to my barracks, I was skipping like a child, and my mates did not believe it. They thought I had lost my mind but I showed them the paper. They were all very jealous, and rightfully so. They still had at least a year and a half to go. Closing the gate behind me one second after 20:00, I stepped out of the military compound with my civilian clothes on, took a deep breath and felt the fresh spring air rushing into my lungs. The ember of hope to make the Olympic team was glowing! My military experience had been tough and sometimes brutal, but I learned to follow orders, to get along, and to tolerate arrogance and sarcasm. However, six months was enough. I was free; *free at last!*

Needless to say, my mother's reaction was tears of joy. Her little son was home again! There was nothing to say or explain because I did not know who had helped me or why, but I reasoned that the team needed a fast canoe paddler. Sleeping in my own bed felt so comfy and relaxing that I had the first good night's sleep since being drafted into the Army. No more straw-stuffed mattresses. My mother's cooking never tasted better. The next morning, I reported to the A-team training site, reclaiming my old single canoe and all the other equipment supplied by the national team. My team members were surprised to see me without my military uniform, and realized that the competition was heating up. The coach gave me the workout schedule and my fellow athletes welcomed me back. After the workout, I surprised my girlfriend and promised to take her to the movies that night to see *Wages of Fear*. I still had two tickets and it was still playing six months later. My girlfriend was very happy to see me in my fancy clothes again, and despite my very short hair, she said yes.

We had two weeks until the first selection race, so my release from the Army could not have come at a more opportune time. The circumstances put me in high spirits. My training was fun but hard, my attitude was outgoing and friendly, and my adrenaline was at an all-time high. To be certain that I was ready for the first race, I did some secret 1,000-meter time trials just to see where I stood. Surprisingly, the results were better than I expected. My confidence grew. A lot was hinging on that first race, but I knew that I would be very competitive.

In the single, winning all the races, spring of 1964.

With great anticipation, the first race arrived. The preliminaries were relatively easy. I did not spend too much energy and had no problem making the finals of the 1,000-meter single-canoe event, which was the Olympic distance everyone was focusing on. The usual faces were in the final, one of whom was the past Olympic champion in this event. For the Sunday afternoon finals, a bigger-than-usual crowd lined the banks to see the outcome of the first event. I was all nerves. I had my lucky 1960 Olympic racing jersey on. Although I was not really superstitious, I thought that every bit would help. The conditions, as I remember, were perfect, with a slight tail wind—which I liked. I reported to the starter and went through the lining up routine. One of the competitors had a false start, and we had to line up again. The second start was good, and I got off very quickly. I kept reminding myself to keep good technique and to force the pace. Passing the halfway-buoys at 500 meters, I looked to the left and then to the right, but I could not see another boat.

The 1,000-meter race takes more than 4 minutes, so it's not a sprint race. It takes stamina, conditioning, and strong will to carry the pace to the finish, and those last 200 meters are agonizing. In the last stretch, I could hear the crowd cheering, but pink elephants began to appear in my vision—a sure sign of exhaustion. All I can remember was that the finish horn sounded. I looked around as my canoe slid through the finish line, and I hunched over in my canoe. The horn was for me—I'd won! Then came the second horn blast and one for each competitor crossing the finish line after that. The second-place finisher, the past Olympic champion, came to my boat and congratulated me, as is customary. At the dock, my fellow club members and many of my friends were cheering; they were just as happy as I was.

After the race, the coach pulled me over and reminded me there would be two more races to go before final selection of the traveling team. I thanked him for the reminder, as if I did not know that. My whole life was hanging on these races. I knew what I had to do, and no reminder was needed. That evening, I celebrated at the club with my friends. I was so drunk I do not know how I got home. I was mad at myself for letting my guard down, but all the feelings of the last six months had boiled to the surface, and I needed that release.

Fortunately, the second and the third Selection Races produced the same results. I was unbeatable in the Olympic 1,000-meter single-canoe event. After the third race, a Hungarian Sports Illustrated issue, *Képes Sport XI. évf. 25 szám, 1964 Junius 16,* featured a picture of me on the cover in my boat with the caption: *Three out of Three, He is back.* (See photo insert pg VII.) It was strange to see my picture on every newsstand all over in the city. People on the street began to recognize me again, and my Olympic dream was rapidly becoming a reality.

Canoeing and kayaking (considered together as one sport on the Olympic program) was inaugurated at the 1936 Berlin Olympic Games. Since then, the Hungarian team has always won at least one medal in this sport. In recent years, canoeing has become the sport that produces the most medals for the Hungarian Olympic team, hence is one of the most popular and the most funded among all sports in Hungary. Recently, two World Championships were held in Hungary (1998 and 2006) and sold out, attracting an estimated 60,000 spectators. The top athletes are recognized everywhere, and they appear in advertisements and on TV regularly. They all have individual sponsors. Canoeing has come a long way, and its popularity is soaring in Hungary.

After the selection races, there was a long season ahead of us. The coach announced the training camp and traveling schedule as follows: three International Races in Copenhagen, Denmark; Snagov, Romania; and Gruneau, East Germany; as well as the Hungarian National Championships, which were mandatory for everyone. I sold more western goods on the black market, which increased my pile of money in our cupboard. A long training camp in September followed, and I had to leave my club, my family, and my girlfriend until the team flew to Tokyo. The Tokyo Olympic Games were scheduled from October 10th through October 24th, 1964. The canoeing events were scheduled to be in the second week with the preliminaries (heats) starting on October 20^{th,} and the finals contested two days later, on October 22nd.

CHAPTER 6
Olympic Defector, Tokyo Olympic Games 1964

The Olympic Training Camp for canoeing in September of 1964 was downstream from Budapest on the Little Danube (a side branch of the river), at a fishing camp. It was not fancy at all, but totally adequate. The water was just like glass all the time, which was the most important thing. The coaching and support staff laid down a buoyed 1,000-meter lane for time trials, which we did twice a week, to monitor progress. We shared dorm rooms, and I was paired with the top kayak paddler. It was a very long and grueling training camp. The past Olympic single-canoe champion, Party János, was also on the team as my training partner and an alternate. He had a lot of experience, as this was his third Olympic Games, and he had medaled in the two previous ones—an excellent track record to lean on. He had not peaked physically earlier during the summer; he was saving it for Tokyo, and he got closer and closer to me with every time trial. I had to beat him each and every time in order to maintain my position as the C1 1,000-meter starter.

The 1964 Tokyo Olympic canoeing competition started mid-October. In contrast, the season ended in the middle of August at the World Championships in non-Olympic years. It was going to be difficult to sustain a high level of performance for two additional months. I asked the coach to give me more rest time, and he said I was lazy and pushed me even harder. I was very unhappy about that, but going to Tokyo and getting a shot at another medal was a huge incentive, making me more motivated than ever.

The closer we got to departure time, the more administrative things we had to do. We got tailored suits and shoes for travel and the parade, as well as workout and competition gear. Every week, reporters came for interviews, but fortunately, we were not in Budapest, so they didn't bother us as much as other athletes. The team chef, Kuruc Tony, came down to the training camp twice a week to prepare special meals for us.

The last week of camp finally came. We all had our uniforms. Pictures were taken, and we had to sign an *Intent to Compete*. Some of the Communist Party bigwigs came with their party propaganda to talk to us about patriotism and how proud we should be to be representing the country. Again, we even practiced how to step up on the podium as we did four years before.

A couple of months earlier, we had our boats shipped to Japan, via train through Russia, and then on a ship to Tokyo. We had identical boats for training, which was standard procedure. The only things we had to carry were our paddles. The last day arrived. We took a bus to Budapest for a farewell lunch in the parliament and a speech by the Prime Minister, then on to the airport. It was a very emotional day for me. My second Olympic Games in a faraway, exotic land. I did not know very much about Japan, but we were provided guidebooks with some basic Japanese phrases in the back. I tried to learn some Japanese, but the language was difficult. In European countries, you can get by with a dozen words and figure out the written words, but not Japanese. It was going to be challenging, but I was eager for it. Another interesting fact was that, for these Games, all Olympians were told to leave their passports at home. Instead, the accreditation card issued to them would serve as their identification and would be used for all public transportation during the Games. Our officials emphasized the importance of always carrying this card.

The Hungarian Olympic Committee, in connection with the government, chartered a Douglas DC-8 airplane from KLM. The Hungarian Airline did not have any long-distance carrier at that time. The Olympic team was split into two groups, the first leaving on September 22 and the second on October 2. The canoeing team was on the second flight because we had our races on the last weekend of the Olympic program. The canoeing finals were a day before the Closing Ceremony.

A big crowd gathered at the Budapest airport to send the second wave of Olympians on their way. The KLM Douglas DC-8 looked shiny and modern compared to the other Soviet-made airplanes we were used to. We were anxious to get on it. My mother and my girlfriend came to say goodbye and kiss me. As it turned out, it was the last kiss I had from my girlfriend. Before we went to the training camp, my girlfriend and I had a serious discussion about our relationship. I was noncommittal but I told her that after the Olympic Games we would make a plan for our future together.

I had seen my father the night before at home, and that would be the last time I ever saw him. He hoped that I would have a good result and keep bringing home that calorie money. Knowing that I might defect at these Games, it was hard to hold back my emotions while parting from my loved ones. They did not know it, but this might be the last time we would see each other for a long time, possibly forever. In order to protect my family, I kept silent about my intentions and left everything I owned at home, including my precious bronze medal and all my hard-earned money.

Finally, it was time for the Hungarian Olympic team to board the plane, and I was one of them! As I mounted the ramp toward the plane's door, I took a moment to have one last glance at my loved ones and my homeland. Now, I needed to leave all those emotions behind and focus on the task ahead. After a very trying year, I felt I deserved to be on that plane and felt a lot of pride in my achievement. Our eighteen-hour flight went from Budapest to Amsterdam, from Amsterdam to Anchorage, and finally from Anchorage to Tokyo. Going over the North Pole was very exciting! We stopped at each city to refuel and to have some exercise. We were told that the flight from Anchorage to Tokyo depended on the weather. If we had a strong headwind, which is usual at that time of year, we might have to stop to refuel in Russia. I was sitting in the seat assigned to me before the flight, between a weightlifter and a fencer. The weightlifter was gross and big, snoring and farting all the way to Tokyo. I spent most of the flight at the back of the plane, moving around, trying to talk with the attractive stewardesses, and looking out the door's porthole, hoping for a glimpse of the North Pole. We got a

Crossing the North Pole Certificate, October 2, 1960.

certificate from KLM for crossing the North Pole, which I still have.

Knowing that Alaska was part of the United States, I wanted to be first out of the plane to step on the land of freedom and my potential future home. Fortunately, they opened both the front and the back doors, and since I was almost sitting in the back row, I was first at the door. The cold, brisk air hit me with a shock. *Wow, America is cool*, I thought. As I descended the stairs, I could see a snowy panorama of Alaskan wilderness beyond the airport. It was just as I imagined Alaska would look like. We disembarked in the mid-afternoon light and did a quick workout in the airport just to loosen up. The airport itself was a disappointment. It was nothing fancy, just a refueling station for over-the-pole flights and the military, and we didn't have a chance to explore. The team leaders kept a sharp eye on us. There was a group of local former Hungarians who had emigrated during the 1956 revolution who came to visit us and wanted to talk, but our officials would not allow it.

The Lake Sagami Olympic Village entrance, October 1964.

After Alaska, the flight was uneventful but long, and I was anxious to get to Tokyo. The captain told us that the wind was in our favor and we did not have to stop in Russia. Sleeping was out of question; I was too excited about seeing Japan. Finally, in the afternoon light, I could see Tokyo Bay out of the window!

OLYMPIC DEFECTOR, TOKYO OLYMPIC GAMES 1964

It was thrilling to step out of the plane at the Haneda airport on October 3, 1964 onto a different, exotic continent. It was seven days before the Opening Ceremony. The Tokyo airport was extremely busy—delegations from dozens of countries were arriving and different languages were being spoken all around me. It appeared to be chaos, and everyone wanted to get to the Olympic Village as soon as possible. Athletes are basically very impatient and always competing. They want to get there first, or at least I did. The canoers had to split from the team because we were not going to the main Olympic Village, but rather a satellite village at Lake Sagami. A couple of the local organizers asked us to identify our luggage and hand it over. We let our luggage go off with them but kept a tight hold on our paddles. We were sure that was the last time we would see our luggage (at least that would be the case in Hungary). Then, we boarded the bus to Lake Sagami. Going through a busy part of Tokyo was an eye-opener, with so many people and so much traffic, despite the special Olympic lane on the highway. However, as we entered the countryside, it was different from anything I'd ever seen before. Small rice fields were terraced into the hillsides, and the landscape looked like a painting. Every inch of the land was cultivated and used; every bit of space utilized.

We were very tired when we arrived at our accommodations, the local schoolhouse. Classes were suspended during the Olympic Games so children could watch. All the different nationalities participating in the canoeing events were staying in that school or the surrounding areas. The female competitors had their own accommodations nearby.

A Japanese hostess escorted us to our room and on one of the beds was my luggage and a sign reading *Mr. Törő András, Canoeing Competitor, Welcome to Tokyo, Home of the 1964 Olympic Games*. On my luggage were several origami objects that the local school children made for the Olympians, a very nice gesture. Also, waiting for me was a small Japanese wooden Kokeshi Doll made by the members of Junior Sports Club at Noruko. Seeing that my luggage had arrived before I did gave me a hint as to the detailed care and organizational skills of the Japanese officials. I still hold the greatest personal admiration and regard for them. In subsequent years, I have been back to Japan for visits and meetings, and I always have a profound gratitude for the Japanese people,

Tokyo Olympic memorabilia.

perhaps because, in addition to putting on a magnificent Games, they gave me the freedom I've enjoyed to this day.

Needless to say, we were anxious to get in our boats and on the water to shake off the traveling stiffness. After some rest and food, we walked down to the boathouse for the first time to find our boats. They were neatly stored on the racks in the section designated for Hungary. We needed to make some adjustments, and it was relaxing to tinker around with our equipment. The organizer brought in a boat builder who had only two tools, a two sided Japanese saw and a mallet. It was first time I had ever seen these Japanese tools. This unusual saw cut on the pull stroke, not on the push, which was the opposite of what I was used to. Our old club boat builder popped up in my mind. How much he would appreciate one of those! This craftsman could make every adjustment and repair that we needed with just those two tools—

perfectly fit pieces of wood together, drill holes to the right size, miter and bevel, you name it. All we had to do was show him our intent (since we could not communicate any other way) and he did it. However, the most impressive moment was the day he brought his young son with him. The boy was about four or five or years old, small with straight coal black hair, cut square in the front. He sat on the floor cross-legged next to his father and watched his every move. We and the other international team members gave him some trading pins and chocolate. It piled up in front of him all day, but he did not touch it. We tried to get him to smile or play with us, but he never did. What incredible discipline! I was very impressed with that small child. I have yet to see behavior like that in any other youngster. Later on, I learned that self-discipline is a virtue of the whole nation.

The canoeing venue at Lake Sagami, 1964 Olympic Games.

The regatta course was only a short walk away from our Olympic Village. As we passed small shops, the locals watched us, and small children hid behind their parents. We realized they may have never seen Caucasians before. We felt like museum pieces. I vividly remember one interesting episode that reflected the Olympic spirit at the small town of Sagamiko. We were walking back from the boathouse to our tastefully decorated schoolhouse. At one street corner was a small store, even by Japanese standards, selling refreshments. We stopped by to get an orange soda. As we approached the counter to pay, the owner indicated with a deep bow that it was all free; he did not want us to pay. Later, we learned through an interpreter that it was a great honor for him that we visited his small business. It really struck me how the Japanese people felt about visitors and how they embraced the spirit of friendship and brotherhood of the Olympic Games. We gave him some of our team trading pins. He was very moved and bowed many times. In return, he gave us a small triangular flag with the Olympic logo on one side and a soft drink ad on the other. By the end of the week, he had a whole collection of pins from different countries. He proudly displayed them on his small counter, glad to be part of the Olympic spirit that had swept the whole country.

The next day, we participated in a flag raising ceremony. It is customary, according to the Olympic rules, that each participating country's flag be flown at the Olympic Village where they reside. Each country had its own flag raising ceremony. Four years before in Rome, I missed this ceremony. This time, we all lined up with the Japanese officials as they raised the Hungarian flag and a high school band played an interesting version of the Hungarian national anthem. With grins on our faces, we paid respect to the high school band and the organizers. It was, again, a Japanese touch that added to our Olympic experience.

Another unusual thing we noticed right away was the Japanese cuisine. We had never heard of sushi, sashimi, or tofu. These dishes, among others, were very foreign to us. At first, we joked about it; but after trying some, we liked it, particularly with wasabi. Many years later, these dishes became some of my favorites. The Hungarian team chef hardly ever made it out to Lake Sagami, so the organizers did everything they could to ensure we had proper nutrition and a high calorie diet with fish and poultry. Before every meal, they politely asked us through an interpreter what we would like to eat.

The Japanese toilets were another new experience! We had never encountered this squatting arrangement, and though everyone joked and teased each other about them, we respected the cultural difference.

The canoe and kayak competitors were about 60 kilometers from Tokyo.

We were out of sight and out of mind for those in Tokyo. However, I believe we had richer cultural experiences through the locals than the athletes who stayed in the sheltered Olympic Village in the city.

Lake Sagami was a magical place with Oriental beauty such as we had only seen in magazines. It was a man-made lake with a spectacular shoreline studded with pagodas and other buildings that were architecturally strange and amazing to us. The morning mist that rose along the shoreline was beautifully surreal. As it would dissipate, views of the bamboo groves and small pagodas along the water, with their unusual upward-curving roofs,

With a local woman in Sagami Village on the way to practice.

would emerge. It was mystical to paddle along this spectacular panorama, and we could almost imagine dragons surfacing as our little canoes sliced through the water. We waved to villagers fishing along the banks, who would bow in response. I still believe that among all the athletes, the water sport competitors got the best of the Olympic experience. We were away from the bustling city in surroundings that I will never forget. It was pleasantly distracting to follow the shoreline in our canoes and not think of the competition ahead. However, in these pristine surroundings, a beautiful race course had been set up with the finish tower and boathouses on the shore to the left of the course.

At our team meeting, the night before the Games started, the coach announced that we were not going to the Opening Ceremony because it was too far away. Here I was in my second Olympic Games, and I still was not going to participate in the Opening Ceremony! It made me sad, but I could not do anything about it. He also announced that we would have several time trials and based on those performances, he would finalize the entries. This created a bad atmosphere within the team. The alternates loved the opportunity to have another chance. The starters hated it, and I was among them.

Gabor Jo (CAN), me, Kovacs Kalman (HUN), and Blaho Kalman (ITA) in front of the boathouse, Lake Sagami.

My performance was getting weaker. I had an elevated temperature, I could not sleep, and my appetite was low, as was my energy level. I pleaded my case that I was overtrained to the coach, but he kept pushing me. The team doctor did not help. They said I had the Olympic jitters and I was lazy. The doctor gave me a shot of vitamin B-12, his favorite medication. According to him, vitamin B-12 cured everything. Clearly, I was overtrained, the season had been too long, and the weekly challenges and time trials had taken their toll. Though I was really afraid that I would lose my starting position, I *had* to back off my training. Fortunately, the organizers allowed only a few coaching launches on the water, so our coach had limited time with us. This gave me some relief, but the time trials would be coming up, and there was no way I could get out of that.

After our arrival in Sagami, a day or two later, the Canadian team arrived and among them was my friend, Elbert Andor. It was a happy reunion and a great relief to me. We had been unable to communicate since I saw him in 1962. He said at that time he would try out for the Canadian Olympic team, but I didn't know if he'd made it, and it was very fortunate for me that he was in Japan. Without his assistance, my plans would be much harder to execute.

We had our previously announced time trials: two times 1,000 meters on the course. It was a staggered start with thirty second intervals between boats in the same lane. The coach decided that I would start first with the previous Olympic champion and my arch rival, Parti Janos, following me. I was very unhappy about this arrangement, but I didn't dare challenge it. I realized that I had to earn my spot again if I was going to compete in my second Olympic Games. All I remember of the time trials is that I gave it everything I had. I collapsed after the finish line and was barely able to count the seconds to estimate the time difference between myself and the champion behind me. I counted *30... 31...* when he crossed the finish line. I knew that it was very close.

The second time trial was a half an hour later with the same routine. It was definitely slower, and I was not sure of the outcome. I approached the coach in his motorboat, and he told me that I won the first one by one second but I lost the second by the same. So, the decision was up to him. I slowly paddled to the boathouse. The whole team was discouraged, as no one had turned in a good time on the course.

**On the tarmac, waiting for my turn to practice,
Lake Sagami, 1964 Tokyo Olympic Games.**

At dinner time, the coach announced the starting team. I was among them and very relieved! However, at the same time, I was concerned about how much this grueling time trial had taken out me physically and psychologically. The coach also told us he had entered the alternates on the official entry sheet, just in case someone got sick. According to the rules at that time, the starting position's name could be changed one hour before the first event. That uncertainty didn't help me fully focus, and there was a nagging worry in my mind that the coach might pull me at the last minute. The weather became rainy and cold, adding to my misery.

Mrs. Francis watching the races with her daughter, Sperry. Lake Sagami, 1964.

In the boathouse, I went to see my Magnificent Seven friend, Elbert Andor. The boathouse, where all the national teams kept their equipment, was divided alphabetically by participating nations. I found him near the "C" nations' area, working on his boat. We had a long discussion, and I told him that if I didn't make the podium, I would defect, and I asked him to help me. He said the best chance would be to have someone on the American team sponsor me and make arrangements with the United States Embassy. He said he would ask around. Later, I saw him talking to a US kayaker, William "Bill" Smoke and his girlfriend, Marcia Jones. I learned later that Marcia's mother, Mrs. Francis, took on the case and called the US Embassy, asking them about the proper procedure for defection. She was an attorney and disliked the communist system, so she wanted to help.

The morning of October 20th, finally arrived. The canoeing competition began. Our coach announced the final starting team, and I got my position. I was in the first heat at 10:50 in the morning with the Russian, Bulgarian, Canadian, Australian, and USA paddlers. I had raced against the Russian and Bulgarian paddler, and I was concerned. Though I had beaten them before, that was several months ago during the early summer when I was in top form. Our report indicated that the rest of the field was not fast. The top three finishers would go directly to the final two days later. I drew lane five, between the Bulgarian and the USA paddler. The Russian paddler was in lane one, farthest to the left. The gun went off and I had a good start, clearly ahead of the Bulgarian. After 500 meters, I looked to the left to see the Russian paddler's position, and he was ahead of me. I wanted to put pressure on him and slowly start to reel him in, but I couldn't do it. He had a good finish and beat me by 1.5 seconds. My time (4:42.31) was the fourth-fastest of the two heats. (The Russian was third-fastest in 4:41.06). I made it directly to the final where anything could happen. After the heats, we had a team meeting where the coaches analyzed the results. They were happy that we had all advanced, but our times didn't promise any podium positions. Since I did not have to go to the semi-finals, I had a day of rest to ponder my strategy.

My final race was on October 22nd, 1964 at 14:40 in the afternoon. It was the third race of the day, and the rain was drizzling with a slight breeze as I slowly approached the start line. My number, 79, was pinned on my jersey. I drew lane three, between the Czech and the Russian paddlers. It was a favorable lane assignment because I could read the Russian's cadence and speed. I knew he had been just a little faster, but I felt I could match and surprise him. The Czech competitor was not much of a threat. I had raced against him in Europe with good success, and his time in the preliminaries was not as good as mine. However, I was very nervous, and I wished that the race had been a month or two earlier when I was in top form. I was now hoping to at least repeat my result of the 1960 Rome Games four years earlier. An improvement on the podium seemed very unlikely.

During my C1 1000m finals race. I am at the bottom right.
Photo credit: 1964 Japanese Olympic Yearbook.

Nevertheless, I was on the start line to have another chance at an Olympic medal. I had sacrificed everything during the last couple of years to be here and wanted it badly. I pushed aside negative thoughts in my head. I took a couple of deep breaths, and I was ready.

The gun went off, and I had a reasonably good start. From the corner of my eye, I saw the Russian paddler taking a slight lead with a higher cadence. I focused on him to keep him within striking distance at the finish, hoping he might burn out. As we approached the 500-meter line, I again glanced to the left. The Russian paddler was still ahead of me and was forcing a fast pace. With about two minutes left in the race I told myself, *I must keep contact*. I always had a good finish and was hoping that the others would fade. I tried to raise my cadence, but my lungs were burning and could not deliver the required oxygen to my muscles. Negative thoughts began to pop into my head. I was struggling, but still fighting. When the horn sounded for the first-place finisher, I was several boat lengths from the finish. As we came through, I thought I was third again, but then I looked to the other side of the course and saw the Romanian and the East German paddler ahead of me. I was fourth. No medal, a *very* disappointing performance. I was crushed. And my promise hit me—*If I do not win a medal, I will defect.* Suddenly, I was confronted with this new reality.

After the race, I was not called to the podium and paddled dejectedly back to the dock. No one was waiting to congratulate me or offer any consolation. I raised my paddle and broke it on the edge of the dock, expressing my frustration. The paddle I broke had been made by my brother, Imre, a couple of weeks before our departure. It was supposed to be for good luck, but clearly it did not work. I walked sadly up to the boathouse, with my canoe on my shoulder, as most of my fellow team members had. Only one of us had medaled—Hess Mihály had earned a silver medal in the K1 1000. There was not much camaraderie in the boathouse, as we were all stung by our losses. When the top three finishers in my race were called to the podium to receive their medals, I remembered the much better feeling four years ago. Hearing the winner's national anthem only rubbed salt in the wound. My mind shifted to the decision I had to make.

After the races, we had the usual team meeting with the Hungarian team officials who had come out to see our event. They expressed their appreciation for our good fight. The final results for the team were one silver medal and three close fourth place finishes. All boats made the finals, but had placed lower in comparison with the results four years earlier. It was very discouraging and disappointing. The team was clearly overtrained, and the coaches had not realized it. They had worked us hard continually from May through October with no plans for peaking at the Games and no value placed on tapering, rest, or recovery. Also, some of the paddlers were getting beyond their prime and they couldn't keep up with the younger, hungrier international athletes (There was also beginning to be some speculation that East Germany and Russia were doping—something new and unknown until then).

After the meeting, as was customary, all the teams packed their boats on trailers to be shipped back to the countries they'd come from. There was a lot of hustle and bustle around the boathouse. My former Hungarian coach now the Italian coach, Blahó Kálmán, and Elbert Andor came over to say goodbye.

Andor said he wanted to see me in the cafeteria at dinner time, and I looked around to make sure that no one heard. I was afraid that if my team leaders became suspicious, they would detain me. At dinner, he told me that it was all set up for that night and asked, "Are you ready?" He told me to be at the Sagamiko railroad station at 6:00 pm to catch the train to Tokyo. Everything was all set up—he and Bill Smoke would accompany me to the United States Embassy.

At the Sagamiko Village railroad station, 50 years later.

Our team had been told that the next day we would move to the Olympic Village in Tokyo to participate in the Closing Ceremony on October 24th. So, everyone was packing and wanting to do some last-minute local shopping. I tried to blend in and appear busy. I put on my team travel uniform and grabbed my small sports bag, which had a few souvenirs in it. I told the coach that I was going to the village to shop and he barely paid me any notice, as he was packing up for the team's departure. I couldn't take more of my belongings with me for fear of attracting his unwanted attention. Then, instead of going to the shops, I headed to the railroad station where Andor and Bill were waiting for me. The train came and as I stepped on I promised myself, *no looking back, whatever happens.* The train was crowded, as I recall, and everyone was looking at us, three Olympians in their respective uniforms, speaking different languages. Since I could not speak English, Andor translated for me. Bill said that Mrs. Francis talked to the embassy officials about my plan and got a positive response. She asked Bill to help me make it happen. The train ride was about 45-minutes long, as I recall, but it felt like an eternity. My friend, Andor, tried to lighten up the limited conversation by translating some corny jokes to Bill and assured me everything would be alright and how lucky I was that Mrs. Francis made the connection with the embassy. I remember he said something like, "The red carpet is rolled out for you. You will be a celebrity." I did not want to be a celebrity; I just wanted to get to the United States. From the Tokyo station, we took a taxi to the embassy. As we walked in, the guard closed the gate, and I was safely on American soil.

This is it, I thought. *I'm beginning a journey that I will remember forever and one that I have to live with forever.* Even though I was technically on American soil at the embassy, I was very anxious to get out of Japan, because I was afraid that the Hungarians might be able to extradite me in Tokyo. My immediate priority was to get on a plane as quickly as possible to make the journey to the United States. No words were spoken between my Hungarian friend and me as we walked into the US Embassy and down a hallway. Every silent moment was loaded with suspense.

We were escorted into a room where a US Embassy official began to ask some questions. My friend, Andor, translated. They looked at my accreditation to make sure I was an Olympian. As I recall, I had to sign a paper that I was seeking political asylum. With that move, I signed my Hungarian life away and realized things would never be the same again. They told me they made some phone calls and I had several choices—I could defect to Sweden, Israel, or the United States. I told them I preferred the United States and was relieved that I had a choice. I did not want to end up in Europe—it was too close to the homeland, and I was afraid that something might happen. I knew of a kayaker who had defected at a competition in West Germany in 1962 who was coerced into returning to Hungary two months later. I did not want there to be any possibility of this happening to me.

Bill Smoke offered to sponsor me and wrote a check for my one-way ticket to the USA. The earliest plane to the USA was a TWA flight to Seattle at about 8:00 that evening. Things were moving very quickly. The embassy personnel said that they had to make some phone calls to the Japanese authorities to grant permission for my departure, but that it should not take too much time. They asked both of my friends to leave and promised to take care of the details.

So, I shook hands with my old Magnificent Seven friend, Elbert Andor, and my new American friend, Bill Smoke, and then they walked out the door and left me alone at the US Embassy. Before they closed the door, they said, "See you in America." I smiled and thought, *I sure hope so*. I sat and absently flipped through some American magazines while thinking of all the things that had just occurred.

There was a certain amount of calm loneliness that settled over me, interwoven with occasional stabs of fear. The fear was for my immediate family, particularly my mother and brothers. What would happen to them now? Would the government make them suffer because of my defection? Would I would be responsible for that? Did I do the right thing in looking out only for myself? I had tried to protect my family by not confiding in them at all about my plans to defect if I didn't medal. They would be able to truthfully say that they did not know and did not help me in any way.

If I hadn't defected and had gone back to Hungary, what kind of life would I have? I would be an Olympian, probably working in the factory barely earning a living wage, perhaps getting married and living with my in-laws for years because of the housing shortage, perhaps continuing my canoeing career or coaching. But would I be content? No. I despised the communist system and all the limitations it put on every aspect of life. No, my choice was to give up that specter of my life in Hungary and trade it for an uncertain future, albeit one in a new society where I could hope to make my own destiny. Even though I was heading to a country where I had no command of the language, knew almost no one, had no money and no special marketable skills except how to steer a single canoe, the alternative looked much bleaker to me. I knew I would never like the Hungarian communist system, which offered advancement only to its members. So, as difficult as it was, I could not see myself returning to my homeland and my family. I realized my choice would cause many disappointments and hard feelings, and I hoped that I would not regret it. I chose the United States of America for my future.

Leaving the US Embassy in Tokyo for the airport.
Photo credit: The Japan Times

I do not know how much time went by before the door suddenly opened and the embassy official reentered with a middle-aged Japanese gentleman. He began to speak in perfect Hungarian. I was so surprised that I blurted out a very innocent question: "Where did you learn Hungarian?" He explained that he was stationed in Budapest before and during the Second World War, working for the Japanese government in industrial espionage. He said that the Japanese government believed the Hungarian scientists and mathematicians were very advanced in nuclear science and were helping the USA government develop a super weapon. But, getting down to the business at hand, he said I should follow him and his instructions. "There are too many reporters at the front of the embassy because the news has leaked, so we will slip out at the back door," he explained. I shook hands with the embassy personnel and followed the Japanese gentleman out the back door to a car.

On the way to the airport, my Japanese interpreter explained that the plane to the USA was parked on the tarmac waiting for me, and we would stop right at the gangway stairs. Without any hesitation, I should rush into the plane where the stewardesses would take me to my seat. We entered the airport through the back gate. At the usual departure terminal, there were already too many reporters, and the Japanese gentleman did not want to take any chances I might be detained by Hungarian officials. I stepped out of the car and looked back at my Japanese friend. He had his thumb up and said, "Sayonara." I responded, "Köszönöm szépen" (*thank you*), and he smiled. I rushed up the gangway, but halfway I stopped and turned around. I saw a lot of different planes parked on the tarmac waiting to depart tomorrow for their destinations—*home*. Then it really hit me hard for the first time: *if I go inside this plane, I will forever be a defector*. My country, my home, will only be a memory, no longer a reality. The words of Captain Bligh to the mutineer Christian Fletcher rushed through my mind. As he stepped into the HMS Bounty's lifeboat, "Mr. Fletcher, I still have a country." I realized what Captain Bligh was saying. When you choose to be a defector, a mutineer, you sever all connections to your country and belong no more. It was a very lonely feeling, and it set heavily on my shoulders.

Then, I turned around and hurried up the steps into the plane where stewardesses led me to the cockpit. I did not have an assigned seat and they did not want me to mix with the passengers, who were intently watching what was going on. As I sat in the pilot's cabin in the assistant radio operator's seat, a saying of my father's flashed through my mind. *Make sure you know where you're going to sleep tonight.* Many questions followed that had no answers. I was about to take off for America, the place I'd dreamt about so many times. I had to pinch myself to be sure this was real. I did not know what the future would bring, but I knew I had the opportunity to chart my life the way I wanted. No more parents to oblige, no more coaching instruction to obey, no more communist propaganda to listen to, no more pressure to perform in my sport. But all other aspects of the future were uncertain. Did I have enough life experience to tell the good from the bad? How would I know if the path I chose was the right one? I realized how sheltered I had been in the first 24 years of my life, always given the necessities and support I needed. But now it was up to me. I was on my own!

I looked out the window as the plane circled Tokyo. The city was bright and sparkling in the darkness, getting ready for tomorrow's Closing Ceremony of the XVI Olympiad. I felt sad I was not celebrating the closing of the Games with the athletes of the world, and I realized that, in these Games, I had not participated in either of the Ceremonies. My heart felt very heavy—my Olympic experience was incomplete, and having another chance seemed like a remote possibility.

I cannot recall most of the plane ride. I was totally exhausted and emotionally drained. A couple of times, the flight attendants woke me up to eat and tried to chat with me. Unfortunately, I couldn't have a conversation with them because I spoke no English. They wanted to comfort me as much as they could. Before we landed in Seattle, each of the plane's crew gave me a dollar bill signed with *Good Luck*. I thought it was a very nice gesture of them. I finally had my own one-dollar bills… legally. They looked the same as the one my father had brought home many years ago, and I felt rich. After all these years, I still have those dollar bills, although once or twice I was very tempted to spend them. I am not superstitious, but I was emotionally attached to them. Some things in life you keep forever.

The Seattle airport was bustling. Reporters had gotten word that a Hungarian Olympic team defector was on the plane, and they all wanted to talk to me. I cannot remember if I had to change planes or not, but I remember an interview with the reporters that was very one-sided because of my lack of English. When I boarded once more, I had a proper seat in the cabin. The flight attendants again took care of me en-route to Baltimore.

CHAPTER 7
First Steps in America, the New World

When I arrived at the Baltimore airport, two gentlemen from the US State Department were waiting for me, and they handled the immigration and customs forms. I did not have any passport because the Olympic accreditation had served as my passport under the IOC protocol. I did not have any luggage, so I breezed through customs as a special case. One of the State Department representatives, who became the handler assigned to my case, spoke Hungarian. I was told that there was a group of news reporters waiting outside and one of the representatives asked me if I would like to talk to them. I said no, I was too tired, and we exited the airport through a back door. The gentleman who was speaking Hungarian explained to me that since my unexpected arrival was two weeks before the presidential election, I had to be detained at a government facility until after the election. Apparently, since President Kennedy's assassination a year earlier, the State Department had become very cautious about entry by communist country defectors. I was emotionally drained from the events of the past 24 hours, so I did not argue. I just wanted to get over all the formalities and go to sleep somewhere. In my head, I heard my father say, "Make sure you know where you will sleep," but at that instant, I did not know and I did not care. I was in the USA and that was all that mattered. They took me to a government safe house somewhere in Baltimore, near the Chesapeake Bay. The reason I know this is because we drove across a long bridge over a body of water I suspected was the Chesapeake Bay. It came in handy to have studied my father's atlas.

It turned out to be a big farmhouse on some acreage with a black couple as caretakers. I was told I would remain here until the election was over and warned not to attempt escape as that would be a federal offense. I told them I was happy to be here and that it looked like a nice place. My handler told me that he would be back the next day with some clothing and a language tape to learn English. That evening, I ate a good dinner, during which my hosts and I looked at each other a lot. We weren't able to communicate much, although I sensed that they were curious about who I was. This was the first time I had ever sat at a table with black people, and it was very unusual and a little thrilling. I realized that many things I would do for a while would be for the first time in my life. After dinner, they showed me to my room, and I went to my bed and quickly fell asleep, exhausted. As I recall, it was not a very restful sleep. There were too many unanswered questions rushing through my subconscious, and I knew I had gone down a one-way street but had to make the best of it without looking back. I wondered when homesickness would hit me, having heard so much about it from my fellow defectors and having experienced it when I was a little boy in Denmark.

I woke up the next morning late, thinking about my team's arrival in Budapest. What would the general reaction be? How would the team leaders explain my absence? Would my mother and family be at the airport waiting for my arrival, as in 1960, not knowing that I'd defected? What a shock that would be for them! Many years later, my brothers told me the story of what happened.

On the evening of October 23, Radio Free Europe broadcast news of my defection worldwide. Although it was still illegal to listen to it behind the Iron Curtain, one of my relatives got the news. The next day, according to Imre, two local communist party functionaries showed up at my mother's house and interrogated her, pretending that they didn't know anything. At the end of their visit, they took my passport. Luckily, they were not smart enough to take my Olympic medal.

They wanted to know if she knew of my intent to defect. My mother could truthfully tell them that she knew nothing because I had purposefully not shared my plan with her. When the Olympic team arrived in Budapest a day later, the official reception was in a small sport stadium instead of at the airport so as not to advertise my defection. At that time, Lajos, who was present, wanted to know some of the details from my teammates. No one would talk to him. However, one of the team members had carried my suitcase with all my competition uniforms and souvenirs and given it to my brother.

My Hungarian Court subpoena, 1964, one month after my defection.

Imre, who worked in my club as a boat builder, was summoned by the club president to his office and, after a long and unpleasant meeting, was fired. He was forced to take a job outside of Budapest in another club. On December 4, 1964, the High Court of Budapest subpoenaed one of my Olympic coaches and one of my team members to testify against me in the court. The court decision *in absentia* was a two-and-a-half-year prison term for my defection. Fortunately, no other major penalty was bestowed on my family, which would have made me very distressed.

When I came out of my room that morning, my Hungarian-speaking handler was already there talking with the caretakers. He brought me the clothes and a tape player with some language tapes and a book. He said that he would try to come every other day to check on me. I passed the time listening to the tapes and watching the children's TV programs he had recommended for learning English. I also got outside for walks around the grounds. The property was large with some shoreline and a small fishing pier where I tried my luck at fishing. The next time I saw my advisor, though, I was driving a tractor cutting grass! Driving a tractor was fun. The caretaker had just turned it over to me in the morning after he started it up. I told him I only had experience driving goats. Of course, he didn't understand, but I wasn't joking either. Nothing to fear, I told myself, as long as I don't have to turn. I guess he was satisfied, because he left me alone. It was natural for him to think that I, as an adult, would know how to drive. (It was actually not until five years later that I got my driver's license.)

My handler told me that, two days after the election, we would go to the State Department for a debriefing. *Now, that should be interesting*, I thought. He tried speaking English to me to see how much I had picked up so far and was not impressed. I tried to defend myself, explaining the letters and the sounds don't match and are always changing. Also, why do they have silent letters? There is no reason to have them if you do not pronounce them. He said that he was not a linguist, but that I better learn English if I wanted to be a citizen. That kind of scared me, so I set my schedule. Every morning, I watched two hours of cartoons. In the afternoon, I listened to the tape with the book and repeated some of the sections. After dinner, I watched TV again, but this time it was the news with my caretakers. They tried to talk to me, but I noticed they spoke a different language than my advisor.

Two weeks went by very quickly, and I was having a great time. I was pleased and thought if it continued like this, it wouldn't be too bad. Then my handler showed up and told me to pack up, because we wouldn't be coming back. I said goodbye to my caretaker couple, knowing I was going to miss the good (southern) cooking I'd enjoyed. It often seemed very similar to my mother's Hungarian dishes.

I got into the handler's huge Chevy station wagon, and it felt like a ship rather than a car. He said he liked to drive this one because it felt safe. An hour-and-a-half later, I was in the US State Department in Washington, D.C., for debriefing.

The room was sparse—one table, with a chair on one side for me and three on the other side for the examiners. On the wall, there was a big mirror—or at least I thought it was a mirror. Three gentlemen came in, my handler, who acted as a translator, and two others, one of whom had a big dossier with him. They asked me if I had anyone to represent me, and I told them my coach was back in Hungary with the team. They asked me to be serious, and then we got down to the real debriefing. I would call it more of an *interrogation*. They asked me about my involvement with the Communist Party and the KGB. They showed me pictures of Russian-looking Generals and civilians and asked if I knew any of them or had any involvement with any of them. After a while, I got sweaty and nervous. I told them that I was an athlete and that although my club happened to be the Army Club, I did not have any involvement with the Communist Party or the Soviet KGB. They asked me if I was willing to take a lie detector test. "Sure, bring it on," I said. "I'm not a spy."

Next, we went to another room full of electronic instruments and a technician. They hooked me up to a machine and told me to relax. How can you relax when lot of electronic probes are stuck to your head? Then they asked me all sorts of questions and showed me the same pictures again. My handler translated for me. After about an hour, my shirt was soaking wet, and they stopped the procedure. The technician looked at the tape. It was a lot of squiggly lines to me, but at one spot the line veered up and had taller peaks. They paid particular attention to that part. They asked me again, "Do you use any other name beside the name you gave us: András Törő?" I told them no, just like before, but then I hesitated. I thought of my nickname, *Vanek*, and how anyone who knew me in Hungary used to call me that. But the people in the room did not know that, so I didn't think I needed to tell them. They asked me a third time so I told my handler that I had to explain something here, and I told them the story of my nickname. They said that it showed up on the tape and that I should have answered truthfully the first time. Since this incident, I believe in lie detectors but fortunately, I have not had any other occasion to test one. After the lie detector, they fingerprinted me "for the file," my translator said. I felt like a criminal having my fingerprints on file, since I had only seen it done in gangster movies.

After it was all over, and I was on file for life, my handler took me to lunch and said I had to see a committee in the afternoon for the results. I was concerned they might reject me. Then what? All sorts of thoughts were rushing through my mind, so I didn't have much of an appetite. Could they change their minds and deport me? I knew the US needed a fast canoe-paddler, but maybe not badly enough.

The committee was nice and accommodating, almost apologetic. They confirmed that since the Kennedy assassination, a new procedure was in place to screen political refugees. They said that I passed the test and asked me what my plan was and where I'd like to go. I told them I would like to go to Hawaii. "Don't we all!" they said laughing. They thought I was very humorous, but I wasn't; I was serious. They had asked the question, and I answered them truthfully. I had just gone through the lie detector experience! Since Hawaii seemed to be out of the question, I briefed them on Bill Smoke, my new American friend, who had promised to pick me up when he returned from his extended trip after the Olympic Games. He had traveled around Southeast Asia for a month. They told me they had had a conversation with Mr. Smoke and that he would be back in early December. That was three weeks away. In my mind, I wondered, *What am I supposed to do? Where am I supposed to sleep?* Again, I had a lot of questions.

The State Department came through for me, though. My handler dropped me off at my new place and gave me his phone number to call if needed. I told him that I did not know how to use the phone, since I'd never had the experience in Hungary. He looked at me very strangely, like I was an alien. I was put up in an Arlington studio apartment and given $40 a week for incidentals. They explained that I could stay in this apartment until Bill picked me up. They also gave me a white piece of paper (3" by 4" size) with a big stamped word on it: *PAROLEE*, which in my case meant *stateless*. On this piece of paper, my name was spelled *T-o-r-o*. I told them that the first "O" had two dots and the second "O" had two bars over it. Names in Hungarian are in the logical order: first is the family name, in my case *Törő*, then the given name, in my case *András*, and finally the middle name, in my case *István*.

They chuckled and told me that those letters do not exist in the English language. They suggested that I could possibly change my name, but it was hard for me to accept a new spelling. It felt like I had lost some of my identity, but I went along. I just wanted to get out of that place. At that time, I did not realize that I would be mistaken forever as either a Spanish bull or a lawnmower company.

This *PAROLEE* paper with my new name was the only official document from the US Government that proved I existed in my new country. (My Olympic accreditation tags had been taken and never returned). I had this *PAROLEE* paper for three more years and guarded it with my life. I still have bad dreams about losing it. I was told that I could travel anywhere in the United States as long as I remained within the borders. Three years later, when I received my green card, I had to give up my precious *PAROLEE* paper. I asked the authorities if I could keep it as a souvenir, but they said it was against the law.

My handler brought me more clothes and a suitcase, and soon I settled down in my new apartment in Arlington. For first time in my life, I had my own place and some money in my pocket. I would have given an eye for a place like this in Budapest!

As I was sitting in my new accommodations, it hit me that I was all alone. Really and truly alone! I had never been alone, always with family or friends; now, I was in a strange country, a strange town, and a strange room all by myself. I reflected on how I had betrayed my country, my family, my sports club, my teammates, my girlfriend, and all my other friends who believed me to be an Olympian and had supported me all those years. I realized that I had defected for myself and myself only. Forever, only I would be responsible for my actions. I knew my life had changed and would never be the same. I had to be reborn to be part of a new life in this strange land.

The Washington Canoe Club from the Potomac, 1910.

From my room, I could see the Washington Canoe Club on the other side of the Potomac River under the Key Bridge. My first excursion with my new freedom was to visit this club and try to get on the water, although it was getting a bit cold at the end of November. Two girls from the club had been on the US Olympic team and had won a silver medal in the two-person kayak 500-meter event. That was a formidable accomplishment considering that American women had never previously won any medals in Olympic canoeing competition. Also, Frank Havens, the 1952 Olympic Champion canoeist, was a member of this club, so I had some Olympic connections there. Hoping to make some new friends, I crossed the Key Bridge and went down to the boathouse. My luck held up as the two medal-winning girls were there and recognized me. They were even all dressed up with their Olympic medals, and told me that they had not taken them off since Tokyo! The younger girl was only 15 years old and she really enjoyed her celebrity. They also told me that the neighboring club, Potomac Rowing Club, had a member who spoke Hungarian and that I should meet him. His parents had emigrated during the Second World War, so he was a first-generation American, but could still speak some Hungarian.

I waited for him the next day at the PRC, and he greeted me in Hungarian. He invited me to have lunch with him at a local restaurant where they had goulash on the menu, and I've never turned down good Hungarian goulash. So, we sat and when the waiters came, he ordered two goulashes and beers. Apparently, he did not know that goulash should be eaten with red wine. The waiter came and presented our order, but it was not anything like the Hungarian *gulás*, I knew! It was a pitiful imitation, to say the least. It had everything in it but the kitchen sink—a hodge-podge of vegetables and noodles with a couple pieces of meat. At first, I thought it was a joke, and when my new friend asked me how it was, I didn't know what to say. I didn't want to hurt his feelings, so I said something like, "It needs some improvement." But I was a hungry Hungarian and ate it gratefully. I thought that if my mother were here cooking fine Hungarian *gulás* in her own restaurant, she would make millions.

True Hungarian *gulás* is a soup of rich broth with square potato chunks, pork or beef cubes, diced onion and red or green pepper. You cannot forget the paprika, which is a major ingredient in almost all Hungarian cooking. The *gulás* is simmered for hours until the broth is just the right color and consistency, then eaten with a spoon and hearty slice of peasant bread and a glass of red wine. It is a very traditional, popular, nourishing dish, particularly when cooked in a kettle over an open fire out in the country. It comes in different flavors: beef, pork, or mutton, depending on the availability of the meat (though I never knew a cook to use poultry). The shepherds on the plains of Hungary claim to have originated this dish. At harvest time, hordes of tourists descend on the plains to taste this unique Hungarian culinary creation.

By now, it was late November, and only a few diehards were still braving the cold waters of the Potomac. One of the coaches, Mr. Jack Ruckert of the Washington Canoe Club, asked me what I was doing for Thanksgiving. Not only didn't I know, but I also didn't know what Thanksgiving was, since Hungarians don't celebrate it. He explained that it's an American family tradition dating back to the time when the pilgrims landed, celebrating the year's harvest and the willingness to live in harmony with the natives. I knew about the Mayflower's voyage and the pilgrims' landing in the new world to establish a colony, because I had read some books about American history. He invited me to join his family for Thanksgiving, and I was grateful for the invitation and curious to see what this national holiday was all about.

My first American Thanksgiving was an eye opener, to say the least. I remember it was a crisp, sunny fall day and he picked me up early in the afternoon. When we arrived at his house, it was already buzzing with people. Cars were parked all along the street and joyful noises, laughter, and delicious fragrances wafted through the whole neighborhood. Young adults were outside shooting baskets and throwing footballs.

Mr. Ruckert had a big family of five kids and, in addition to other relatives, there must have been over thirty people at his place, including one lonely Hungarian. Entering the dining room was a shocker—I had never seen so much food in one place in all my life. The huge, beautifully decorated table was heaped with all sorts of culinary creations I did not recognize. The table settings with shiny utensils, cloth napkins, and many different glasses, were impressive. Each side dish and relish was in its own bowl, heaped high with an accompanying spoon or fork. There were so many delicious smells in the air that it was hard to distinguish any particular one. *I have to try everything*, I thought. Banners that said *HAPPY THANKSGIVING* were hanging on the walls, with turkeys, Pilgrim hats, and other decorations created by the children.

I was introduced to the family as a newly arrived pilgrim. Everyone around me wanted to know my story, with young and old asking all sorts of questions. Unfortunately, I did not have enough command of the language to explain well enough, so Mr. Ruckert came to my rescue and explained my situation. I became an instant celebrity and a popular addition at the Thanksgiving feast. In the meantime, more people were arriving, bringing more food! I was beginning to wonder what would happen with all the leftovers. The adults were standing around with their pre-dinner drinks in their hands, discussing politics and the upcoming football games.

Then, the big moment came, and Mr. Ruckert called everyone to the table. I was seated with his kids. He bowed his head and called for a prayer, and we all held hands, following his lead. From the corner of my eye, I looked around and felt the genuine spiritual connection—it was Thanksgiving in its purest form. After saying grace, the table exploded in the sound of utensils, eating, and talking. I was interested in all the rituals, slicing the huge roasted turkey, heaping piles of stuffing and mashed potatoes on my plate, drowning it all with gravy, and politely passing the food around. There was so much food, and it was all delicious. I was very glad I had come! During the dinner, Mr. Ruckert raised his glass and toasted me on my first Thanksgiving and wished me a good stay in my newly chosen country. I was moved by his kindness and could hardly hold back my tears. I said, "Thank you, thank you, thank you." Pointing to my plate, I raised my thumb to indicate my hearty approval of the food.

After the main meal, the table was cleared and the climax of the dinner followed—the desserts. The ladies took over the table, cutting into the many different pies—pumpkin, pecan, chocolate, berry, and so on—and serving them with a healthy scoop of ice cream or whipped cream. It was surreal to see so many calories passed around. Of course, coffee and tea followed for those who wanted it.

The kids were excused early and went out to play baseball on the back lawn. They asked me to join them. I didn't know anything about baseball, though I had heard of it, of course. I was impressed by how much the professional players made, even then. At that time, I could not have imagined that in my future I would meet and serve on the US Olympic Committee with one of the most well-known and controversial figures in professional baseball, Mr. George Steinbrenner. When my turn to bat came, beginner's luck smiled upon me. On the second pitch, I connected and the ball disappeared into a thicket. The kids all thought I was good!

The Ruckert house in College Park, Maryland, backed up to a forest park, so there was lots of room to play and lots of leaves to rake. I was really surprised that there were no fences between the properties. How did people know where to stop raking the leaves or stop shoveling the snow? It was fun to play outside in late November, but as the sun started to go down we all moved inside, where a big fire was already roaring in the fireplace. We all had more pies and ice cream, and I came to the conclusion that Thanksgiving was not a bad holiday. Hungarians should have a celebration like that. Perhaps when the Russians leave the country, we would celebrate. *That would be a real Thanksgiving*, I thought.

Mr. Ruckert asked me if I would like to stay with them until my friend picked me up. He said I could stay in the basement where one of the fireplaces was. I did not really want to give up my new apartment, but living alone was not much fun either, and I wanted to have more conversations to learn the language. So, I moved into their basement and that weekend they invited me to a Maryland University football game. I don't remember who they played against, but it was the first time I saw an American football game. They tried to explain the rules, like the downs and the ten yards, etc., but it was too much to learn. I could not understand why it was called football either. The only time they kicked the ball was when they stopped the action, totally opposite of the European football I loved. However, I enjoyed the halftime show when the marching bands took the field. I liked all the different formations and the music. They explained that every university, college, and high school has a football team, a stadium, a band, and cheerleaders. That was a huge surprise to me and later, I learned that he had forgotten to mention the professional teams.

Life was good with the family and I began to pick up the language. Everyone addressed me in English, so I was forced to respond in kind. Then, on December 15th my friend, Bill Smoke, showed up with a big Streamliner camper. He learned at the Washington Canoe Club that I was hanging out with the Ruckert's. I said an emotional goodbye to my first American family, and we left to go back to Michigan, where Bill lived with his parents. But Bill was not in a hurry; he said we'd stop by Philadelphia to visit his rowing friend, Jack Kelly. Bill had been a lightweight rower before the Olympic Games and switched to kayaking to make the Olympic team. I had heard of Jack Kelly from my old canoeing partner. In the 1956 Melbourne Olympic Games, Jack was rowing the single and he took third place behind the Russian, Ivanov and the Australian, Mackenzie. His family was cheering for him on the shore, including his sister Grace Kelly, the film star. I was hoping I might have a chance to meet her as well! Unfortunately, that didn't happen, but I had a good visit with Jack. (Later on, Jack and I crossed paths many times over the years, and were good friends from the time he was the vice president of the USOC until his untimely death in 1988).

Bill suggested that we also stop by in New York City and see the Statue of Liberty and the Empire State Building. He gave me a big tour and I was impressed with the city and appreciative of the chance. New York, of course, is every Hungarian's dream city. It is the city of opportunity and fortunes as well as tragedy, but in the end I was disappointed. It was too noisy and crowded for me; the people seemed unfriendly—aggressive and faceless. I had many more occasions to visit New York City over the years, but my first impression has never changed. I have always felt very uncomfortable and insecure there. We spent two days in New York. At the New York Athletic Club, I saw the America's Cup in the trophy room. I knew about the Cup and its history, but seeing it in person was very special. We also visited the United States Olympic Committee headquarters, the Olympic House, at 57 Park Avenue where we met Mr. Bushnell, the Secretary of the USOC (The USOC was headquartered in this location until they moved to Colorado Springs in 1978). He had just returned from the Games, and he knew about my defection. He wished me good luck and asked me to "please continue to support the Olympic movement." At least, that was how I understood it. Little did we know that twenty years later, I would step into his shoes as the newly elected Secretary of the United States Olympic Committee and continue to support our lifelong passion for the Olympic movement.

Finally, we got back on the road and headed for Michigan. We stopped to sightsee at Niagara Falls, and Bill said he would like to take a shortcut to Detroit through Canada. It would save lots of time and miles, but I told him I could not risk it. The State Department was very specific about not leaving the country. He said that they didn't check everybody, and we should take a chance. I didn't want to take any chance! I had to hang on to my *PAROLEE* paper. Grudgingly, he agreed to go the southern route around Lake Erie. By the way, Niagara Falls was spectacular. I had heard of this natural wonder, but seeing it was breathtaking. We walked all the way down the Mist Trail to the lower platform, and I marveled at those brave (crazy) people who made it over the falls alive in a barrel. *What courage!*

The original USOC headquarters in New York, 1921-1978.

As we made our way to Michigan, the most popular song on the radio waves was Petula Clark's "Downtown." It seemed to be on almost every station, and by the time we arrived in Detroit, I knew the song phonetically. Even now, when I hear that song, it reminds me of that first trip to Detroit.

Bill's parents lived on Grosse Isle, a small island in the Detroit River. As we were crossing a small bridge, we stopped to pay a toll, and it was strange to me to pay to cross a bridge. Then, Bill told me that his family owned the bridge! Now that was even stranger. My friend, Elbert Andor, had told me that Bill's family was well off, and I began to believe it.

Smoke's house on Grosse Isle in the Detroit River of Michigan.

The Smoke's home was spectacular! It was a three-story, brick, Tudor-like castle with a four-car garage, servant's quarters, and a waterfront right on the Detroit river. His grandfather had come to America from Poland around the time of the First World War and established a florist business in the Detroit area. They changed their name from an unpronounceable Polish one to Smoke. The family business put on the Hudson Department Store's Christmas flower show every year, using flowers from all over the world, as well as from their own greenhouses. It was a spectacular show, with beautiful floral displays in the middle of the cold Michigan winter. Christmas was only a few days away, so immediately after our arrival, Bill and I were kept busy delivering poinsettias all over the Detroit area in a big, covered panel truck. The Christmas flower business was good. Bill was the oldest of four brothers, and they all helped out in the business, particularly at Christmas and Easter. Since I did not have any winter clothes, he gave me an Eddie Bauer down jacket. It was a short cut jacket almost like a parka, but very warm, and I kept that jacket all through my Michigan years.

At the Smoke's house, the Christmas decorations were not only inside the house, but also outside. It was like a fairy land! All the outdoor decorations would glitter in the snow when we returned after a long day of flower delivery. Inside, all the fireplaces were going and the house was warm and cozy. Beautiful, large red and white candles were lit in many of the rooms, while red and gold ribbons and stars covered the walls. In the solarium, a glass extension of the house looking over the river, stood a Christmas tree. It was

My first American Christmas with the Smoke family, 1964.

an unbelievable sight, but I felt sadness in my heart, thinking of my family and our poor Christmases as I grew up.

In Budapest, we almost always had a Christmas tree, not the biggest one but the prettiest, in my mind. We set it up in one of our two rooms, on a chair, decorating it the day before Christmas or on Christmas day. My mother used to buy a box of *solon* candy for the holidays. Each piece was wrapped in thin, colored foil and tissue paper, and we'd hang them on the tree with hooks for decoration. This candy came in all kinds of flavors, including vanilla, berry, marzipan (my favorite), and of course, chocolate. When Christmas Day came, the candy all appeared to still be hanging on the tree, but there was actually no candy inside the paper foil. My brother and I had perfected the art of taking the candy out and redoing the wrapper so it still appeared to have candy inside. We both denied removing the candy, and our father swore every year that next Christmas we would not get any, but my mother always bought some just the same. We had several colorful decorative balls and a shiny star, which we placed on the top. On Christmas Eve, we also had sparklers to light. Sparklers were my favorite things, though we had to be careful not to accidentally start a fire. We kept the Christmas tree until January 5th when, according to tradition, we took it down. Usually, we cut it up and burned it in our stove. We never had any individual Christmas presents that I can remember. We didn't need them; we were happy without. Mother always made a nice Christmas dinner, ending with desserts and pastries. My all-time favorites were her poppy seed and walnut rolls (*beigly*). In the evening, we sat down to sing Christmas songs, and it always felt very festive and moving, no matter how poor we were. My last Christmas tree in 1962 was really just a branch. Only my parents and I were at home then, and my father didn't think we needed a tree. "It costs too much," he explained. But my mother still got a small branch anyway. As my brothers grew up and left home, I started going to my Canoe Club on Margaret Island to have a holiday celebration with my second family as well.

On Christmas Day 1964, my first American Christmas, I sat down with the Smoke family to open presents, beginning with the stockings. Everyone had a big, fancy, decorated stocking. They even had a makeshift stocking for me. I was not familiar with this stocking custom and they explained that these presents were from Santa Claus. In Hungary, Santa Claus visits on December 5th, *Miklos* (Saint Nicolas) Name Day, and December 25th is strictly a religious celebration of Jesus. In America, they all mixed together. I eventually came to realize it is all for marketing purposes and capitalism.

Back on Grosse Isle, after the stockings came the main presents. There were all sorts of delicately-wrapped boxes with colorful ribbons and bows piled up under the Christmas tree, each tagged for its lucky recipient. Just the wrapping paper cost a fortune, I thought. Mrs. Smoke brought in some eggnog and cookies to make sure we had enough energy to open all the presents. It was overwhelming, to say the least. I had never seen such a display of abundance. Everyone was unwrapping their presents at once and thanking the givers for their kindness. I was pleased to receive some nice new clothes, which I really needed.

One detail I vividly remember was when the youngest boy in the Smoke family, 15-year-old Paul, was unwrapping a present, he found a stack of stock certificates inside. "Not these damn stocks again," he cried. He wanted something more fun. Bill tried to console him, saying "It's for your future, Paul. You'll be thankful for them." Here was something new again. I just vaguely knew about the stock market and about owning shares in a company, but giving stocks to kids at an early age was a very novel idea. At that time, I realized I had many things to learn in this strange country about money management, the monetary system, and the basic rules of capitalism.

After settling into my new place with the Smoke family, I felt happy that things were going so well, and that my sponsor was an understanding and well-off family. A couple of days before Christmas, there had been some nice unseasonably sunny days in Detroit. Otherwise, Detroit's early winter weather was much like Hungary's—cold rain or snow with freezing temperatures. But this particular day was really nice. The black top driveway in front of the big garage was clear, all the snow shoveled to the side. Above the garage doors, a basketball hoop and backboard were mounted. I thought at the time that this was unusual, but later I saw that almost every home in the USA where boys were growing up had a hoop. Paul challenged me to a one-on-one basketball game. I accepted, being anxious to do some physical exercise. Since leaving Washington D.C., I had had three square meals every day (my favorite being hamburgers) but very little exercise.

Paul was taller than me already at fifteen and ended up over seven feet tall when he finished high school. We started to play, though I did not know any of the rules. I just bounced the ball and tried to score any way I could. On one play, I pushed him a bit too hard, and he almost fell to the ground. He turned around, and with anger in his eyes, looked around make sure that no one else could hear him and said, "You're a nigger!" I had no idea what he was calling me, as I'd never heard this word, *nigger*. From his expression, I could tell that he was not pleased and it was probably a bad word. After we finished playing, I looked it up in my always-handy Hungarian-English dictionary in my room. The dictionary told me that the word referred to black people, but was used as a derogatory term, particularly in the south. I was kind of pleased that Paul thought that I was a black person. We, Hungarians, had great respect for black athletes and admired them, particularly during the Olympic Games. The Hungarians I knew had no color prejudices. After the Second World War, one black US soldier had stayed in Budapest. He worked for many years as a waiter in the New York Coffee House, a very prestigious establishment usually frequented by writers and actors; the elite of the Hungarian society. Everyone wanted to see him and he drew a crowd. I hadn't seen him myself but I had heard about him. It took me several years to fully understand the meaning of *nigger*, and what it meant in that context.

Bill's father was a tall man. He had played semi-professional basketball in his youth and liked all kinds of sports. He was at the Tokyo Olympic Games to see Bill race. He related to me because of his parents' struggle through their early years in the USA. After Christmas one dinnertime, Mr. Smoke asked me what my plans were. I told everyone I would like to learn English as quickly as I could so I could then enroll in a place of higher education, perhaps in a university. They all agreed that was a good plan. They told me that just outside of Detroit, in Ann Arbor, the University of Michigan had an English Language Institute (ELI) for people just like me to learn English. Bill, who was dating Marcia Jones (also on the US Olympic team in Tokyo, winning a bronze medal in the single-kayak event) said that Marcia's mother, Mrs. Francis, had already contacted the institute to see if I could enroll. She would provide me with a scholarship. Mrs. Francis herself was a graduate of the law school, and one of the early female graduates and a loyal alumna.

The Smoke family also told me there was a large group of Hungarians living in a section of Detroit. Many of the older folks came before World War II and the younger ones left during the 1956 revolution. I told the family that I would actually like to stay away from Hungarians so I could learn English and merge into American society more quickly. They thought that was also a good decision.

CHAPTER 8
My Years at the University of Michigan

My luck smiled on me again. On January 5, 1965, Bill drove me to Ann Arbor and helped me find lodging. He rented a room in a boarding house, where I had a roommate—an American boy of Greek heritage. Bill helped me take care of the paperwork and gave me $20 for incidentals. I enrolled in the University of Michigan English Language Institute, though the term had already started. Bill gave me a map of the campus and showed me how to get to my language class. For a long time, I did not deviate from this original route to class.

On arrival day, we had lunch with Marcia's sister, Sperry, who was in graduate school and running on the track team for U of M. She suggested I work for my food at one of the dormitories as a busboy. After lunch, Bill took me back to my room and said goodbye, promising that he would be back in two weeks. I was alone again!

Winter in Michigan was just as bad, or perhaps worse, than Hungary with damp, cold, slushy snow, and below-zero temperatures. Luckily, I had Bill's Eddie Bauer down jacket, which was much warmer than my Olympic overcoat, the only other thing I had. I wore that Eddie Bauer jacket for many years and was sad to part with it when it fell apart. That jacket saved my life.

So, there I was beginning my new life in America in an unfamiliar place of higher education. I didn't know if I should cry or be happy. Everything was going so well so far, happening so quickly. The next morning, I went to my class along the route Bill had showed me. My class was a small group of about ten foreigners from Greece, Turkey, Colombia, and Japan. There was also another class parallel to ours at the same time; we were all there to learn English as a second language. We had four hours of class each morning with a teacher. *Repeat after me*, was the order of the day. I heard "repeat after me" so many times that it hurt and I could mimic her like a parrot. In the afternoon, we went to the English lab, where we listened to tapes and had more *repeat after me* exercises. It was intense and relentless, this pounding of a new language into my head, but it was very effective. After the first day of *repeat after me* exercises, my head was spinning. I told myself I had to do it to be a citizen and to attend the university later in pursuit of that brighter future.

The second day in Ann Arbor, Sperry got me a busboy job at one of the dormitories. Busboy is a fancy name for dishwasher. I received as much lunch and dinner as I could eat and a very small salary. It was a good deal, I thought, trading physical work for food. I worked with Jack, an old black man, who was a full-time busboy. He earned his living and supported his large family by being a dishwasher. He talked to me all the time, but I could not understand a word of what he was saying. Was he speaking English? It didn't sound at all like what my English teacher was saying. I wondered if there was more than one kind of English spoken in America, and my suspicions were confirmed later as I traveled around the country. Almost every state has its own dialect of the language. The alphabet may be the same, but it sure is pronounced differently. Later, Jack invited me to his church on Sunday, where he said there would be lots of gospel music, dancing, and singing. Unfortunately, I never took advantage of his offer. Later, I really regretted this because I could have learned a little about the religious aspect of the black culture. So, there I was, a decorated Olympic medalist washing dishes and learning a new way of life. It was not demeaning, though, and I found it exciting because everything was new and everything was for the first time.

Bill came back two weeks later, as he promised, and noticed my language improvement. I could say simple sentences, though the English-Hungarian dictionary was always at hand. He said at Easter he would drive to see Marcia in Oklahoma City, where she lived with her mother, and that I should go with him. That meant a one-week break from my language class, which I really couldn't afford, but the chance to travel and see more of America was too enticing. Bill often took trips and liked to stop in Ann Arbor to pick me up throughout the years I lived there.

In the meantime, Sperry took me down to the indoor track where she trained, so I could run with her as a "rabbit." A *rabbit* in this sense is a faster runner who helps a slower runner train by always being a little ahead. It was good cross training for me. I wanted to get back in shape because I hoped to paddle again and eventually make the USA team. According to international rules, I could not compete for two years internationally, but I could enter races domestically. So, things began to shape up as far as my conditioning and future hopes to get back in the boat were concerned.

Down at the sport complex, Sperry introduced me to many university athletes. It was fun to see the swimmers and divers recently returned from the Tokyo Olympic Games, as well as the football and basketball players. Cazzie Russell was the big basketball star at Michigan at the time, and I went to see some of his games. He turned pro and went on to have a very successful career. Through athletics at Michigan, I met many outstanding athletes and coaches who would later come back into my life.

Things were going along fine at the English Language Institute, when one day they called me to the administration office. *This is strange*, I thought. *My tuition is paid! Why would they want to talk to me?* There were two local FBI agents there, and they wanted to ask me some questions about Lee Harvey

English Language class, March 1965. I'm in the foreground.

Oswald and his wife, Marina Oswald. I knew about Oswald, President Kennedy's assassin. I remember the day well: November 22, 1963. I was traveling on a streetcar in Budapest on leave from the Army when I heard the news. People were crying in the streets. We could not believe that such a terrible thing could happen. President Kennedy was a very popular and respected person in Hungary. He stood up to the Russians, and that gave Hungarians hope in resisting their oppression.

But I didn't know anything about Oswald's wife. It turned out she was in the other English language class meeting at the same time as mine and the FBI wanted to establish whether or not there was any connection between the two of us since we were both from Eastern bloc countries. *That's interesting*, I thought. The US Government was checking out all possibilities as the Cold War raged on. Later, I did see Marina in the class but made sure to stay away from her. The last thing I wanted was to be associated with her and get deported. On January 5, 1965, the *Detroit Free Press* had an article on Marina saying that "her book agent advised her not to grant any interviews during her eight week stay at the U of M English language Institute in 1965."

My classes were going great. I was slowly beginning to understand people and engage in limited conversation. The teacher kept telling us that the more we practiced, the better we'd get. For me to be admitted to the university, I had to achieve a total score of 72% on my final three examinations, which were oral comprehension, reading comprehension, and writing. The finals were scheduled for the first weekend in May.

Spring comes with a bang in Michigan. From one week to the next, with temperature changes and more sunshine, nature really takes a leap, and everything suddenly becomes green. The dark gray trees are covered with bright green buds, while the crocuses and other bulb flowers begin popping out of the ground. It is the most beautiful time of the year after a long, hard winter. In 1965, an early spring came the first weekend of April, and flowers I did not know existed bloomed. All the students were outside on "the Diag," short for *the Diagonal*, which was right in the middle of the campus in the front of the main library. It was a large open space with benches, green lawns, and tall trees crisscrossed with sidewalks and was a favorite gathering place for the

The old canoe livery, Argo Pond, Ann Arbor, 1965.

students. Some of the classes had even moved outside with groups of students sitting on the lawn.

With warmer weather, Sperry invited me to go down with her to the Huron River (a section called Argo Pond) between two dams, where an old canoe livery was located. She kept her single kayak there and was going to begin practicing on the water. The river opened up earlier than usual and was ice-free. This place, the old Wirth Canoe Livery, which dated back to 1898, became my favorite spot in Ann Arbor. I loved that place and spent all my spare time there practicing and informally helping with canoe rentals on the weekend. The livery rented touring canoes—old strip-planked canvas-covered Old Towns, Peterborough boats, and Grumman aluminum canoes—to students on the weekends for pleasure boating on the river. The livery was a two-story wood building built right over the river on stilts. I was told that, many years previously, there had been a very cold winter with lots of thick ice on the river. Spring rains raised the water level, and the ice floes knocked some of the pilings out of the river bed. This explained why the livery did not have any level place. All the floors were slanted and nothing was square anymore, which gave real character to the building. The owner's family lived upstairs and told me that, back in the 1920s, the livery had reached almost all the way across the river with a large dance hall. It was the place to listen to big band music and dance. What remained from that era were the coin-operated *orchestrions*, *melodeons*, and other antique mechanical music boxes. These were popular in the early part of the 20th century in small town saloons where music bands did not visit. The livery still had four of these music boxes, which fascinated me. You could hear the big drum *orchestrion* a mile away.

On a sunny weekend day, this place was buzzing with students taking out canoes to travel up river for picnics. It was a lively place to be, particularly if you were a canoe-paddler. But I needed a training boat, and buying one was out of the question as I did not have the money for it. Some of the sports magazines that Sperry brought along advertised the new Danish racing models, but all I could do was salivate.

At Easter, we had a couple days' vacation, but our teachers emphasized the need to continue practicing. Bill came by as promised and told me that we were going to Oklahoma City to see Marcia, now his fiancée. His camper was all loaded up with potted Easter flowers for Marcia's mom. I was reluctant to go because of my studies, but tempted by the opportunity to see Oklahoma City and the home of my benefactor. So, I grabbed my bag and soon we were rolling down Highway 66. We listened to the radio and talked. I did practice conversation. He said he would like to make it to Marcia's in twenty hours, which meant we had to drive non-stop. In the middle of the night, somewhere in Kansas, he got very sleepy and asked me if I would like to drive. He knew that I had never driven a car, let alone a stick shift camper. I figured that sooner or later, I'd have to learn and now on the open, deserted highway might be as good a time as any. So, we switched places, he showed me how to shift gears, and then he fell asleep. I was cruising along pretty good, keeping it at 75, listening to the soft music of WJR 69.5 when it started to drizzle. It was just a light cold rain, but enough to make the road wet and slippery.

There were not too many stop lights on Route 66, but there were some in Kansas. I saw the light about a half mile ahead of me and it was green with no other cars in sight. As I was getting closer, it changed. My first reaction was to speed through it, but I reconsidered and slammed on the brakes. The pavement at the light where all the cars had stopped and leaked oil was like an ice rink. The camper began to fishtail and I lost control. Holding on to the steering wheel and with a foot frozen on the brake, the truck slid down into the ditch on the passenger side. We almost rolled over, and the flower pots shifted and then spilled over to the low side of the camper. The vehicle stopped, as did my heart. Bill woke up and said a couple of choice words. We got out and opened the back doors to see the wreckage inside, and not one flower pot was standing.

The locked back tires had dug a deep trench into the soft embankment, so we got the shovel out and begin to dig. A car stopped by and asked if we needed some help. In all my many travels in the United States, I have always admired the willingness of fellow travelers to help, particularly during the night. I learned to do the same. However, Bill thought that we could dig ourselves out of this one on our own. He tried to rock the camper out of the trench, but it only got deeper and deeper. About a half an hour later, a tow truck came from the opposite direction. The fellow who stopped must have alerted the gas station attendant ahead of us. The tow truck pulled us out and, with our van undamaged, we continued our way. Bill said that I was lucky and praised my skill at keeping the truck upright but there had been no skill at all—it was pure luck.

In Oklahoma City, I met my benefactor and Marcia's mother, Mrs. Francis. She lived alone on a ranch of several hundred acres in a relatively modern house with a swimming pool, horse barns, and an electric gate. One day, as we were driving around in the city, she pointed out some oil wells in front of the state capitol building. She said, "Those mosquitoes suck the juice out of the earth." She invited me to come down after graduating from the English Language Institute and spend some time in Oklahoma. I mentioned to her that I would like to make a racing canoe and get back into competition, and she liked my enthusiasm for canoeing. Perhaps this was because both her girls had decided to try to make the US Kayak team for the 1968 Olympic Games in Mexico City. She said she would sponsor my boatbuilding, and it was an offer I couldn't refuse.

I did come back to Oklahoma City in the summer of 1965 and built my first single canoe. I tried it out in Mrs. Francis' swimming pool. It wasn't the prettiest thing, but it would give me a chance to get on the water and start training. We took it back to Ann Arbor and I kept it at the canoe livery. In addition to building my canoe, I took driving lessons that summer from an instructor financed by Mrs. Francis. Bill had told her about our adventure, and she felt it was important that I know how to drive. I didn't get my license, though. In fact, it would be another five years until I did that.

In the spring of 1965, Bill and Marcia got married in Oklahoma City. I was invited as a special guest to sing at their wedding because Bill had admired my renditions of "Downtown" when I sang along with Petula Clark on our first trip to Michigan. Sadly, "Downtown" did not meet the approval of the bride, so I chose a nice Hungarian song instead, which I practiced with the piano accompanist, who didn't have the sheet music. The wedding was very festive, with beautiful flowers and tasty American food. I felt very lucky that both families embraced me as a new member, and Mrs. Francis promised to support me as long as I studied at Michigan. This security blanket eased my financial anxieties, but at the same time, it put some pressure on me to perform well. After the wedding, Bill and Marcia moved back to Michigan where Bill was attending a community college. I went back to Ann Arbor to finish my first term at the English Language Institute and was glad they were nearby.

Testing out my first self-designed and self-made canoe in Oklahoma, July, 1965.

Back at the ELI, my first examination period came in early May, and I had to do 72% or better to have any hope of attending University of Michigan. I was very excited and nervous. It turned out to be very tough for me and I failed both my oral and written comprehension tests. My total score was only 68%, and I was very disappointed, while my mind raced with questions about the future. It occurred to me that I might not have the ability to graduate from an American university, and that I didn't have a trade to fall back on. In Hungary, I had high school training as a draftsman for steel structures, but how useful this was in America, I did not know. I told Bill my results, and he was very encouraging, suggesting I take another half semester. The English Language Institute offered a half-semester course in the summer, so I signed up with the financial help of Mrs. Francis. I was a very lucky man, but the pressure was on even more—I must not fail the second exam. It was hard to focus now that summer had arrived and the boathouse was waiting. Some of the paddlers training with me were talking about going to the Nationals, which were held in Washington, D.C. that summer of 1965. It was very tempting, but for now my education took priority.

English Language Institute
THE UNIVERSITY OF MICHIGAN

This is to certify that **ANDRAS TORO**

has attended the **INTENSIVE COURSE IN ENGLISH**

offered for the period **January 8 to April 23, 1965**

and has made satisfactory progress in English Language study for this period.

Ann Arbor, Michigan, U.S.A.

J. C. Catford
Director, English Language Institute

April 23, 1965
Date

Robert F. Dakin
Coordinator, Intensive Course

My English Language Institute Certificate, April 1965.

I buckled down and studied. The final examination came at the end of the half semester in July. I was as nervous as before the Olympic finals. A lot was at stake—if I failed again, I would disappoint many people who had been helping me and believing in me, not to mention myself. I would be a failure forever. I put lots of pressure on myself. Even now when I have a bad dream, I dream about taking my language exams and failing! With sweaty hands, I waited for the results. It was 82%. I did it! Now I had the privilege (and anxiety) of figuring out my next move.

Bill and Marcia stopped by one day and invited me to go with them to the National Championships. I decided I could afford to take a break and celebrate my success at the ELI by going with them to see my first big race in the States. We piled into Bill's camper and headed to D.C., but the US Canoeing Nationals was very disillusioning. The competition was held on the Potomac River in front of the Washington Canoe Club, which had produced many Olympic athletes. The course, if it could be called that, was a couple of plastic milk jugs floating on the river, indicating the approximate finish line, and I couldn't believe my eyes. I'd had a great vision of straight buoyed lanes with flags and banners, tents set up for the competitors and spectators—the usual pageantry that I was accustomed to in Hungary. Bill and Marcia explained to me that canoeing was a totally amateur sport, with no financial support, and consisted of a club system that struggled just to stay alive. The American Canoe Association (ACA) is the oldest sports federation in the USA founded in 1880, but its main focus is recreational canoeing, not Olympic-style competition.

They urged me to become a member of the ACA because it was a requirement to compete domestically and internationally for the USA. I signed up for it and have been a member ever since.

I didn't race in the 1965 US Nationals because I didn't feel prepared, but I promised myself I would be back next year. The canoeing competition was very weak, and many events went directly to finals due to the lack of entries. However, the women's kayak division was strong with the returning Olympians. Marcia did well against her competition. The officials spent more time bickering on the shore than running the races. I came back to Ann Arbor with the resolve to help US Canoeing in the future as much as I could.

After returning from Nationals, I decided I needed to work. The dorms had closed for the summer and I was out of cash and food. I stopped by a local construction site and asked the foreman if there were any openings. He asked me about my skills and what tools I owned. My answer was very honest if unimpressive—I had no experience and no tools. The next day I bought a hammer, just in case, and upon returning to the site, I was hired to install fiberglass insulation. The following morning at seven, I showed up for work. We off-loaded a truck with rolled-up fiberglass insulation and then began to hang it. The work was simple, but very itchy and unpleasant with all the fiberglass pieces floating around in the humid Michigan air. Speaking of humidity, if you have not experienced it, you do not know what it's like. It is brutal in Michigan from June to September, both day and night, and you cannot escape it. The air is dense with moisture, making breathing a challenge. I cannot recall my hourly wages, but it must have been the absolute minimum. The foreman urged me to work faster. It was a dirty, exhausting job, but I had to do it to make money and survive. It also solidified the idea that education would assure me of a better future.

Visiting the West Engineering building, 50 years later.

That Friday, I received my first real paycheck. I noticed there were some deductions for Social Security and other taxes. I did not like it much, so I asked my coworkers about it. They said, "Welcome to America." Then the foreman pulled me aside and told me that since I was not a union member, I should give him 10% of my hard-earned money to protect my job. This really pissed me off, but he was bigger and I realized that I couldn't do much about it, so I paid him. Perhaps it is the American way, I consoled myself. Back at my apartment, I sat down and tried to figure out how many years it would take to be a millionaire with my small paycheck. My calculation was very discouraging—without factoring in any living expenses or taxes, I had to work over 200 years. That simple calculation gave me even more determination to go back to school and get my higher education.

I began to earn some money, but it came in the form of a check, and I had never dealt with such a monetary system. Bill suggested I open a checking account at the local bank and came with me. I was reluctant to give my hard-earned money to an institution that I did not understand, but Bill assured me this was the way the capitalist system worked. I realized there were a lot of things to learn in this strange country before I would feel comfortable. My father's banking system of cash-in-the-cupboard was not the American way.

Towing tank at U of M, where I worked from 1965-73.

At U of M, the West Engineering Building enclosed the northwest end of the Diag. There was an archway in the building for students to pass under to get from the Diag to the city streets beyond. I passed through it every time

I went to my ELI class and always heard woodworking machinery sounds coming from that building. One day, I looked through the window and I saw workers making wooden boat models. The place turned out to be a shop for the Hydrodynamic Laboratory of the Naval Architecture Department. It was a research facility that also did commercial testing; they made model boats to test in the towing tank. When the West Engineering Building was built at the turn of the century, the Dean of the school was a naval architect, and he insisted on having a towing tank and a woodworking shop as part of the Hydrodynamic laboratory. A towing tank is a long, narrow pool of water, relatively deep, which has an electrically-driven carriage traveling the full length on a track above it. The boat models are attached to this carriage and dragged through the water to measure resistance. By extrapolating to full scale, they could measure the power needed to propel a boat.

I could do woodworking, as I'd helped my brother build boats at my club back in Hungary. So, one day I worked up the courage to go inside to talk with someone about possible employment. With my broken English improving, I explained that I knew how to do that kind of carving. The foreman said that there was no opening, but luck smiled on me again. Professor Couch (everyone called him "Dick"), a cigar-smoking gentleman who was head of the laboratory, was standing nearby and heard my inquiry. He told me that they were looking for a carriage driver, but the person must be a student. I told him that I was at the English Language Institute right now, but when I finished I hoped to enter the university. He hired me as a carriage driver, a job I held during all my U of M years. Professor Couch became my mentor and advisor, a father figure to me. He believed in me—something I appreciated very much.

I gladly quit my insulation installing job and started working as a carriage driver for the U of M Naval Architecture Department. It didn't pay much, but the work hours were flexible as long as the data collection was completed. I worked late at night and went to the canoe livery for training during the day. I figured that the income was enough to survive.

I proudly told Prof. Couch that I had passed the English language test and asked him what it would take to be a university student. He said that he would put a committee together to test me for university entrance. The time for the regular admission tests that year had already passed, and a couple of days later he invited me to take the test. There were three professors in the room—Prof. Couch, Prof. Hun Cho Kim, and the Dean of the Engineering Department. Needleless to say, I was even more nervous than at the start line of the Olympic finals. First, they tested my English and my ability to read and comprehend. I must have been acceptable, because they continued. Mr. Kim handed me a paper with a simple differential equation written on it and asked, "Can you solve it?" I had never seen a differential equation in my life. I knew they existed because my high school math was pretty decent, but I'd never reached that level. I handed the paper back and, with trepidation said, "No, I can't." I was afraid that that was the end of my higher education. But instead, Prof. Couch said, "Okay, you are a freshman. You may register at the beginning of the academic year in August." He sensed that my ability was there, and he wanted to give me a chance. (I was surprised by how much importance was given to mathematics.) The first semester was to begin in only a few weeks. Right away, I proudly told Bill I was enrolling, and two days later, Mrs. Francis covered my out-of-state tuition. Again, the pressure to not disappoint them was huge.

In August of 1965, at 25 years of age, I began my freshman year at the University of Michigan. I spent the next seven years getting my bachelor's and master's degrees from the School of Naval Architecture and Marine Engineering. It was the best seven years of my life. As a freshman, I was quite a bit older than my classmates, but that did not bother me at all. I was working at the Hydrodynamic Laboratory as a carriage driver, learning about resistance and the dynamic behavior of ships and getting paid for it.

Mrs. Francis' lawyer friend, who took care of the affairs of many elderly widows in town, found me a place to live. My new place was in an old two-story house on Thompson Street where I had the whole upper floor to myself. This house was just behind the Student Administration building, where President Kennedy delivered his famous speech where he said, "Ask not what your country can do for you, ask what you can do for your country."

My landlady was a frail 92-year-old widow of a geology professor. She lived alone in that big house and needed a caretaker. I had to do some housework for my stay, but it wasn't much and I could fit it into my schedule easily. My

MY YEARS AT THE UNIVERSITY OF MICHIGAN

The house I stayed at on Thompson Street, Ann Arbor 1965-69.

new home was only short walk to the campus and not far from the boathouse. I stayed in that place until she passed away four years later. Then I moved to the place of another 90-year-old widow. This house was even fancier than the one before and had an elevator. I am fortunate to say that during my university years, I only paid three months' rent, which saved me a lot of money for my future.

Through my friendship with an athlete on the campus, I got a busboy job at the Kappa Kappa Gamma (KKG) sorority house. This time *busboy* was a fancy name for *servant*, but I received free lunches and dinners during my school years, as well as a small stipend. The work was easy—about 45 minutes each time, the food was good and plenty, the girls were pretty, and there was the eternal hope of fringe benefits. However, the house mother had a strict rule that we busboys could not date any of the girls in the house. The girls liked my Hungarian accent and the fact that I was an Olympian with a medal, and somewhat older than themselves. They liked the way I announced, "Dinner has been served." I have many great stories and memories of being a busboy at the KKG house.

There were six tables with ten girls at each table. One table of girls was notorious for only dating the athletes, or *jocks*, as they called them. Friday night was a particularly difficult time to serve that table because there was either a game or party or both. They would come down, fresh from the shower, smelling good with their hair curled and without makeup. We pretended not to recognize them and jokingly mixed up their names. They did not want to eat; they just wanted to get out of the house. We had to hurry to clear everything away, and there was a lot of food left that had to be thrown out. I hated that, remembering the food shortages during and after the war when a spoiled piece of bread was a delicacy. I still frown on wasting food, and I taught my kids not to do it.

In the fall of that year, I was training with Sperry on the track at Yost Field. I saw the football team practicing and the punters kicking the football. I thought, *I can do that.* Working up my courage, I went over to the kicking coach and told him, in my limited way, that I played soccer and was a pretty good kicker. He showed me the football and asked if I had ever kicked a ball like that. No, I hadn't but I wanted to give it a try. We went to the 20-yard line and he gave me three balls to try to kick through the uprights. I put the first one on the kicking tee and took a sideways swing at it soccer-style and I blasted it through the uprights. The coach was really surprised and said he had never seen a football kicked that way. The next two balls went the same way, and he told me to come to practice the next day.

The following day, the coach took me to the equipment manager and told him to suit me up. "We have a new kicker." I practiced with the team for about a week before my old soccer knee injury came back and sadly, I had to quit the team. Interestingly, Pete Gogolák, a refugee from the 1956 Hungarian Revolution, was just introducing this unconventional style of kicking to the AFL at the same time.

Money-wise, summers were always tough on me. I had no bus boy job, which meant I had no food. I remember the summer after freshman year coming back from the boathouse after practice one day. I was very hungry as I was passing my favorite hamburger joint, Crazy Jim's. It was a small place, but served the most delicious hamburgers I've ever had, with a slice of grilled purple onion. I am salivating now just thinking about it. I looked into my wallet and all I had left were the four one-dollar bills that the pilots and the stewardesses gave me on the plane from Tokyo to the US, signed *Good Luck in America*. I was so hungry, I was tempted to spend them then—and on several other occasions—but I never did. Those one-dollar bills brought me so much luck, I had to keep them. Instead, I went to a friend's house for some leftovers and paid for it by washing his dishes.

Time was going by quickly, and I started thinking about entering the US Nationals and the North American Championships that second summer. I got excited again about canoeing and the possibility that, in the future, I might represent the USA at the World Championships and, perhaps, at the Olympic Games. I knew that I would not be eligible for the 1968 Mexico City Games because I would not yet have US citizenship. I had been pleased to learn that the IOC was now allowing athletes to compete for a second country, because in the past, it would not have been possible.

I began conditioning and on-water training at the canoe livery in the boat I'd made in Oklahoma at the end of the previous summer. Things were looking very promising, and my training on Argo Pond with Sperry went well. Even though we didn't have a measured distance, my times on our improvised course improved all summer. I was confident that I would do well at the Nationals and qualify to represent the US at the North American Championships. I did do well by winning both the US Nationals and the North American Championships in Toronto that year in the single canoe 1,000-meter event. I was the best in the USA and in North America! One disappointment was that I didn't see my Magnificent Seven friends who were Canadian paddlers now. I was told by their former teammates that they had not made the team this year.

When I returned to U of M for the fall semester, I talked to Prof. Couch about getting my permanent residency, the green card. He promised that he would make some calls, and a month later a local government official called me up and asked me to come in for an appointment. I went with Prof. Couch to the meeting. They asked me some questions, and Prof. Couch vouched for me as a good citizen. Two weeks later, I got my green card. I was very happy to give up the *PAROLEE* card and to almost be an official citizen. It granted me the right to pay taxes and vote in the local elections, but not in the national election for the presidency. They told me that I also could apply for a re-entry permit to the USA, which was almost like a passport. If I did that, I could travel almost anywhere in the world. The government official also told me that

I must register in the next two weeks at the local Selective Service office. Prof. Couch explained it was for the military draft, and I got scared that I'd have to go the US military after having just finished with the Hungarian Army. So, with great reluctance, I reported to the local Selective Service Office, but my good luck followed me again. Eligibility for US military service is up to age 25, and I had just passed that age limit. I received a 4-D classification and a certificate that read *Registered, Over Age*. Getting drafted into the military would have been disastrous—not only would it have delayed my education and training, but the Vietnam conflict was heating up.

Then in the mail, I received my Social Security card. At first, I did not understand the purpose of it. As I asked around, friends explained to me the significance of Social Security as a federal plan to provide financial assistance to retirees. Years later, when I was an independent business owner, I was responsible for taking Social Security out of my own earnings. Now that I am retired, I've earned the benefits of my contributions each month.

With my green card and Social Security number, I qualified to pay in-state tuition for the university. I was very happy about it, and I told Mrs. Francis I'd like to "stand on my own feet" and take care of the tuition myself. She very much appreciated my independence. She came to visit me and we had a nice dinner in the Lord Fox restaurant, which was Ann Arbor's finest at the time. We had a long talk about my future, and she was impressed by my English. She promised her continuing support if needed.

I wrote to my parents about my permanent residency and my re-entry permit. They told me that in my absence, I was sentenced to two-and-a-half years in prison for my defection and I should not try to come home. Half of this sentence was eventually commuted in 1976 and the other half in 1982. When I first returned to my homeland in 1986, I was still very apprehensive. I did not trust the Hungarian government, even though my trip was an official visit to sign the Sports Cooperation Agreement between the USOC and the Hungarian Olympic Committee, which I drafted while I was an officer of the USOC.

Back at the University of Michigan in 1967, my studies were going all right. I tried to take full course loads but ended up dropping half of the classes at the last minute because I still had some comprehension problems, and the training, competing, and jobs took a lot of time. It was slow going, particularly during the first couple of years. It did not help that Bill was always traveling and picking me up to accompany him to Florida, Canada, Oklahoma, and California, and so on. I always obliged, as I liked to travel, but it did not help my studies. On the other hand, I did learn a lot about the American landscape.

After the first year, I really settled into the U of M Naval Architecture Department. All the professors and Hydrodynamic Laboratory staff (where I was working) began to know me, and I felt like I had a new family. It helped that my communication skills started to improve. As a matter of fact, one of my friends said, "you were nicer when you did not speak any English." The Naval Architecture Department was located at the 4th floor of the West Engineering building and included a very large drafting room. This drafting room became my second home. I spent countless hours, day and night, studying and socializing with my fellow naval arch students. The drafting room was always open year-round. In the semester breaks and holidays, only a few stranded foreign students hung around, and we bonded together.

On the perimeter of the drawing room were the professors' offices, which were always open for consultation, as well as the department office for official help. We all knew each other and had no hesitation in discussing any issues. I felt very comfortable in this environment to pursue my goal of being a naval architect graduate. The drafting room had many shipyard-size drawing boards that were assigned at the beginning of each semester to

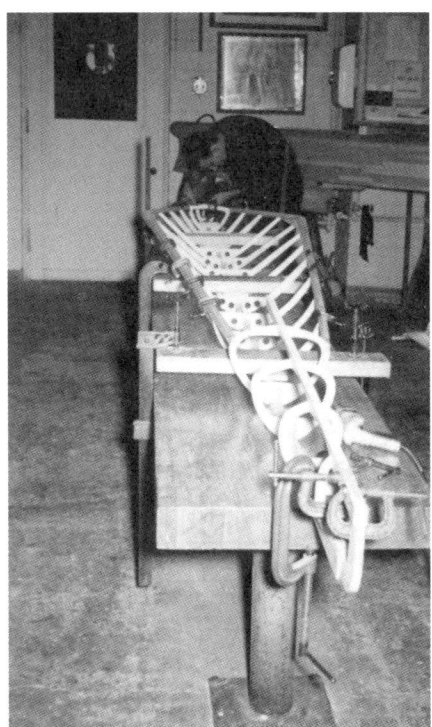

Building my self-designed racing single canoe at U of M woodshop, 1966.

one or two students. Each graduate student had a table to themselves, and it reminded me of my old Hungarian Canoe club locker distribution system. We could leave any books and projects on the table or take a short nap. It was very secure, although the door was open 24 hours year-round. Some of the regulars, like me, had a key to the West Engineering Building front door, which gave us access to the whole building. In later years, it came in handy when I started to build canoes in the model-making shop. Only a couple of times did I get into trouble by not cleaning up on time when I worked late on Sunday night, or for using some fiberglass resin that smelled up the whole building. Luckily, Professor Couch always came to rescue me.

As you entered the drafting room, on the end wall was a tenth scale model of an Americas Cup yacht—a very impressive display reminding you of the pinnacle of the profession. Also, one of the offices was the VULCANS Quarterdeck Society meeting room, a naval architecture student group. I became the Commodore (President) of the Quarterdeck Society in my senior year. All around the room were bookcases for technical reference books that you could use at any time, a table with several chairs and a sofa in the corner, which was almost always occupied by a sleepy student who had pulled an all-nighter. Occasionally, I took a nap there as well. It also had a small table with a coffee pot, which was on most of the time. Needless to say, the quality of the brew was not up to standard, but at least it was warm. It survived on a five-cents-per-cup honor system donation, and I must confess that I started to pay my share only during my senior year. There was also usually a box of cream-filled cookies or some other treats supplied by the student society. This came in handy for me, particularly during the summer and holidays when I did not have the bus boy job. I never liked coffee too much, but that kind of cookie is still my favorite. I often took advantage of this snack bar; it was survival for me.

On many occasions, the professors had small jobs for the students, doing illustrations or calculations, which paid well. I was always available, and they liked my work, as I was good at drafting. On one of the tables in the drawing room was an old hand-cranked mechanical calculator, which was noisy but used all the time. Naval architecture requires a lot of numbers and calculations, and all the homework assignments had to be turned in on time. So the pressure was on to see who got to the machine first. If you didn't get access to it, you had to do all your calculations by hand and slide rule. It was a competition. Then modern times arrived in the early '70s, and the department got an electronic calculator with screen display. It was a novelty and quickly became very popular in the department. Soon, students were able to afford their own hand-held calculators, and the old slide rule era was gone forever.

Then, in 1971, one of the professors pinned a notice on the board that the American Society of Civil Engineers (ASCE) would hold an annual intercollegiate National Concrete Canoe Race. That really got my attention—an event that was right in my area of expertise. I quickly organized a team of more than twenty students and asked the professor to enter The U of M Concrete Canoe Team in the race. Although we were not civil engineers, we got permission to race.

Drafting room in U of M Naval Architecture Department, 1969.

Some innocent non-engineers said that a concrete canoe could not float. They did not understand the hydrodynamic effect and Archimedes' principal. The rules of the competition were very simple, as I remember. The cost had to be less than $200. I designed one canoe while the other students designed the second, as we needed two canoes to train against each other. I set the training program and drilled the team on proper conditioning and paddling technique. It was an opportunity for me to get back into the canoeing competition. We built the molds for each canoe and covered them with chicken wire, and troweled the concrete aggregate into it. Then we took it off the mold and smoothed the outside. Both canoes performed well and were relatively light.

The race was at the University of Illinois, and we packed up our canoes and drove to the race site. Some of the teams brought a crane along to handle their canoes. Our boats were very sophisticated by comparison. The regatta was a total success for us—we won all the distances and categories, except the faculty race. The professor who steered that canoe claimed that he was a voyageur and did not need my instructions on how to get around the turning buoy quickly. They lost, which spoiled our clean sweep. One of the students wrote a paper on the design and construction of the canoes for the Society of Naval Architects and won the student award for it. I was very happy to contribute to my alma mater and canoeing at the same time. It was a small feather in my canoeing cap, but not an insignificant one, because it showed me that I could motivate others to get involved.

In the late '60s, I was introduced to professional canoe racing, which is very popular during summer and fall in the northern states and Canada. This canoe racing is different from the Olympic style. It is a sit-down, modified traditional-type canoe for two people. The boat has strict specifications for length and width, which is checked by the race organizers before each competition. Some of the local professionals asked me to paddle with them, but I didn't want to jeopardize my amateur status for future Olympic competition. I needed to remain a true amateur, and there wasn't much money in it anyway. However, I joined the Michigan Canoe Racing Association's amateur division for marathon paddling, and I got involved in many of the local races in Michigan and Ohio. In later years, I even designed and built my own marathon racing canoes. This provided me with an additional source of income when I sold my winning boat after the race. Some of the paddlers whom I recruited from this group went on to be Olympians.

The period during the late sixties was a very interesting time to be in America, and to be an American. It was a turbulent time with the Vietnam War in full swing. It was very unpopular with the youth. Many demonstrations and acts of civil disobedience were occurring all over the country, particularly on college campuses. The government had reinstituted a military draft, and many students were burning their draft cards or going to Canada to escape their service. The hippie movement was blossoming, and American youths were looking for alternative lifestyles. All the popular music was about love and freedom, and some of the greatest songs written in that era are still popular today. The Woodstock Jazz Festival was an acclamation of America's expression of *free love* and freedom. San Francisco's Haight Ashbury region became the hot bed for the movement. The *flower child* generation captured the imagination of the American youth and challenged the established government order. Experimentation with mind-altering and recreational drugs became common in certain circles.

The country was very much divided—conservatives supported the capitalist establishments, and the rebellious youth wanted change. This division shaped America's future, both in domestic and international policy, for years to come. Many laws were passed by Congress to provide equal opportunities for the masses. The Civil Rights Act of 1964 was passed by Congress, which, for me, was an eye opener. I could taste the individual freedoms and democracy at work.

On January 13, 1968, Bill called me with the sad news that Mrs. Francis had passed away during a tragic house fire. I was shocked to hear it, as only a few days earlier we were together in Florida on a houseboat, vacationing with Bill and Marcia. On New Year's Day, we watched the Orange Bowl Parade together, and later that day, I accompanied Mrs. Francis shopping. Bill said that he would make arrangements for me to go down to Oklahoma City for the funeral, and I was saddened to lose a true friend and benefactor.

1968 rolled around, the year of the XIX Olympiad in Mexico City. The US team trials were in Long Beach, California. I had several paddlers whom I coached in Ann Arbor beside Marcia and Sperry Jones, and all of them made the Olympic team. After the trials, we went to Lake Tahoe and Colorado to do some high-altitude training in preparation for the altitude of Mexico City. Team processing was in Denver, Colorado. I was already helping the Olympic Canoeing Team as an unofficial coach, so I volunteered to help the USOC with athletes' processing, which meant handing out uniforms and other chores. During my stay, I befriended Dick Dunham, who was on the administrative staff for the USOC and was responsible for the transportation of the US Olympic Team. He knew my history of defection during the Tokyo Games and appreciated my continued involvement for the US athletes. He offered his help, and I asked him if it would be possible for me to get on the chartered flight with the team to Mexico City. Bill was already driving down to Mexico City with Marcia's boats and had promised he would bring me back to the states if I found a way to get down there. Mr. Dunham said there would be some empty seats on the last plane and he had no problem with me joining him. Sure enough, I got on the last charter flight to the Olympic Games. Here I was again going to the Olympics, not as part of the official delegation, but going just the same.

With Billy Mills, 2016.

During my stay in Denver, I also met Billy Mills, the great track athlete and 10,000-meter Olympic Champion in Tokyo. He was invited to give a motivational speech about his Olympic experience to the athletes before they left for the Games. He was (and is) my all-time hero of Olympic competition. His story is well-documented in many books and the movie, *Running Brave*, which tells Mills' story of as an Oglala Lakota Indian. He and I roomed together in Denver and had many conversations about his tribe and the struggle of his people, which I truly enjoyed because of my fascination and respect for North American indigenous peoples' culture. We became lifelong friends.

As we landed at the airport in Mexico City, I had a little problem convincing the authorities that I was officially an unofficial assistant. Then, Mr. Dunham came to my rescue and talked to the authorities, and they quickly obliged. I was in! I joined the team on the bus and we went to the Village. We easily drove through without anyone checking for accreditation (I did not have one). In those days, security was lax!

Contrary to my usual good luck, the first people I ran into at the cafeteria on the first night were my old Hungarian teammates and coach. The coach right away started to ridicule and discredit me. I tried to ignore him, and told my old mates that I was here unofficially as a coach. That was stretching

At the 1988 Mexico City Olympic Games at the Xochomilco canoeing venue in my USA uniform.

the truth a bit, but I had to show off my commitment to my new country, the sport, and the US Olympic team. I had a chance to talk to one of my friends privately, and he told me that I should not write anything controversial in my letters, because they were being opened and censored. He also told me that after Tokyo, all my team members were questioned separately and had to sign a statement explaining what they knew about my defection. Later, I learned that two of my Tokyo teammates had made negative statements about me.

In the Village, I slept on the floor of one of the canoeists' rooms for a couple of nights until I met up with Bill. He had a big camper on that truck I almost rolled over going to Oklahoma. Bill parked his camper at the Regatta course in Xochimilco (meaning *the hanging flower garden of Mexico City*), so I stayed there with him for the rest of the Games. Xochimilco is a beautiful, colorful place with many canals and small flat-bottom, human-propelled tour boats selling flowers, pottery, and silver jewelry. One of the canals had been dredged and widened to accommodate the rowing and canoeing course. I was happy because I could paddle on the water after the official workouts were over. I felt that I could still do it—I could still compete at the Olympic level. I was only 28 years old.

The competition was very tough, and the Hungarian team did exceptionally well. I found myself rooting for them. The US team made the finals in the women's kayak single (Marcia Jones Smoke took fourth place), and double event (Marcia and Sperry, seventh place). Because of the high attitude, many athletes had trouble breathing, particularly in distances over a minute. The organizers' medical staff was in great demand during these Games.

I went to see the Modern Pentathlon and Track and Field events. I could get into any event with the athletes because I was wearing a US uniform that I acquired in Denver, and security usually didn't check for accreditation. There were many memorable events I had a chance to witness: Bob Beamon's world record long jump (8.90 meters), Dick Fosbury's new high jump style (his signature jump became known as the *Fosbury Flop*), Kipchoge Keino's 1,500-meter victory, and the well-publicized victory of Tommy Smith's 200-meter sprint and his Black Panther salute during the medal ceremony.

Two weeks went by very quickly. I wanted to attend the Closing Ceremony, but there were no more tickets available. On the day of the Closing Ceremony, we packed up the boats, and while the team was at the ceremony, Bill got an idea. "Let's collect some souvenirs, like the flags and banners around the racing course and on the poles." We were leaving the next morning, so why not? We proceeded to liberate some banners, which Bill stuffed behind the seat of the truck. I started to shimmy up the poles for the flags, but the organizers had greased them, so it was tough going. I was on the top of the third pole when I heard "Alto! Alto!" and the click of a rifle as a bullet was loaded into the chamber. I looked down and saw a soldier holding Bill and pointing the gun at me. Suddenly, my whole life went foggy. I climbed down slowly, holding the banner in my hand. *Caught red-handed*, as the expression goes. Bill tried to speak to the soldier. "No speak English," was his response as he shoved us and held a gun on us as we proceeded to the police office near the boathouse.

The head officer wanted to see our accreditation. We had no such IDs, and we were not part of any official delegation. As such, the situation became more complicated, and I visualized myself in a Mexican salt mine doing hard labor, without parole. Bill had his briefcase with him and began to search for documents and hand out some souvenirs. He told the officer that we were collecting souvenirs for our team and that we were the boat transport crew. He showed Marcia's picture and tried to explain that she was his wife. The officer began to soften. He remembered Bill's camper van parked along the race course. Earlier, he had given Bill permission to park there during the competition.

Bill pulled out some twenty-dollar bills and some leftover pesos, and the officer softened some more. As Bill emptied his pockets, I stood there with nothing to give. The officer wanted to see the truck, and luckily, everything was hidden behind the seat in a compartment. The officer looked around in the truck but not very thoroughly. Bill gave him a couple of US Team shirts and US baseball caps. Bribing ourselves out of the situation worked, and the officer motioned with his hand and let us go. We said with relief, "Gracias, Señor." He smiled. We got in the truck and drove away. Bill broke the silence, "Consider yourself the luckiest son of a gun on the face of the earth." I forced a smile and could have wrung out my shirt.

I could hardly wait to leave Mexico City behind and begin our journey back to Michigan. Crossing the border in Laredo, Texas, was uneventful. The border guards were interested in talking with Marcia about her Olympic experience.

I had skipped the fall semester for my first US Olympic experience, which was certainly memorable and almost disastrous. Winter was approaching and I did not like that very much. California paddlers told me that their climate was nice and warm all year around, and I couldn't understand why people would live anywhere else. Michigan had very tough winters, colder than Hungary, and almost unbearable summers with high temperatures and humidity. I promised myself that as soon as I graduated, the very next day, I would be on my way to California.

In 1969, I learned that my father had passed away at 65. I was sad that I did not have a chance to see him again and find out what happened after I left the country. Was he proud of me or mad at me? I will never know. My oldest brother moved into the house that our father built with my calorie money. This brother had taken care of him in the last months of his life. My mother was still doing very well, living alone, and doing the gardening, which she loved. The notice of his funeral from my family came too late anyway, but I wouldn't have risked going to Hungary for it.

My senior year (1969-1970) was a very memorable year. The U of M Naval Architecture Department was full of excitement. The academic curriculum required that each graduating student complete a ship or boat design from the conceptual to the builder's drawings. My class broke up into two to three student design groups. I chose my classmate Paul Gow to be my partner. We proposed to our academic counselor to design a salvage tug. Both of us liked smaller crafts, and we were happy to learn that our counselor approved our concept. We divided the design task among ourselves, sharing responsibilities and cross-checking our calculations and drawings.

In the middle of the term, our professor announced that the senior class was invited to present their final designs to the Gulf Section of the Society of Naval Architects and Marine Engineers (SNAME), sponsored by the Section. We were all excited to go to New Orleans (the headquarters of the Section) before our final exams. To make our presentation better, I made a model of our

At my graduation with Marcia and Bill Smoke.

My University of Michigan diplomas.

salvage tug and tested it in the towing tank. We packed it up and took it with us.

New Orleans was fabulous; the Society really rolled out the red carpet for us. Some of the local design companies took the opportunity to interview some of us for employment. We stayed in a French Quarter hotel, had lobster for lunch, and in the evening, walked Bourbon Street and listened to the famous Preservation Band. New Orleans reminded me of European cities, and I felt at home.

Our presentation was a success, the model was a big hit, and a couple of days later, we returned to Ann Arbor to graduate. I received my diploma from the University of Michigan with a Bachelor's degree in Naval Architecture and Marine Engineering. During the graduation ceremony, I looked back over the past six years at my accomplishments at the University of Michigan, from "repeat after me" in the English Language Institute to the final naval architecture design course. It was not easy to keep my focus on getting my education, learning my profession, and coping with everyday life. The Pinocchio Syndrome was always very tempting. A couple of times, I bordered on flunking out, but help always arrived in time to save me.

Bill and Marcia came to my graduation and took me out to dinner. I was very happy, but with a bit of sadness that my mother could not be there. I knew how proud she would be, and I sent her a picture of me with my graduation gown on. I was not the best student the university ever had, and had received every kind of grade they ever issued, from A to F with dropped classes and so on, but I had a good enough average to get me into the master's program with the help of Professor Couch. So, I decided that I would continue my studies in the graduate school that fall.

Before graduate school started, I finished my research paper on the behavior of planing crafts (speedboats) in shallow water. I built a fast speedboat model for my study and tested it in the towing tank for different depths of water. The result was unique and useful data for speedboat designers. I wrote a paper and presented it at the Southeast Section of SNAME for the student paper competition. I received the SNAME Student Paper award for it. I was very gratified to be recognized among my peers in my profession.

That summer was my first opportunity to become an official member of the US Canoeing Team and represent the US at the 1970 Canoeing World Championships held in Copenhagen, Denmark. Previously, the Canoeing World Championships occurred every four years, but in 1970, the International Canoe Federation decided to have World Championships every year. I was excited to go to the trials to make the team. At the North American Championships and the trials, I won the 10,000-meter C1 events and qualified for the US team.

We had to cover our own expenses because the American Canoe Association did not have the money to support us. I had saved up enough money that I could afford to pay my own way. I was nervous about using my re-entry permit the first time, but at the immigration checkpoint, the officer looked at my book and stamped it. I was very relieved.

At the World Championships, there were lots of new faces on the Hungarian team. Some of them had just been juniors when I was still home. They remembered me. I talked to the long-distance single canoe paddler who was from my former club, suggesting that we work together during the race, and he agreed. I thought that I could draft on him, which was legal to do by the rules. He was faster and the favorite to win, so I was looking forward to collaborating during the race. I had a good start and was slowly working my way toward him when the Japanese boat hit my stern and spun me around. Suddenly, I was facing the wrong way! When I got my boat back on track, the whole fleet had gone by. I was really mad, but I did not give up, since I still had 9,500 meters to go. It was the hardest hour I have ever paddled in my life, and on top of all that, the weather was very hot. I was so dehydrated it took me a week to get saliva back in my mouth. I never did catch up with the Hungarian, but I finished seventh. That was the best result for the whole US Canoeing Team. It was a weak consolation for my effort. My Hungarian friend won the race and asked me what happened. I told him about the incident and that he could not have helped me after that. I had wanted to show my Hungarian coaches that I was back in competition and I would be someone to reckon with in the future.

Just before the team had left for Copenhagen, I had received a letter from my brother Lajos, saying that he might have a chance to come to the World

Championships as a tourist. I was excited to see him, and he would be the first family member I would reunite with since my defection (I was very glad to hear that the Hungarian government had eased up on travel restrictions). Sure enough, one day he showed up at the boathouse where we stayed, and with tears in our eyes, we embraced.

There were so many things to ask and talk about. We spent much time together, and I learned about my mother's misfortune—of my father leaving her and taking my calorie money, and the retaliation of the government due to my defection (Luckily, they were only summoned to the local authorities to be questioned shortly after the Games, but all our correspondence was censored for many years). I learned about my new nephews and nieces. My brother was there for a week and we saw each other whenever I was free. Our farewell was very hard, but I promised that I would visit home as soon as I could.

Returning to Ann Arbor, I enrolled in graduate school. I had saved up enough money to pay for my higher education, and my advisor, Professor Couch, encouraged me. In my second year as a graduate student, one of my other professors approached me to ask if I would be interested in teaching the Small Craft Design class. My final design and my speedboat research paper had impressed him. I gladly said yes! I knew it would certainly help my bank account which needed some improvement. Luckily, I had kept very good class notes when I had taken this course a couple of years earlier, which helped me to prepare my lectures.

Teaching was a very interesting experience. From the first moment I opened the door to my class and walked to the desk facing the students, I felt the power of communication and the responsibility to be credible. I felt the same anxieties like before canoe racing, except this time it was not physical, it was intellectual. I outlined the course, the exams, and the grading system for the students. At the end of the course, each student had to submit a conceptual design for a small craft and would be graded on that. I had a hard time grading the papers. I wanted to be fair based on their performance. I succeeded in giving only a few B's.

In October of 1971, one of my classmates from Australia handed me a magazine article about a five-day, 403-kilometer, sit-down marathon canoe race in Australia called the Murray Marathon. This was a yearly fundraising event organized by the Australian Red Cross. The race started at the town of Yarrawonga on Boxing Day and finished at Swan Hill on New Year's Eve. Each participating team had to raise $500 Australian and must have a land support crew. I wrote a letter to the organizers to let them know we were interested if they could waive the fee, and their response was positive.

I was excited for the opportunity to travel to a country that I'd always been interested in and to race in another discipline of canoeing. So, I set out to design a boat to meet the requirements. My partner, Doug Soules, and I made the canoe in the naval architecture woodworking shop, but in order to take it with us, I had to make it sectional. I had seen sectional rowing shells in Europe, so I followed the same technique with watertight bulkheads. When it was all dry, we cut the hull between bulkheads, which left us with four pieces; we then folded the pieces into each other, so it became two separate packages that we checked on the plane as luggage. We wrote to our newly acquired friend in Australia that we were bringing our boat and paddles with us. Through Doug's relatives and a radio station solicitation, we raised enough money for the tickets.

A week before Christmas, we drove to Los Angeles to try out the boat and depart for Australia. It was a long flight to Melbourne, and we had to stop in Fiji to refuel. It was exciting for me to land on a Pacific island, which had long been my ultimate dream! Our Aussie friend was waiting for us at the airport in Melbourne. He wondered where our boat was, and when we showed him the two packages, he couldn't believe it. We had to go to his house right away to reassemble it in his living room to prove it to him. We stayed at his house and practiced on the Yarra River at his club, the Fairfield Canoe Club, then left the day before Boxing Day to drive up to Yarrawonga. It was a fantastic drive on a winding road through bush country with many new sights along the way—kangaroos, wallabies, kookaburras, and so on. The dry, hot weather was a shock, coming from Michigan's frozen winter.

We did not have the required land support crew, so the Royal Australian Air Force volunteered to take care of us. They pitched our tent and cooked our food, which consisted of two things—steak and beer. On the eve of the race, the organizers had a big, mandatory briefing about the race rules, the course, and river safety. They emphasized that we should not paddle too close to the shore or under tree branches because "the world's most poisonous snake" lurks in the trees along the river bank. We were also informed that there would be at least two checkpoints each day where we could get some water and provisions.

Our race started at 7:30 am. We were in the second group of boats, fifteen minutes after the first group. The sun was just beginning to rise, and it was already getting hot. We wore loose net racing shirts, shorts, and caps with large flaps at the back and sides to protect our necks from the sun. Some racers showed up in *white pajamas* that covered their whole body. We thought it was a joke, but later we understood the reason for this odd outfit. We took one bottle of water, two rolls of lifesaver candies, and an orange, and planned to get more supplies at the first checkpoint.

Our strategy was to push hard for the first hour and see where we were, then adjust our tempo accordingly. Ten minutes after the start, we were way ahead of everyone in our group and catching up to the group that started before us, so we felt good. After two hours, we were seemingly all alone on the river, with no boats ahead of us and no one behind us. Scanning the shore, we could not find the first checkpoint where it should have been (Later, they told us that they were late to arrive and set-up, since they didn't think anyone would be so fast). It was the beginning of an eight-and-a-half-hour day. The two sticks of candy and the orange were all we ate that day, and we resorted to drinking out of the river. The river was beautifully clear, calm, and wild. We saw a naked aboriginal family spearfishing from the shore, and kangaroos sipping water out of the river. Suffice it to say, the scenery was quite different from rivers in North America.

We arrived first at the finish line of the first stage (day) with the much faster class of boats just behind us. Everyone was very surprised by our performance, and the Air Force guys were quite proud to be taking care of the winning team. The last thing I can remember seeing that night was Doug, my partner, with a huge steak in one hand and an ice-cold Fosters in the other. They woke us up the next morning and asked us if we were ready, but we did not think so. I couldn't force my hands open and my shoulders and back were aching.

"Let's have breakfast, mate," they encouraged us. The breakfast consisted of an omelet with beef steak and beer. But we came to race, and there were four more days to go. On the second day, a motorboat followed us to make sure that we were not cheating. After two hours, we asked them to leave us alone; it was too noisy and disturbing, not to speak of breathing in the fumes.

Over the next three days, our bodies adapted to the brutally hot temperatures, and we carried more water to keep hydrated, put on sunscreen, and our hands toughened-up. The organizers adapted, too, by making sure that they were set up at the checkpoints in a timely manner. We won all four days' stages in a total of about 32 hours of paddling, with a very large time margin between us and the second place in our class.

On the final day, the stage was handicapped by time so that the Lipton Cup Trophy could be awarded to the first arrival at Swan Hill. We had not known about this. We wanted to win that Cup and could have kept the winning margin closer if we had known about this handicapping. They started the slowest boats first and handicapped the rest, so there were only a handful of

Racing in Australia, New Year's Day, 1972.
Photo credit: Fairfax Syndication, Australia.

fast Olympic kayaks behind us. They told us it would only be about a five-and-a-half hour day, and we paddled very hard, catching all the boats ahead of us. We got the last boat about half an hour before the finish. Our relief didn't last long, and the Olympic kayaks started to catch up. Two boats went by before the last bend to the finish line, and we ended up third on arrival, but way ahead of our class. We set the class course record for each stage, which had not been broken for over ten years.

Our final time for all five stages was 35 hours and 7 minutes (about 5 hours ahead of the second-place finisher in our class). Our memento for that epic race was a quarter-sized medal, the smallest I'd ever received for the longest race I had ever paddled. In the Australian canoeing circles, though, we became legends. They bought our boat and made a mold of it, and my design became the standard class boat for the two-man canoe for the Murray River Marathon and acquired the name, *The Toro Boat*. We spent one more week in Australia sightseeing before we returned to the freezing temperatures back in Michigan.

Forty-seven years later, in 2018, I learned that there was an annual race called *The Great Toro Race* from Picnic Point to Barmah. This section of the river is the third stage of the Murray River Marathon. The Great Toro Race was open only to Toro boats molded after the original boat that I had left in Australia. I was truly honored to find that I had contributed to long-distance marathon racing on another continent! My wife, Jane, and I decided to participate that year. So we flew to Australia, met up with old and new paddling friends, and were able to race in the original *Toro boat*. We had a fabulous time and won our class on a windy, blustery Murray River day.

One reason I have included this Australian race in my story is to illustrate the different disciplines of canoeing and my passion for the sport in general. My Olympic-style canoeing skills, experience, and fitness would carry over to other canoeing disciplines—marathon, whitewater, slalom, dragon boats, outrigger, SUP, etc. Canoeing is a lifetime sport with many disciplines, but there is a common thread of loving to be out on the water in nature.

My father, Törő János, and my mother, Kis Julianna, on their wedding day, 1930.

Our only formal family portrait, 1947. From the left, my brother Lajos, my mother Julianna, my brother Imre, my brother János, myself in front, and my father János. Note the typical Hungarian jacket that my brother and I wear.

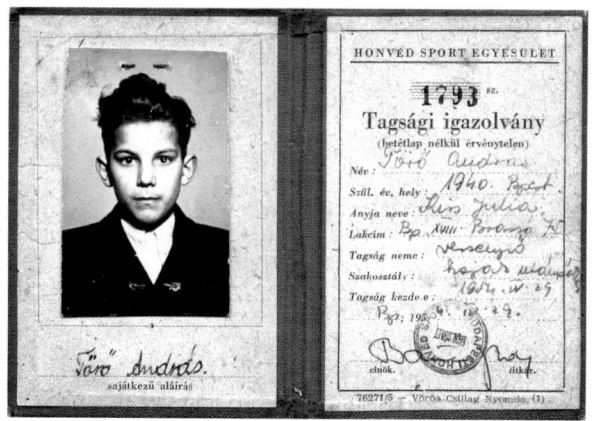

My first Honvéd Sports Club membership ID, 1954.

Starting the Big Loop tour in the war canoe, 1955. I am at the back of the canoe on the left side.

Winning the canoe (C1) Hungarian Junior National championship, 1958.

The clubhouse (Sirály) on Margaret Island where I spent many hours, 1954-1964.

Departing for an international competition, 1960. I am at the door.

Winning an international race in the double canoe (C2) with Farkas, 1960.

At the Olympic training camp, in our new boat, Rackeve, 1960.

In my Olympic uniform departing to the 1960 Rome Summer Olympic Games.

Medal Ceremonies for Men's Canadian Double (C2), 1,000-meter event, during the 1960 Rome Summer Olympic Games. Third place finish (bronze medal), Farkas Imre and Törő András, Hungary. Photo credit: Petrovits László, MTI.

Olympic flame arrives at Lake Sagami.

Getting ready to practice at Lake Sagami canoeing venue, October 1964.

My race at the 1964 Tokyo Summer Olympic Games, Single Canoe (C1) 1,000-meter event, Heat 1, Lane 5. I am a close second at the halfway point in the race. Photo credit: 1964 Japanese Olympic Yearbook.

My 1964 Olympic Diploma for my fourth place finish.

1964 Sagami Olympic Village entrance.

Marcia Jones and Bill Smoke in Lake Sagami, Tokyo.

Andor Elbert (Tonya) and his C2 partner, 1964. He is in the back of the boat.

Newspaper article reporting my defection and giving my first American interview in the Seattle airport. Photo credit: Seattle Times.

One of the dollar bills I received from the pilots and flight attendants on my way to America.

Working at the U of M Naval Architecture towing tank, from 1965 to 1973, West Engineering Building, Ann Arbor, Michigan.

Winning one of my first North American championships, Tupper Lake, New York, 1969.

Winning my first international race—Dominion Day Regatta in Toronto, 1966.

My race at the start line, 1972 Munich Summer Olympic Games, single canoe (C1) 1,000-meter event, Heat 1, Lane 7. Photo credit: 1972 German Olympic Yearbook.

Reunited with my mother in the Olympic Village at the 1972 Munich Summer Olympic Games.

Chuck and I practicing in Lake Placid before the 1976 Montreal Olympics.

Discussing the 1980 Olympic Boycott with President Carter's National Security Advisor, Zbigniew Brzezinski.

Toasting the Olympic sponsors at the 1988 Seoul Summer Olympic Games.

Officiating at the 1996 Atlanta Centennial Olympic Games.

Racing double outrigger canoe with my wife, Jane.

In Rome at the Hungarian Embassy celebrating the 50th anniversary celebration of the 1960 Olympic Games. My canoe partner, Farkas, and I are in the middle.

In Tokyo for the 50th anniversary celebration, 2014.

My family, Tamás (my son) holding Elijah (my grandson), Marissa (my daughter-in-law), Jane (my wife) holding Oliver (my grandson), myself holding Emily (my granddaughter), Katalin (my daughter), and Benjamin (my son-in-law), 2016.

CHAPTER 9
Making the US Olympic Team, 1972 and 1976

I was doing a lot of marathon canoe racing in Michigan and Ohio, so I was in relatively good shape and looking ahead to the next Olympics. The graduate studies were going well, and my pay at the naval architecture research lab was adequate enough to survive. I also got an opportunity to earn some money teaching.

I knew that I wanted to keep training during graduate school. The 1972 Olympics were coming soon, and I definitely wanted to make the US Olympic Team and fulfill my dream of marching in the Opening Ceremony. I had a strong feeling that without experiencing the Opening Ceremony, you were somehow not a true Olympian. So, with a couple of friends, Toby Cooper and Doug Soules, I began a two-year training program.

The Olympic year arrived in January of 1972. I set my goal to represent the United States in the upcoming Games, complete with an official U. S. Olympic uniform and participation in both the Opening and Closing Ceremonies in Munich. I decided, along with Doug Soules, to suspend my studies for the winter semester and go to California to get in some extra on-water training. I'd begun serious conditioning training the preceding fall by going to the local gym on campus. There were about four of us who trained together from the Hobo Canoe Club, which I had established. It wasn't really a club, as we had no formal papers; it existed in our minds only. The gym had an indoor track suspended above the basketball courts, which was used by university students and the local girls AAU track club, the Michigammes. They were coached by the famous Red Simmons, so named for his red hair. We went almost every afternoon to train in this gym, and my favorite thing was showing off my rope climbing talent. I could still climb the rope using only my arms while holding my legs in an L-shape. Since my high school years back in Hungary, this has been my signature move. They all admired that, even Coach Simmons. Among the Michigammes were two young red-headed girls running track. One was Jane Marie Babcock, my future wife, who was running hurdles and sprints. I talked her into joining the Hobo Canoe Club and taking up kayaking. She loved the outdoors, the water, and the canoe livery, so it was natural for her to pick up kayaking. I made her a boat and a paddle, and in the first month of 1972, and she joined us in Newport Beach, California for spring training.

Before we departed, I asked for an audience with the U of M Athletic Director, Mr. Donald Canham, to plead my case for financial support, which I very badly needed. Training three months in California cost a lot of money. My pitch was that I was still a student of U of M, an athlete in an Olympic sport, and a potential Olympic team member. Any financial support would be very helpful for my preparation to make the team. In the Athletic Director's office, there were several other coaches when I entered, all drinking coffee and Coca Cola. I presented my case, and they listened for a while, but responded that canoeing was not an NCAA sport and not supported by U of M. I was very disappointed when I left that office.

Before I closed the door, I heard someone say, "Canoeing is for recreation," and they all laughed. It discouraged me that the top athletic administrators at the U of M had the notion that Olympic-style canoeing, the most difficult and challenging sport of all Olympic events, was a joke—a *recreational* activity. My disappointment clouded my vision and, at that moment, I cursed the U of M Athletic Department, wishing that the football team would lose all future Rose Bowls. My curse must have held up pretty well, because over the next 20 years, from 1972 through 1992, the U of M football team made it to the Rose Bowl eleven times and won only twice—in 1981 and 1989. Thinking back, I regret cursing my alma mater, but in the heat of the moment, I had to do it.

After Christmas, when Michigan's weather was getting very cold, we tied our boats on my new (used) van (Ford Econoline 300) and left for Southern California. I took a semester off from my graduate work, and Doug did the same. Jane graduated from high school early, so we were free as birds. The van was my first vehicle, and I was pretty nervous about the expense, but we needed transportation that could carry all the boats.

Doug, an experienced car owner (and Detroit boy), helped me with the selection and purchase. He was surprised when I pulled out $800 in cash from my pocket, which was a lot of money for me. Doug suggested that I get insurance as well, another expense, and then there was the gasoline, which was about twenty cents per gallon. When the gasoline price went up a penny or two, Doug always cursed it as *highway robbery*. We worked on the van, bolting a rack on the top for the boats and made a fold-out bed in the back. Underneath, I had storage containers for food and water, so it was not fancy, but it was adequate for our needs. We outfitted the van the way we wanted, and I felt great pride in my first automobile, even though it wasn't much to look at. Doug also mentioned that I had to get a driver's license.

I have an interesting story about my first experience with the DMV. The Ford van that I purchased had only one seat, on the driver's side. It was a panel van for deliveries. I wanted such a van so I could outfit it as a camper and haul my canoe. So, when I went to the DMV for my driver's test, I set a regular dining room chair on the passenger side.

When the DMV examiner came out to the car, he asked me "Where should I sit?"

"On the chair, sir," I replied, pointing to the loose chair. He was not amused, and couldn't tell if he was dealing with a stupid foreigner or a joker.

He said, "You better come back with a proper seat bolted to the chassis."

So, Doug and I had some more work to do. We went to the local junkyard and got a proper front passenger seat and bolted it down to the chassis. Eventually, I passed all the tests. That van served me well for many trips and was maintained with guidance from Doug. We rebuilt the engine and fixed the clutch and the brakes. It was almost like new when we finished, and we called her "Big Bertha."

We took off in early January for Newport Beach, where we rented a small house for three months. Our private training camp was very productive, and there were several other paddlers training there at the same time. I was willing to make the US Olympic Team either in the single or the double canoe. The year before, in 1971, I went with the USA Team to the World Championships in Beograd, Yugoslavia and did the double canoe with Andreas "Andy"

Weigand, a very good left-handed paddler. We finished fifth on the C2 500-meter race and seventh on the C2 1,000-meter race, which was the best American result in two-man canoeing for many years and still is. We had a good race, but I felt we could have medaled if we'd had better conditioning and more time together. The prospects were good for next year's Olympics. Andy Weigand and I practiced together in Newport that winter and were to paddle together at the Olympic trials later in the year. However, after I left California, he teamed up with another paddler whom he thought was faster. I was very disappointed but could do nothing about it, and felt that I lost an opportunity to earn another medal.

Andy Weigand and I training in my homemade C2, January 1972.

Doug, Jane, and I had to go back to Michigan by the middle of May, because we ran out of money. We detoured north to see San Francisco and my old friend, Andor, who in the meantime had come to the US from Canada and settled down there. It was a happy reunion for both of us. He was about to open his own printing shop, and I admired him as an entrepreneur. He suggested that, after my studies, I should consider coming to northern California. A couple of days after our visit, we were back on Highway 80, driving to Michigan. It was a nice trip despite the fact that we got snowed in at the Laramie Pass in May for two days, where our canoe paddles came in handy for digging us out of a snow bank.

The Olympic Trials were in Indiana in July. I still did not have the proof of citizenship that was required to enter the trials, and I asked Prof. Couch to help me again. He called up the US Immigration Office in Detroit and expedited the procedure, explaining my potential Olympic participation. Just a couple of weeks before the trials, the Immigration Service called me to appear. They said there would be a short test and an oath to take. I got nervous again about the test part, and I agonized over the possibility that I might not pass. I couldn't fail and lose this opportunity to be on another Olympic team for my adopted country, so I tried to stay relaxed.

My citizenship paper, 1972.

We went to the US District Court building in Detroit on July 11, 1972, only two weeks before the Olympic Trials. The exam was in the office of the clerk of the court. He sat on one side of his desk with Prof. Couch and me across from him. It was a short test. One question asked during the exam was: *What are the two legislative branches of Congress?* I completely blanked out I was so nervous. Professor Couch came to my rescue. He said, "You know those people in Washington." "Oh yes, the Senate and the House of Representatives," I responded. I passed the test and then took the Oath of Allegiance to my new country.

My Citizenship Certificate was presented to me in a nice folder. I was very proud and relieved. After almost eight years in the US, I was finally recognized as a citizen. Bill and Marcia took me out for lunch, and my Hobo Canoe Club members did a barbeque for me at the old canoe livery to celebrate. One of the girls in the club made me a US flag shirt to wear for the celebration (I still have it). I took my Citizenship Certificate to the trials and guarded it with my life. I still do.

My citizenship celebration with my Hobo Canoe Club teammates, July 1972.

MAKING THE US OLYMPIC TEAM, 1972 AND 1976

Getting ready to race in the 1972 Olympic Trials with Doug Soules.

At the trials, I showed up with my newly designed and built single canoe and my citizenship paper. As a newly graduated naval architect, I felt obliged to design and build my own boat. I entered the single (C1) 1,000-meter event and the double (C2) 1,000-meter event with Doug. On the day of the single C1 race, we had a bit of a headwind, which I never liked, and my new canoe did not have any splash rail at the front deck. I had not had the time to finish all the details. During the race, the canoe began to fill up with water, and I worried I might capsize or sink before the finish line. I had to slow down, and finished in third place. In the double, Doug and I got second place. The Olympic team selection was based on a point system, which included both races, and there were five team positions to fill. Both Doug and I got on the team, and I was designated to race the single (C1) 1,000-meter event while Doug was an alternate. Jane also tried out for the Olympic team in the K1 women's 500-meter event and made the final, but failed to make the team.

Needless to say, I was very excited about my first official Olympic competition with the USA team. We were outfitted at the processing center in Washington D.C. and flew directly to Munich, Germany. In comparison with my Hungarian experience for team processing, it was different. Although they altered our parade uniform to fit, it was not tailor-made but commercially made by the Olympic sponsor, Sears, Roebuck and Company. We got a lot of stuff and our huge team suitcases filled up very quickly. I had never received so much apparel, and I was very happy with all that new gear. However, it reminded me how much more precious my first hand-me-down sweats in Hungary were.

With my Olympic teammates getting ready for the 1972 Olympic Opening Ceremony.

The Munich Games were held between August 26 and September 11, 1972. The canoeing competition took place at the end of the second week of the Games. Finally, I had a chance to participate at the Opening Ceremony.

The pageantry began at the Olympic Village, where the Organizing Committee provided buses for all participating national team delegations to travel to the assembly area just outside of the main stadium. Each country gathered behind their flag, held by an attractive girl. Everyone was wearing the parade uniform provided by their Olympic Committee's sponsor just for this occasion. (I still have mine in my Sears, Roebuck and Company suitcase).

In the assembly area, several marshals anxiously encouraged the teams to line up in marching formation, but it was almost impossible. Everyone wanted to mingle, meet new faces, and greet fellow competitors (I went over to see the Hungarian team). They were surprised to see me in a USA uniform. I told them I was competing. The energy was palpable. We could hear the loud cheering from the stadium as the Parade of Nations started, and teams began to enter the stadium in the alphabetical order of the host country.

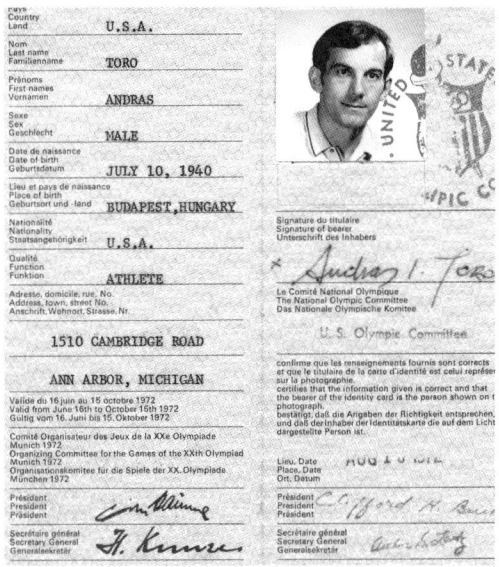

My accreditation for the 1972 Munich Olympic Games.

Olga Fikotova Connolly (the former Czechoslovakian 1956 gold medalist discus thrower) was chosen to carry the US flag. After the Games in 1956, she was married to an American athlete named Harold Connolly and was eligible to compete for the US, much to the frustration of her former country, where she was considered a traitor. I felt a kinship with her.

The moment was approaching for the US Team to enter the stadium. Most everyone broke rank as they tried to mug for the TV cameras at the entrance. As we came through the tunnel, the stadium erupted with a thunderous roar—a thrilling sensation. I felt very proud of my last eight years of achievement in my adopted country. Looking around the stadium, all I saw were colors, waving flags and hats, and cheering spectators. They were all here to witness this global quadrennial spectacle, and I was a part of it. It is hard to describe the emotions I felt as I kept step with my teammates. It was an overwhelming combination of awe, excitement for what was to come, and pride in my achievement of making it this far.

This was my moment—the third time around, and I had finally made it to the Olympic Games Opening Ceremony. I marched into the sacred place where only Olympians could go. I wanted this almost more than anything else. Being an Olympian is an earned distinction that only few can claim. This celebration is one of the highlights that all athletes take away from the Games. It binds us as together Olympians. It felt clear that the Olympics were about much more than just winning a medal.

Suddenly, I felt sadness in my heart, thinking about how magical it would have been to experience such exuberant pageantry twelve years earlier at my first Olympic Games with the Hungarian team in Rome. It will always be a black hole in my Olympic experience. At that time, the coaches forbade us from participating, but with the US team, participating at the Opening ceremony was mandatory.

Marching on the track, where many records would be broken and new Olympic heroes would be crowned, I brought my mind back to the present. This was my moment, and I wanted to enjoy it, soak it in, and preserve it.

After a lap on the stadium track, we all lined up on the infield to await the Olympic Flame. However, everybody soon left their designated areas and lined up at the edge of the track to watch the flame pass. The crowd exploded in a deafening ovation as the Olympic torch entered the stadium.

As the cauldron was lit, the Games were officially open, and we all became Olympians. Our faces reflected the joy of fulfilling our dreams. I felt the energy that bonded us together—sportsmanship, comradery, and the beginning of a lifetime association with something unexplainable called the Olympic spirit, which becomes part of your being and defines you for the rest of your life.

This was my third Games and my first Opening Ceremony, and it gave me a new experience and perspective that I'd never felt before. The Opening Ceremony is a very uplifting experience—all the athletes and coaches of the different participating nations stand united on the field with the hope that in the following two weeks their dreams of being champions, or at least medalists, will come true. However, no matter what happened on the playing fields, they would be Olympians forever.

For me, the greatest surprise of all occurred after the Opening Ceremony. As we returned to our living quarters, I found my mother standing there with a German Olympic Official! She wrote me a letter prior to the Games saying she might have a chance to come as a tourist visitor, but I couldn't envision that happening and didn't hold out any hope of seeing her. Apparently, the Hungarian government organized a train full of Olympic visitors to come and she was lucky to be included, despite her defector son. My brothers helped her with

Finally marching in the 1972 Olympic Games Opening Ceremony. I am somewhere among my teammates. Photo credit: USOC Archive.

the finances, and needless to say, our reunion was full of tears and joy. After eight long years, I was hugging my mother! We spent as much time together as my training allowed. She stayed only for a week, so she didn't see any of my races, but I promised her that I'd visit her as soon as possible, depending on the Hungarian government. Our separation was equally tearful.

Unfortunately, the Munich Olympic Games experienced a very tragic and sadly memorable event. It was the first time in the history of the modern Olympic Games that a terrorist attack was carried out on athletes. I will never forget that morning as long as I live. We were returning from an early morning practice on September 5th and found the Olympic Village locked down. Military personnel came on our bus with heavy weapons and searched everything, but we didn't know what was going on. Security was already tight, but this was too much.

We soon learned that, during the night, Palestinian terrorists had invaded the Village, occupied the Israeli team headquarters, and were holding members hostage. We heard rumors that some Israeli athletes and coaches had been killed. From our rooms, we could see the Israeli team accommodations and caught a glimpse of a ski-masked terrorist on the balcony. The Olympics were in turmoil, and all competitions were postponed until further notice by the IOC.

We were in limbo, waiting in our rooms, tensely following the events on TV. *Would the Israeli athletes survive this? Would the Games be completely canceled? Would there be any competitions held at a later date?* Mark Spitz, the decorated Jewish-American swimmer, requested to leave the Village immediately and was flown home, fearing for his safety. Some other athletes also left the Village to stay with their families in hotels. We were allowed to move around the Village and go to the cafeteria, as long as we stayed away from the cordoned-off war zone.

Negotiations with the terrorists began soon after, and the rest is well-documented history. It will be forever remembered as *The Black September Games*. This act of terrorism forced implementation of very strong security measures at future Games, which made them less vulnerable but also less enjoyable for athletes and visitors. In addition, the Games have become extremely expensive for the host country, due to all the added security measures.

Two days after the terrorist attack on the afternoon of the 7th, Mr. Avery Brundage, President of the International Olympic Committee, summoned all athletes to the Olympic Stadium and led us in a memorial for the eleven slain Israeli athletes and coaches. Then he declared, "The Games will go on."

The atmosphere in the stadium was very somber—there were a lot of teary eyes and sad faces all around me, not only for our slain friends but for the purity of the Olympic Games and Olympic spirit, which had been spoiled forever. In the end, though, I believe that this terrorist act brought Olympians even closer together with the goal of preserving the peaceful existence of the Games.

We had to get our minds back into the competition, as the Munich Games resumed on September 7. Our boats were provided by the organizing committee—brand new, wooden, Danish-made and -designed canoes. We brought all our own paddles and knee cushions with us from home. The race course was divided into two sections so the rowers and paddlers could practice without much interference. I looked at all the faces of the paddlers going by, but eight years had passed since I left my old country, and I hardly recognized anyone on the Hungarian team anymore.

The man-made Olympic regatta course was a brand-new venue built just for the Games. It was outside of Munich, at *Oberschleissheim*, close to the infamous concentration camp, Dachau, with its evil sign reading *ARBEIT MACHT FREI* hanging over the gate. I visited this camp after the competition and have some shocking memories of the exhibits showing the brutal treatment of the Jewish population.

My race was the single canoe 1,000-meter event. I remembered how nervous I had been eight years before in Tokyo, and thought of how much change had occurred in my life since then. Now, here I was again in Olympic competition, but wearing different colors. I certainly hoped that I could make the finals again this time. My preparation had been adequate, but my focus was divided between my new adult life in America, studying, and canoeing. I was 32 years old and in my third race at my third Olympic Games, and I was sure it would be the last one.

Looking left and right at the start line, I saw faces that I recognized as juniors from Hungary in 1964. As usual, the Hungarian team showed up with a very strong squad. My old coach had passed away, and the new generation of coaches and competitors were more sophisticated about preparation, conditioning, and technique. I made it to the semi-finals, but then the competition was very tough. I finished sixth in the semifinal, thirteen seconds behind the victor, a Romanian who went on to win the gold medal in the final. Obviously, I wanted to do better to prove to myself that I was still competitive internationally. Despite my disappointment, I realized how fortunate I was to still be competing at this level and representing the USA for the first time in Olympic competition.

The Closing Ceremony was very memorable. As we filed into the stadium, you could see that most of the Olympic flags had a black ribbon attached in memory of the eleven fallen Israelis. There was no jubilation. All the athletes were milling around the field saying goodbye to each other, hoping that this tragedy would never repeat itself. Again, I felt that the purity of the Olympic movement had been tainted and would never be the same again. In the history books, there would be always an asterisk to explain the unfortunate events. Terrorism invaded the Olympic movement—political factions used the Games to propagandize their cause.

Leaving Munich and the Olympic Games left a hollow feeling in me, and I realized that this was my last Olympics. I could not imagine my life without canoeing or preparing for competition, and I didn't want to quit all together. I had invested so much in the sport and the physical preparation of my body. There was no future in paid coaching in the USA, so only going back to school and finishing my master's degree assured me of a better future. However, I still had a lot of questions, decisions, and opportunities to weigh.

Completing my master's diploma in 1973 signaled another milestone for me. I decided that as soon as I graduated, I would get in my van with all my possessions, and point her West, not stopping until I reached the Pacific Ocean. I had a great time in Newport Beach the year before, and I'd always wanted to be a Californian. I would never regret spending eight years in Michigan, but that was enough. I needed a change, and a consistently warmer climate appealed to me more and more.

MAKING THE US OLYMPIC TEAM, 1972 AND 1976

Miki Kossa and I, 1978.

In May, 1973, after getting my master's degree in naval architecture from the University of Michigan, I closed the drafting room door behind me for the last time. I had tears in my eyes. I felt just like in Tokyo—closing the door on the past and opening another one for new experiences and a better future. I knew that the opportunity ahead would be challenging, but I welcomed it. Leaving Michigan behind and settling on the West Coast presented an uncertainty, and I hoped that my good fortune would follow me to California, the place I always wanted to be.

Two years earlier, I had met Miklos "Miki" Kossa, also a Hungarian and a Michigan naval architect graduate, in private practice in Berkeley, California. We met in the hydrodynamic towing tank where he tested a tug-barge concept. He told me that when I graduated, I should come and join him, so I did. I arrived in early June 1973 at his Berkeley home with my van and canoes on the top. He was working out of his house, so I stayed with his family for a couple of weeks until I moved to a former classmate's house in Walnut Creek, California, just on the other side of the coastal hills.

Miki and I never had a formal business agreement; he was independent and I was as well. I got a certain percentage of the total from the projects we jointly worked on, and that was it. This arrangement worked for more than twenty-five years, until Miki suffered a severe stroke and I was forced to continue the business alone. Miki's wife, Connie, and their two daughters, Christina and Susie, are like family to me. We spent many memorable years together. Miki was a good skier and a master rower, a sport he continued to practice as a coxswain even after his stroke.

Although I was on my own, I was emotionally attached to Michigan, where I'd left my young American love, Jane Babcock. She was enrolled at the University of Michigan at the time, and we had some very serious talks about getting married. I was not yet established in my business and she was still going to school, so our financial situation was not the best, but we decided to marry, anyway.

At that time, the University of California at Berkeley also had a naval architecture department, and I met a Greek student there through Miki. I helped him in the UC towing tank, testing his final design. One evening in August, he invited me to his home for dinner. He mentioned he was taking a job in New York City with a Greek ship owner, and in two weeks he'd be moving, and needed to sell his house. I told him I was about to get married around the same time, and had no place to stay with my new wife. He said that he had $16,000-equity in the house, which he wanted to carry with him to buy a new home in New York. The total cost of his house was $32,000 with a 4.5% assumable G.I. loan. I had $16,500 in my bank account saved up from working in Michigan.

My house in California since 1974.

MAKING THE US OLYMPIC TEAM, 1972 AND 1976

We went to the local title company and he signed the house over to me, and I turned over my hard-earned life savings to him with no real-estate agent, no middle man. I have never been so scared in my life. I had a new house and a piece of California to my name, a loan to pay each month, a new life with a wife, and a seriously depleted savings account. As I later learned, there were many more expenses to owning a house than just the loan payments—property taxes, utility bills, sanitation bills, insurance, and general maintenance, which all add up.

That weekend, I got in my little red truck (I had gotten rid of the big gas-guzzler, Bertha) with a small homemade plywood camper on the truck's bed and $500 in my pocket—my whole life savings! I drove to Ohio, and we got married on September 14th, 1974, under the maple tree on her family's farm near Oberlin, with her extended family standing by. My Hobo Canoe Club friends, Toby Cooper (my best man) and Doug Soules, stood by as my witnesses. Bill and Marcia came, and they were the closest family I had. It was a very nice country wedding, the way we wanted it. No one on my Hungarian side could come, so it was a little sad for me. I would have given anything to have my mother there to see her little son getting married. But that was impossible (It took another eight years to bring her to the States to see my first-born child, Katalin).

With Jane and her family at the wedding, September 14, 1974.

After the wedding, we all gathered for a potluck meal on the lawn, and it was a very festive occasion. My father-in-law, Jarvis Meach Babcock, who had served President Johnson on the staff of the Council of Economic Advisors and also taught in the University of Michigan Economics department, persuaded me to be a Democrat and vote whenever I could. This was a small price to pay for marrying his daughter. Although I did not know much about the US two-party political system, as it turned out I made a good choice.

My father-in-law was a well-read, educated man with a photographic memory, particularly when it came to weather, baseball statistics, and farm history. At dinner time when we all set around the table, he dominated the conversation with many historical facts and anecdotes. Both the English and French dictionaries were always at his side, as well as any other pertinent reference materials. He enjoyed telling stories and good, clean jokes. I never saw him drinking any alcoholic beverages, but he smoked many cigars outside of the house on the porch. He loved his family's farm, which dated back to the mid-19th century. When his father died, he left his teaching job at the University of Michigan and moved back to the farm to take care of it. Every summer, especially after we had kids, we went back to visit the family homestead. Just like in the children's story books, Grandpa's farm was always there for us. It is a special place for me and my family.

Arriving back in California after our honeymoon trip across the country, I carried my wife over the threshold into an empty house after I got the key from the neighbor where my Greek friend had left it. Jane transferred to UC Berkeley to study landscape architecture and I went back to work with Miki. The house slowly began to fill up with donated furniture and pieces I made. Looking at the house now, I cannot visualize it ever being empty. It's a small house, just under 1,000 square feet of living space, with two bedrooms and one bathroom on a 100- by 75-foot lot with couple of fruit trees in the back yard and a small garden.

Jane was recruited for the women's rowing team that was just being organized at UC Berkeley that fall. It was exciting to have her involved in this sport, and it kept me closer to the water as well. I trained, occasionally, in my newly designed and built single canoe, but the intensity was no longer there.

MAKING THE US OLYMPIC TEAM, 1972 AND 1976

Aerial view of the Babcock family farm in Rochester, Ohio.

After the 1972 Olympic Games, coaching become my passion. I wanted to give back all the knowledge, technical information, and experience I had gathered over the years in my sport. The opportunity came in 1975 and 1977, when I became the coach of the US National Junior Canoeing Team. I took both teams to the Junior World Championships. The first one was in Rome, Italy on the 1960 Olympic course where I got my bronze medal seventeen years earlier, and the second one was in Vichy, France. It was a challenging opportunity to work with young athletes to develop their skills. They did not do too well, as a lack of domestic competition and unfamiliarity with Olympic-style canoeing was too much of a handicap against the European competition. However, one young athlete, Greg Barton, showed real potential and I continued to work with him. Later on, his Olympic feats became legend.

There was a lot of buzz among my canoeing friends about the 1976 Olympic Games in Montreal, Canada. One of my local, nationally-ranked whitewater canoeing friends, Chuck Lyda, approached me and asked if I would be interested in trying out for the US Olympic Team with him in the flat-water double canoe. It was in early spring of 1976 with not much time left for serious train-

My Junior World Championship Canoeing team, 1975.

ing. He was a strong left-handed paddler, perfect for doing the double canoe with me. I told him I'd have to think about it and discuss it with my wife. I knew it would be a huge time commitment and that I'd have to take time off from my job. I had to look at the single-minded pursuit of Olympic participation in a different light now. I was 36 years old with a lot of experience, but I had not practiced any sprint racing since the last Olympics. I decided that I would give it a try, but set a time standard to achieve before actually going to the US Olympic trials. I designed a new two-man Olympic racing canoe and we built it in my garage just in time for the trials. We began our practices twice a day in a borrowed canoe four months before the Olympic Trials, with a training schedule that I put together. The training was going well and other paddlers joined us at the Berkeley Paddling and Rowing Club. We achieved my self-imposed time standard by mid-May. The Olympic Trials were back in Ohio in mid-June, so we had to get on the road and travel across the country again. Qualification consisted of the best combined placings out of three consecutive races over two days. We won the first race and came in second in the second

My Junior World Championship Canoeing team, 1977.

one. In the third race, we had to be ahead of the boat which beat us in the second race no matter where we finished overall, and we did that. I was on the Olympic team again for the fourth time! There are very few athletes in any Olympic sport who have competed in four Olympic Games for two different countries. I am proud to have achieved such a feat.

Just before we departed to go to Lake Placid, I promised Chuck that I would race in the US National Whitewater Championships with him on the South

BPRC boat house, Berkeley, California.

US Whitewater Championships with Chuck Lyda, 1976.

Fork of the American River (Chili Bar). Chuck was one of the top U. S. whitewater paddlers and was eager for the opportunity to race whitewater with me. We were stacked up against a very strong team that had been winning these races consistently over the past eight to ten years. Earlier, we made a boat that was kind of a proto-type but legal and served the purpose. All I remember of the race was a big drop at a rapid (Class 2-3) about 750 meters from the finish. The crowd on the shore was yelling to encourage us to speed up because we were behind by 3 seconds. It is not much, but on a moving river, it is hard to make up. We entered the rapid and suddenly were vertical (doing an *ender*), but the turbulence at the bottom of the rapid spit us out, luckily right side up. We sprinted there to the finish and won the race by two seconds. I was able to add another feather in my canoeing hat as a US National Champion in a different discipline of canoeing, whitewater downriver.

The US Olympic team was summoned to Lake Placid where we were outfitted and again, we received a suitcase full of stuff donated by the sponsors, mainly Montgomery Ward (I still have most of it in the same suitcase). Then, a couple of days before the Opening Ceremony, we were bused a short distance across the border to the Olympic Village in Montreal. The drive was very boisterous with all the athletes from different sports on the bus.

It felt good to be in the USA uniform again. Some of my teammates claimed that I just made the team to have another Olympic uniform. I must admit that there was some truth to that. However, the Olympic dream was still burning in my soul, and I had to give it another chance. It took a lot of sacrifice on both the family and professional levels. I knew that this would be my swan song. We trucked in our boat from the trials, and Jane came to be with me. She stayed with one of my Magnificent Seven friends on the outskirts of the city.

The 1976 Montreal Olympic Games (July 17th to August 1st) were still exciting, but the magic for me was gone. Realistically, just making the final would be a great accomplishment. We went to the Opening Ceremony, the second and surely the last time for me as a competitor. The theme of the Opening Ceremony was the great Canadian frontier with its diverse indigenous people. The North American Indian culture and history came alive on the stadium's field, and it was a great spiritual show inspiring the participants and guests. I was moved and thrilled by this, due to my lifelong fascination with the North American Indians, their spiritualism, and their canoeing culture. Leaving the Opening Ceremony, I was re-energized.

The canoeing competition was scheduled for the second week, as usual. After our daily training session, we had a chance to visit other competitions. There was a lot of discussion in the papers about the East German team's performance in all sports. Allegations surfaced that there was widespread, organized doping, and their team's sudden and dramatic improvement raised a red flag. The IOC and the International Federations were alarmed and there was almost unanimous agreement that doping must be stopped. The results were tainted and it appeared that the organizer's testing facility was not adequate to keep up with the pharmaceutical industry. Many athletes and team leaders felt that the future of the Games was in jeopardy.

At the Olympic Opening Ceremonies, Montreal, 1976.

The US Canoeing team, 1976 Montreal Olympic Games. I am in the front row, first on the left.

On July 29th, the canoeing competition began. Chuck and I were in the second heat on the far lane. The weather conditions were good, and our heat included the Russian and Hungarian teams, who eventually finished with the Gold and Bronze. After the start, we fell behind, and the Russian's boat wake hit our canoe, causing it to turn toward them. I had to make some hard steering strokes in order to not leave our lane and be disqualified. We slowed down considerably but finished the heat in our lane. I did not want my Olympic experience to end with a disqualification. We came in last but made it to the *repecharges* (a second chance to qualify for the semifinals). Our time was 4:21.18, second to last over all, not too promising. In the afternoon, we had our *repecharge*, and improved on our time, but it was not good enough to advance further. My Olympic competitive career was over. It was sad, but I had to realize that time and age were not on my side. I had lived up to my promise to my partner and to myself to make the Olympic team, but this is where it ended.

Two days later, at the Closing Ceremony, I wanted to capture all the sights, emotions, and spiritual connections the Olympic movement had given me over the past sixteen years of my life. Here I was, marching into the stadium with my fellow Olympians all around me, dressed in our national uniforms and coming together as friends instead of the rivals we'd been for the past two weeks. Formerly fierce competitors were now celebrating with true camaraderie in the spirit of Olympism. There were athletes with teary eyes waving flags, athletes dancing about with big smiles on their faces, some riding on the shoulders of new friends, others trading souvenirs with each other, and some seeming to be in a daze as they contemplated the end of the Games. Though there were many languages being spoken on the field, there was one sentiment—peace and brotherhood. I had never had such a feeling of perfect inner equilibrium.

Then, suddenly, the party was over, and the Olympic caldron, which had burned so brightly and had symbolized the Olympic spirit for sixteen days, was extinguished. The crowd did not want to leave; they desperately wanted to hang onto this unforgettable moment. Eventually, we filed out of the stadium in hopes that our feeling of peace, friendship, and harmony would last long after the Olympics. Many would also be hoping to repeat the experience in four years, but for many like myself, there would be no returning as an athlete.

I realized that in the past 16 years, almost one half of my life, I was involved in the Olympic movement mainly as a competitor. This global celebration of humanity and sports had captured my soul at an early age and inspired me to be a part of it. I had been touched by the Olympic Spirit which is an elusive concept, and I am still searching for the words to describe it. This global phenomenon every four years inspires new generations of athletes to pursue their dreams. The individual triumph of being an Olympian also frees the human spirit to share universal values in this diverse world, creating peace through sport. Despite the tendency for the media to pit nation against nation, camaraderie and friendship as well as fair competition unite us as athletes on a stage where only a select few can participate.

Being an Olympian is the joy at the end of a long, hard journey. The journey is different for each and every Olympian, but nevertheless, the dream to be one is the same. The Olympic journey is guided by a vision to reach this ultimate goal. Olympism does not end with the last competition. It continues throughout life. I strongly feel that we Olympians have an obligation to carry the Olympic torch and promote the values of Olympism to the end of our days.

The next day, I was driving back to California with Jane in my little truck and homemade camper. Having sold my canoe to a Canadian club, I had some money to finance the trip home. During the long days of driving, I felt at peace. I knew that I had done all that I could for myself as an athlete and my competitive life at the Olympic level was over. Though I hoped to contribute to the Olympic movement in some other way, it was time to settle down now and have a family. As it turned out, my hope became a reality, and a better one than I could have dreamed of.

CHAPTER 10
My Years in the Olympic Movement

After my last Olympic Games, I decided to stay close to my sport and the governing body to share some of my knowledge and continue to participate in whatever capacity I could. Olympic volunteerism captured my soul and became my passion. The late '70s were challenging times for amateur sports in the US, however. Two major sport associations, the AAU and the NCAA, governed all of US Olympic sports, but athletes had no voice at the administrative level in these organizations. Some spirited, well-known athletes expressed their dissatisfaction, wanting to have their voices heard and their issues considered.

In 1978, the US Congress began to work on the Athletes Bill of Rights, spearheaded by Senator Ted Stevens of Alaska. This Senate bill was advocated for by some well-known Olympians, including Miki King (diving 1968-1972, gold 5-meter springboard), Donna DeVerona (swimming 1960, gold 4x100 relay), Bill Toome (track and field 1968, gold decathlon), and Kenny Moore (Track and Field 1976, marathon 4th) just to mention a handful. If you are an Olympic sport fan, you will recognize these names. These athletes began their crusade after the 1976 Olympic Games and worked very diligently to be heard. The Olympic athletes' goal was to have more voting power on each National Sport Governing Body's Board and have representation on the US Olympic Committee's Board as well. They were asking that a minimum of twenty percent of the boards consist of currently-competing Olympic athletes. The athletes also demanded that they have their own Council (Athletes Advisory Council) under the US Olympic Committee's Constitution and By-Laws. These proposals were very controversial, at both the sports' National Governing Bodies and the USOC level.

Historically, the United States Olympic Committee Board members were affiliated with the Amateur Athletes Union (AAU) and its selected Olympic sports. However, the AAU did not include all of the Olympic sports under its membership—canoeing and rowing, for example. As such, the cause was very personal for me to fight for canoeing to be represented at the USOC level. The bill, as it was stated, would disenfranchise the AAU and would establish a new independent sports body for each of the AAU sports. The debate was very animated at each meeting, but the athletes prevailed, and the Athletes Bill of Rights was passed by the US Congress in October 1978. Passing the bill was one thing, implementing it was another.

The Athletes Advisory Council was actually formed even before the bill was passed by Congress. In 1977, I was asked to become a founding member, fighting alongside other distinguished Olympians for the Athletes Bill of Rights. I never dreamed of being a leading figure in the US amateur sports movement, but the cause fit my character. It was a controversial issue with heated discussions shaping the future for US athletes and their role in the administration of their sports and in the Olympic Movement. My devotion to the work of the Athletes Advisory Council took high priority in my life, with much traveling and time commitments. Life was also getting more complicated. Jane and I welcomed a baby girl into our family on October 23, 1978 and named her Katalin (Katie). Jane stayed at home taking care of her, so I had a young family to support, but was self-employed and barely making enough to live on.

In 1979, the USOC Constitution and By-Laws were amended to formalize the AAC's existence and

My young daughter, Katalin, 1979.

to give athletes twenty percent representation on the US Olympic Committee's Board of Directors. The Athletes Advisory Council voted amongst themselves for who would be on the USOC Board. Six AAC members were voted onto the board, and I was one of them. This honor—to represent all of the US amateur athletes on the USOC and be a full voting member of the USOC Board—was the greatest I had ever received in my sports career outside my Bronze medal. The way I looked at it, the medal was earned by physical prowess on the playing field, but this honor was respect I had earned from my peers. I served six years on the Athletes Advisory Council and ten years on the USOC Board of Directors, four of which I was the Secretary of the USOC.

In 1978, I was appointed the US National and Olympic Canoeing Coach. This coaching position was voluntary, with only travel expenses reimbursed. My responsibility was to coach the canoeing and kayaking teams for the 1979 World Championships in Copenhagen and the 1980 Olympic Games in Moscow. My excitement was beyond belief! I wanted to prepare my team well and show the international canoeing community that I was a good coach—and show the Hungarians that I had made it in America. My position as US Olympic coach would really make my Hungarian counterparts and the sport leaders envious. However, I had a strange feeling about traveling to Moscow. Although my defection was sixteen years earlier, the prison sentence for my defection was still on the books. I tried to reassure myself that the Olympic Games were special and I'd be protected as a citizen of the US, but strange things can happen behind the Iron Curtain, so I remained uneasy about entering the Soviet Union.

During the 1970s and 1980s, the Cold War was raging between the Soviet Bloc countries and the western world, mainly the United States. The Soviet Union invaded Afghanistan on December 27, 1979, and the US government was frustrated with diplomatic efforts to negotiate with them. The US Administration urged the United Nations Security Council to pass sanctions against the Soviet Union and tried every possible way to retaliate for the Afghanistan invasion. On January 20, 1980, President Jimmy Carter announced in a press release that "I have given notice that the United States will not attend the Moscow Olympics unless the Soviet invasion forces are withdrawn from

Afghanistan before February 20th." Each and every Olympic hopeful became very concerned by this message from the White House. The Athletes Advisory Council had an emergency meeting, and it was very somber. We did not know what to do except wait until February 20th. Some of us were convinced that the US Government was bluffing, since they had just approved the Athletes Bill of Rights guaranteeing athletes the right of participation.

The Carter administration sent its legal counsels, Lloyd Cutler and Josef Onick, to the US Olympic Committee's headquarters to discuss the mandate of non-participation. The USOC officers strongly objected to this plan. But the word got out that there had been no discussion—the lawyers were simply delivering the message from the President that the US team would not participate.

Coaching with my daughter Katie in Florida Olympic Training camp, 1980.

I was in Florida coaching my team at a conditioning camp when I received a summons as a member of the Athletes Advisory Council to the White House for an Executive meeting to discuss the Olympic boycott situation. My team encouraged me to do whatever was needed to protect their right to compete. When I arrived in Washington, the press was clamoring for interviews with us. Just before we went to the White House, the AAC decided to show a unanimous front against the boycott, although there was actually some dissension among us.

We filed into the press room of the White House where the press secretary, the legal counsel and Mr. Brzensinski, the US National Security Advisor, briefed us on the Soviet invasion, the international situation in the Middle East and the consequences of a Soviet expansion in that region. It was a bunch of propaganda and a geopolitical lesson we were not interested in. From the tone of their lecture, it was obvious that the President, who was the next speaker, would announce his executive decision. President Carter entered the press room, and the athletes did not stand up as a protest of the edict to come. To my knowledge, and I was told this by one of the White House staff, it was the first time that an audience did not stand for the President. I was proud, and still am, that I was there and defied the President of the United Sates. The President's speech was short and to the point. In closing he said, "Our Team will not go." The room was dead silent. Needless to say, we were devastated. Our heads hung low, and we looked at each other with disbelief. He asked us to endorse his decision. Counselor Cutler recommended the athletes form a small, five-member committee to continue dialogue with the White House but, in fact, the final decision was the US Olympic Committee's by Constitutional mandate.

President Carter's words were picked up by the worldwide media and on the news in no time. Local newspapers and TV stations interviewed the athletes. The national polls were running very high in favor of the boycott, and the athletes were portrayed as selfish, un-patriotic, un-American spoiled brats. The public quickly forgot the most spectacular Olympic victory only a month earlier at Lake Placid, during the 1980 Winter Olympic Games, when the US Hockey Team defeated the heavily favored and unbeaten Soviet team en-route to the gold medal. The whole nation celebrated this victory, and it was propagandized as an ideological victory as well. Within a month, all such sentiment reversed, and the whole nation turned against its own youth, taking sides with the Carter administration propaganda. The best political and military weapon that the US Government could come up with against the Soviet invasion of Afghanistan was to boycott the Olympics and take away the rights of 600 amateur athletes.

The government propaganda machinery did everything possible to justify the boycott of the 1980 Moscow Games. They referred to the boycott as a

My button protesting the 1980 Olympic boycott.

National Security measure, but as history proved, the boycott was ineffective and foolish—Soviet forces occupied Afghanistan for nine more years. The State Department sent an envoy to other nations to urge them to join the US boycott effort (They were partially successful, but 70 nations ignored the call and showed up at the Moscow Games anyway). A bill was introduced on the floor of the House of Representatives and the Senate to vote on the boycott, and it passed overwhelmingly. The athletes' cause was doomed, but the USOC still had to make the final decision. The last hope for the athletes was that their own governing body would stand by them and defy the executive order. Discussion was still going on between the US Olympic Committee, the athletes and the White House.

The five members of the Athletes Sub-Committee [Anita DeFrantz (Rowing, 1976), Fred Newhouse (Track and Field, 1976), Larry Hough, Ed Williams, and myself] were summoned to the White House again for a final briefing before the US Olympic Committee's House of Delegates voted on the boycott. The meeting was in the White House conference room with the President's counselors and Mr. Zbigniew Brzensinski. They repeated their propaganda and we proposed several alternatives, but all of them were deemed unacceptable. They were only looking for our endorsement of their boycott, and we could not do that. I argued that it was exactly the same kind of propaganda and government intervention that I resented in my old country. Brzensinski countered that the difference was that I could openly argue with the White House without the fear of reprisal. I was not certain of that, but I did it anyway. Needless to say, we left empty handed and with heavy hearts. The following week, the US Olympic Committee was scheduled to vote on Olympic participation.

My wife, Jane, with daughter, Katalin, on the White House lawn with the President's daughter, Amy Carter, 1980.

Vice President Walter Mondale showed up at the Antlers Hotel in Colorado Springs to deliver the administration's message with no surprises—the boycott was on. This historic meeting was held on April 12, 1980 on a bitter winter day that got even uglier for the athletes as the day went on. There was only one item on the agenda, a resolution to decline the International Olympic Committee's invitation to participate in the 1980 Summer Olympic Games in Moscow. After Vice President Mondale's address, the USOC President called for limited discussion and a secret ballot vote. Many athletes and representatives wore the button that I made up for the event, which read *we will go*. It did not help. Among the speakers was USOC Treasurer, William E. Simon (former Secretary of the US Treasury) who told us in his speech that, "It is somewhat incredulous that a group of mature persons whom I consider to be among the most patriotic of Americans, our Olympians, can seriously discuss defying the president of the United States on a national security issue." I did not believe that running, swimming, or paddling had any relationship to a national security issue, and I still don't.

My 1980 Olympic canoeing team with the trophies won during our international tour.

After the discussions, which were limited, the votes were counted and it was 1,704 to 697 in favor of the boycott. In other words, the United States Olympic Committee voted against its own right and Charter not to participate in the 1980 Summer Olympic Games in Moscow. The 1980 Games were over as far as the USOC was concerned, but not to some athletes. Anita DeFranze sued the USOC over the decision, but her suit was thrown out of court. The last straw had broken. For many great athletes, this Summer Games was the only opportunity to pursue their Olympic dream. Years of training and personal sacrifices were thrown away by our government for a bogus national security

On the White House lawn with Jane and Katie, 1980.

reason. What was really troubling to me was that a peanut farmer President, frustrated that his administration failed to achieve the release of 52 American hostages in Teheran and stop the advancing Russian Army in Afghanistan, coped by sacrificing American Olympians. No words can describe my disappointment and frustration.

    I returned to my team at the Florida training camp and announced that we would still have an Olympic Trials and select an official Olympic Canoeing Team as required by the USOC Charter. All other Olympic sports did the same. This Selection Race was held on a weekend in early May in Craftsbury, Vermont during a light snow storm. After two days of competition, we had a team selected and I forwarded their names to the US Olympic Committee. The USOC told me that the team could go to an international race with all expenses covered. I felt very empty in my heart and felt great sorrow for my athletes, some of whom quit paddling after the trials, never having the chance to compete at the Olympic level. They were denied the opportunity to compete at the highest level and be called Olympians by the very organization that was supposed to protect them. The canoeing team decided to go to Spain, but my Olympic coaching debut was never to be.

However, there was still a small ray of hope. The International Olympic Committee extended the entry deadline and some of us hoped it might just be possible to enter as individuals. However, the IOC would have to change its charter in order to do that. That was a tall order, and when the US got wind of our idea, they threatened to withdraw our passports and notify the IRS if we attempted to participate as individuals. They had the whole nation's support, so the athletes were alone and doomed (It took 36 years for the IOC to accept individual entries by forming a refugee team for the 2016 Rio Olympic Games).

As a consolation prize for the 1980 summer Olympians, the USOC and Levi Strauss (the official apparel sponsor of the 1980 Olympic Team) organized a party for Olympic team members, their spouses, and their children in Washington D.C., including a White House visit and picture-taking with President Carter and his family. At first, the Athletes Advisory Council decided to boycott the White House visit, but the athletes were not united on this issue. So, the decision was made to leave it up each athlete. President Carter wanted to show a united front to the nation and world on this issue. However, many team members did not show up for pictures with the president on the White House lawn. (My canoeing team declined, and I was proud of them). The athletes were very grateful to Levi Strauss for their commitment to the athletes, and we all received the official uniform and all the accessories that we would have gotten anyway. The party was a huge extravaganza, with live entertainment and fireworks, but a very poor substitute for the Olympic competition. I went with my family and attended the festivities with a heavy heart. My eighteen-month-old daughter, Katalin, had a chance to swing on Amy Carter's swing on the side of the White House with Amy looking on. Very few kids can say that.

The bottom line on the Olympic Boycott was that we did not go, and for compensation the athletes got two Tiffany medals, a party in Washington D.C., and a consolation prize regatta—a very poor substitute for not going to

*USOC Commemorative Medal for the 1980 Olympic Team members.
Made by: Tiffany & Co. New York.*

the 1980 Moscow Games. I still think that the USOC felt guilty about voting against its own constitution and the athletes they were supposed to protect.

It later came to my attention that since the USOC declined the invitation to participate in the Moscow Olympic Games, the IOC would not recognize the selected 1980 USA Olympic Team. In other words, the USOC-selected 1980 Olympic Team members were not Olympians as far as the IOC was concerned. They don't even appear on the list of Olympians in the IOC's history book. This was a double-blow to the 1980 USA Olympic Team as they did not have a chance to compete and were not registered as Olympians in the international arena.

In my case, I was forced to miss my fifth Olympic Games. It bothered me not to find out how good a coach I was and what the results would have been. This bitter Olympic experience made me disillusioned with the US government. I told my family that we might have to move to Australia or somewhere with less government control. However, I realized that there was no such place, so I would have to make the best of it and stay. Over the next ten years, I became more deeply involved with the Olympic movement, and I did my best to make a difference on the USOC Board of Directors where I was a voting member. I introduced several changes at committee levels and at policy levels.

During the late 70s, there was an urgent feeling among athletes that the US was losing its competitive edge against the Soviet Union and its satellite countries. The Soviet Union held, on a quadrennial basis, a successful *Spartakiade* in all Olympic events. In 1978, the USOC announced its first US Olympic Sport Festival, modeled after the *Spartakiade*—a mini-Olympics. The US Olympic Festival, as it was called, would be awarded to a city annually, except in the Olympic years.

The USOC covered all the participant expenses (travel, room, and board), the local organizing committee was responsible for the venues and the National Sport Federations (NGBs) staffed and ran the events. To increase national competition, the country was divided into four regions (East, West, North, and South), each having its own colored uniforms. It was a media-friendly event and well-covered locally and nationally. In the beginning, most NGBs brought their top athletes to the Festival and used the competition as a pre-selection or trials for upcoming Olympic Games or World Championships.

I was excited about the opportunity for my sport to participate in the Festival's program. It would bring another high-quality race to our athletes' calendar, and media exposure to the sport, which was badly needed. Fortunately, I was at the highest level of the USOC and could speak for canoeing and protect the sport when sometimes threatened due to inadequate facilities at the Festival sites.

The early success of the Festivals was encouraging. However, as the years passed, the Festivals became a financial drain for the USOC especially when the top athletes declined to participate and the sponsors withdrew their support. Some of the high-profile sports began to use the Festival as a junior-level development event. "The USOC could not guarantee marquee names to host cities that needed such attractions to lure sponsors and sell tickets," wrote a *Chicago Tribune* journalist. In 1995, the USOC decided to end the festivals. "The goose killed the golden egg."

One positive thing emerged in organizing the US Olympic Sport Festivals. Some states formed a state sport organization to run state sport festivals (like the Empire State Games in New York) or have a state sport council to develop amateur sports. Some of these entities are still in existence helping local Olympic athletes.

I was disheartened at losing the US Olympic Sport Festival despite my efforts to save it. Canoeing lost an opportunity for athlete development and for public awareness of an otherwise minor Olympic sport.

In 1982, I proposed *Operation Gold*, an athlete's incentive program to provide direct financial support to medal-winning athletes who want to continue to compete at the international level. This was the first and the only proposal presented to the USOC that directly benefited athletes monetarily. At first, this proposal ran into some opposition, but in later years it was adopted and it's still the only direct financial support for athletes from the USOC.

Encouraged by my Athletes Advisory Council success, I decided to propose a similar athletes' representation at the International Olympic Committee level. I wrote a letter to Mme. M. Berlioux, Director of the IOC in Lausanne, with my proposal attached. To my surprise, she answered me. I continued to pursue the subject and was asked to present my proposal to the IOC Executive Board in Los Angeles, California on February 24, 1981. I was granted a fifteen-minute time slot for my presentation. I flew to Los Angeles and nervously waited outside of the IOC's meeting room. As I entered, there in front of me were the members of the most powerful amateur sports organization in the world. They all had a translator's headphone on, and everyone was looking at me. I took a deep breath and handed out my one-page proposal paper and, after formal introductions, read it to them. I wasn't too sure what kind of response I would have. However, in mid-June I had received a letter from Mme. Berlioux saying, "The IOC considers the inclusion of athletes in this Congress to be of utmost importance, in that their views on the three themes in question may be heard." I was glad that my effort was fruitful.

I learned later that Mr. Peter Talberg, the Finnish representative on the IOC Executive Committee, had great interest in my proposal and wrote his own proposal to set-up an athletes' office in Los Angeles during the Games. Consequently, Mr. Juan Antonio Samaranch, the President of the IOC, requested that the Los Angeles Organizing Committee set up an athletes' office in the Village. I am glad that I had a part in establishing the athletes' voice at the highest level.

During the 1984 Winter Olympic Games in Sarajevo, I was a member of the US support crew for the US Olympic athletes. Four of us from the USOC arrived a week early to set up the Village for the athletes. This was an interesting experience for me, being on the other side of the fence—an organizer rather than a competitor—and at the Winter Olympic Games, too.

The US team supplies were flown into Zagreb and then trucked to Sarajevo. At the Olympic Village, we got the news that the trucks had been stopped there by the Serbian customs officials for inspection. One of the team leaders said to me, "Go and get it, Andy. They are your people. You speak the language." With some trepidation, I took our official car to the Sarajevo customs office.

The office was a hole-in-the-wall kind of place. Five workers were crammed into a cubicle, which was so full of cigarette smoke that I could hardly see the wall where General Tito's picture was hanging. The head man greeted me in broken English, with a cigarette hanging out to the side of his mouth. I responded in my broken Russian, glad that my seven years of mandatory Russian instruction was finally paying off, and that this guy and I could "understand" each other to a degree. He showed me a stack of papers, which were the inventory lists of our supplies, and he conveyed to me that we must go through each and every box individually.

If he was serious, we would be inventorying until next Christmas, I thought. As we were going out to the trucks, I got the idea that first we should open the USOC Executive Director's box of personal supplies. He was also a smoker. The custom officer's eyes were like saucers when I popped open the box of Marlboro cartons. He had never seen that much treasure in one place. So, I started offering it to him. He looked around as he stashed the packs into his pockets. Eventually, I gave him the whole box and a couple of bottles of Jack Daniels as well. I was out of there in ten minutes with all the inventory lists stamped "Approved." A week later, the Executive Director asked me what happened to his personal supplies. When I told him the story, he reluctantly agreed it was worth it.

During one of the USOC functions in Sarajevo, I was approached by a member of the nominating committee to see if I'd be interested in becoming one of the six officers of the USOC for the next quadrennial (1984-1988). My heart stopped, and I could not believe what I was hearing. *It was an honor even to be asked*, I thought. For me, a poor Hungarian defector, to be one of the officers of the most successful and prestigious amateur sports organizations in the world was unbelievable. I could hardly contain my enthusiasm, but I told him that I had to think it over and would let him know in the next few days. The following day, I told him, "Yes!"

The Sarajevo Winter Games were a success for the USA, and I have good memories of meeting some of the winter athletes and mixing with International Olympic Committee members and TV broadcast personnel from ABC. During the Games, I organized a dinner honoring the athletes, and John Denver showed up to entertain us and the event was televised live.

I have many wonderful memories in connection with the Sarajevo Winter Olympic Games. Marching with the team in the Opening Ceremony was one of them. Compared to the summer Games, it was smaller because of the number of participating countries. However, it was just as colorful and had the same pageantry. The enthusiasm of the athletes and the anticipation of the official opening were just the same. With these Games, I was an official, not an athlete, so my frame of mind was different. However, I could not help but be caught up in the athletes' exuberance that surrounded me. We were all one—Olympians.

During the Games, I befriended many of the USOC's managerial staff, the "behind the scenes" workers helping the athletes. I was proud to contribute to the overall effort. This experience helped me for the next four years when I became the Secretary of the USOC.

Several months later, the 1984 Summer Olympic Games were in Los Angeles, California. The Russians and their allies boycotted the Games as payback to the US for four years earlier. I was on the jury for the canoeing competition, an official position with the International Canoe Federation (ICF). Two years earlier, I was elected as a Continental Representative to the ICF Board of Management. I held that position for ten years, and one of my responsibilities was to present the medals at the podium for World Championships which were held every year between the Olympic Games. Over the next 12 years, this assignment took me to many foreign places. So here I was, back at an Olympic Games but as an official. The Los Angeles Games were a financial success because the organizers used existing facilities, and American TV paid a large sum of money for the rights to broadcast the Games to home audiences with a lot of airtime for advertising. After the Games, there was a surplus of money that was distributed among the sports' national governing bodies. This was the first time in the history of the Olympics that had happened. Interestingly enough, Los Angeles was the only candidate to host the 1984 Olympic Games. With the Soviet boycott, the international sports community sensed that the Olympics may be victim to political posturing, which could mean the beginning of the end for the modern Olympic Games. The Olympics did change, but they were far from over. The 1984 Los Angeles Olympics Games were a showcase in every respect, but the Olympic movement was tainted again by a boycott. I felt sorry for the Soviet athletes who needlessly suffered for a senseless cause.

Presenting medals at the 1994 Mexico City World Canoeing Championships.

With my young son Tamás, 1982.

During the 1984 USOC Quadrennial Congress meeting in October, the USOC Nominating Committee put forward a slate of officers for approval. My name was on that list as Secretary of the USOC for 1984 through 1988. It was an honorary, volunteer, unpaid position. I was now glad I had not left the country four years earlier to defy the boycott. This great honor was bestowed upon me by my peers in the organization. There was no challenge from the floor, so Congress voted in the new officers for the next four years. Many of my peers congratulated me and wished me good luck. With the many highs and lows in my involvement in the Olympic movement, this was definitely one of the high points.

I returned home to California as the new Secretary of the United States Olympic Committee. Though the position was as a volunteer, it was almost a full-time job with much responsibility and time commitment. I sat down with my wife and young family to discuss this situation. I now also had a son, Tamás (Tommy), born on May 22nd, 1982. Being self-employed, taking leave from work would stress our finances even more than they already were. During the discussion, I sensed that Jane felt my strong commitment to the Olympic movement, as well as my urgency to continue supporting my sport and US athletes in general. Reluctantly, perhaps, she supported me. I did not know at that time how demanding my role would be. It turned out to be a very exciting and intense four years, attending many sport meetings, both domestic and international.

The Executive Committee of the International Fair Play Council. I am in the back row, first on left, 1988.

This quadrennial, John Kelly was Vice President of the USOC. I had met him twenty years before in Philadelphia, but by now we were very close friends. He appreciated my Hungarian heritage and my continued involvement in the Olympic movement. He asked me if I would be interested in taking his place on the International Fair Play's Administrative Council. Jack believed in Fair Play, and once said, "Without fair play, sport is no longer sport." I was honored to be asked, and during my four-year tenure with the Fair Play organization, I met many distinguished sports leaders. The yearly council meeting was always during the Roland Garros Tennis tournament because the President, Mr. Jean Borotra, was a French champion tennis player. The actual Fair Play Award was presented at UNESCO each year. I was a relatively young member on the Council, but I took my position seriously and with diligence.

The Pan American Games in 1987 were held in Indianapolis, and as Secretary of the USOC, I was a liaison to the organizing committee. Canoeing had never been part of the program for the Pan American Games, and I took on the challenge to convince the organizers to include it. I promised the organizers that I could deliver ten American continent canoeing teams to compete, and the first gold medal of the Games would be in canoeing for the USA. Luckily, the canoeing team delivered! I was very pleased to play a major part in providing an international competition to paddlers in the Americas and introducing audiences to a *new* sport.

With my children at the 1987 Pan Am Games, Indianapolis.

Indianapolis was very close to the family farm, so I invited my in-laws to join Jane and the children at the Games with me. They were there for the duration, which made my participation more enjoyable. I was happy to give back some lost time to my family, which I had spent over the last years with my volunteer work for the Olympic movement.

An Olympic year arrived again. First came the 1988 Winter Games in Calgary, Canada. In my USOC position as the Secretary, I had an obligation and honor to be present at the Games and march with the US delegation in the Opening Ceremony. I took my family with me to Calgary, and they had accreditation to attend all events. The Opening Ceremony was bitter cold, as I recall. My wife and children were sitting in the first row of the stadium waving at me as I paraded by. It made me feel important and gratified to share with them the rewards of all the hard volunteer work I did for the USOC and

With the family at 1988 Calgary Winter Games.

the American athletes. My family had sacrificed, too, in the many days that I had been away from them while the children were growing up. I hoped that in this moment they also felt that their sacrifices had been worth it. We had a wonderful time seeing many events and enjoying the warm hotel room at the end of the day.

In the fall of 1988, the Summer Olympic Games were held in Seoul, South Korea and were unique and beautiful. The Koreans did a magnificent job of organizing, and the colorful choreography and pageantry of the Opening Ceremony was spectacular. My wife, Jane, joined me in Seoul. We went to see the canoeing events, where I was a jury member again. One of the USA kayak paddlers was Greg Barton, whom I had coached as a junior. Four years earlier in Los Angeles, he had won a bronze medal in the 1,000-meter single-kayak event. He was favored to do well again, but this time he wanted to race both the single- and the double-kayak 1,000-meter events, which were scheduled just forty minutes apart. It was a very hard combination, and only a couple of paddlers in the history of the sport had attempted it.

Greg was initially declared second in the single-kayak 1,000-meter race until the photo finish revealed that he had won by 0.01 seconds. Then, hurrying from the podium (in canoeing, medals are awarded immediately after the race), he hopped into the double kayak, which was waiting at the dock with his partner, Norm Bellingham, already in it. Incredibly, Greg and Norm won the double against all the other fresh and strong competitors, again by a very close margin (0.03 seconds). After the race, Greg jokingly said, "We won the double by twice as much." He made history accomplishing a feat that no one

Marching with the USA delegation in the 1988 Winter Games Opening Ceremony. I am a step behind.

Marching with the USA delegation at the 1988 Seoul Olympic Games—one step ahead.

had done before and no one has repeated. Bud Greenspan, the Emmy award-winning Olympic documentarian, captured this race in his *Sixteen Days of Glory*. Greg's race is the opening segment of this movie, which includes an interview with me as Greg's development coach. I was honored that I had a part in Greg's legendary Olympic performance.

During my four-year tenure as a USOC officer, I got deeply involved with the organization, serving on many of the standing committees and always giving the athletes' causes priority. As secretary, I was appointed to work with the Olympic Bid Committees. They were groups from various US cities bidding to bring the Games back to the States. Atlanta was chosen as our US bid city for the 1996 Centennial Olympic Games, and Salt Lake City for the 1994 Winter Olympic Games. Both cities won their bids at the IOC level. It was a very unique opportunity for me to have firsthand experience in the bidding process and lobbying. I met many of the most prominent sports leaders in the world, which gave me insights into the global picture of amateur sport.

Through the USOC, I became a delegate to many international sport organizations, like the Association of Summer Olympic International Federations (ASOIF) and the Pan American Sport Organization (PASO). These sport organizations have regular meetings to resolve issues within their domain. As a delegate, I attended many meetings and used my voice to protect the interests of US amateur athletes. I felt that I had a unique position for understanding the issues because of my dual country background. When my term as USOC Secretary was over, I had to leave these organizations.

During one of the international sport meetings, I approached the Hungarian Delegation about establishing an Olympic sport exchange program between the US and Hungary. I was the chairman of the USOC's International Relations Committee which I had established several years earlier. For a long time I thought that this kind of sport exchange would benefit both countries' athletes, mainly in the minor sports. The Hungarians encouraged me to draw up a proposal. I did this with the help of some staff members and presented it to the USOC board for approval. The board had a favorable response and encouraged me to set up the meeting.

In the beginning, I was reluctant to make this first visit back to my homeland. I did not trust the Hungarian government officials. Although my sentence had been commuted several years earlier, I felt that it might not assure me a safe visit. After much soul-searching, I decided to take a chance and go with the USOC delegation (as the USOC Secretary, it was my duty) to Budapest to sign the exchange agreement. I rationalized that if anything happened, it would be a diplomatic affair which the Hungarians would want to avoid. Still, it would be very unpleasant to be detained.

We were picked up at the airport in Budapest by an official state car with Olympic flags on the fenders and escorted to the hotel. I was pleased that the Hungarian Olympic Committee rolled out the red carpet for a defector. My mother visited me with teary eyes and said, "I hope they do not arrest you." I

Signing of the USA-Hungarian Sport Agreement, October 18, 1989 Budapest, Hungary. In the front row: Schmitt Pál, President of the Hungarian Olympic Committee, IOC member; Robert Helmick, President of the USOC, IOC member. I am in the back row third from the right. Photo credit: Koppány György.

told her that I was not too sure. Needless to say, I slept uneasily that night. The next day, both parties met at the Hungarian Olympic Committee's headquarters and had a reception before the official signing ceremony.

The presidents of both Olympic Committees, several State officials, and a US Embassy representative were present. I felt relieved to see some high US officials. After the formalities, we had a nice lunch and very lively discussion about the future of sports in general. All the newspapers and the Hungarian TV covered the event. I stayed two more days to visit my family and my old club on Margaret Island. That brought back good memories. After returning to California, I felt good about the exchange program. However, due to financial and scheduling difficulties, it never materialized in the way I had envisioned.

Two years before the Atlanta Games, I got involved with three California paddlers who asked me to coach them for the upcoming Games. They had dual citizenships, USA and Antigua Barbuda, so they were eligible in both countries. They faced two problems. One was that Antigua Barbuda did not have a domestic canoeing federation and due to that, they were not eligible to compete for that country. The second was that the IOC had established a qualification criteria based on performances at the previous year's World

Championships, or at a Continental qualification race. So first, we had to work on establishing an Antigua and Barbuda Canoe Federation and applying for membership in the ICF. Through my connection with the Pan American Sport Organization, I was able to form a new canoe federation and acquire membership.

The second problem of qualifying at a competition proved to be more demanding. After only nine months of practice, the very green competitors (one two-man canoe team and one single-woman kayaker) from Antigua Barbuda entered the 1997 Duisburg Canoeing World Championships. Those results were not up to par, so they did not qualify. However, the 1995 Pan American Games were in Mar del Plata, Argentina, and they were eligible to compete. So, I went with the team (all self-funded) to Mar del Plata as the coach and manager for the new Antigua and Barbuda Canoeing Team.

The weather was dreadful as I recall, with 20-knot side winds and close to two-foot waves on the course. Both boats struggled to stay upright, but they made it down the course in their respective races, qualifying for a wild card invitation to the Olympic Games. The official ICF invitation came in early June for the Antigua and Barbuda Canoeing Team to participate at the 1996 Centennial Summer Olympic Games in Atlanta! Needless to say, we had a big celebration. For me, this was the third country that I would officially represent at an Olympic Games. I was the coach and team leader. We got the official Antigua and Barbuda uniform and a few other sponsor items; not nearly as much stuff as the US team gets.

Unfortunately, a couple of days before the competition, my team members were in a bus returning from the racing course when the bus was involved in an accident and they were injured, preventing them from racing. They were devastated, and I was very disappointed for them. However, they enjoyed the Opening and Closing Ceremonies and got a taste of the Olympic spirit.

The competition was fierce and no US boats made the finals, so I cheered for the Hungarian team, which did very well. As it turned out, these Centennial Games were the last in which I coached and was involved with the development of athletes at the international level.

STATE OF CALIFORNIA

Senate

RULES COMMITTEE

RESOLUTION

By

Senator William Campbell

Relative to Commending

Andras Istvan Toro

WHEREAS, A man of outstanding athletic achievement, Andras "Andy" Istvan Toro is deserving of heartiest congratulations and commendations; and

WHEREAS, Mr. Toro, a native of Budapest, Hungary, immigrated to the United States in 1964 and became a naturalized citizen in 1972; and

WHEREAS, He attended the University of Budapest, and he received his Bachelor and Master of Science degrees in naval architecture and marine engineering from the University of Michigan; and

WHEREAS, Mr. Toro is an independent naval architect and marine consultant, and since 1973, he has worked as a consultant with Miklos M. Kossa, a naval architect and marine consultant; and

WHEREAS, He was a lecturer at the University of Michigan and at the California Maritime Academy; and

WHEREAS, Mr. Toro has been involved in canoeing since 1953, and he was a member of the Hungarian National Team from 1958 to 1964 and he won numerous national championships and competed in the 1960 and 1964 Olympic Games and the 1962 World Championships; and

WHEREAS, He was also a member of the United States National Canoeing Team from 1965 to 1976 and won numerous United States and National American Championships, and he competed in the 1970 and 1971 World Championships and the 1972 and 1976 Olympic Games; and

WHEREAS, Mr. Toro served as the Athletes Liaison for the 1984 Winter Olympic Games, and as head coach of the 1973 North American Championships, the 1975 Junior World Championships, the 1975 Regatta of the Americas, the 1977 Junior World Championships, the Nationals from 1978 to 1981, and the 1980 United States Olympic Team; and

WHEREAS, He is a member of the American Canoe Association and the International Canoeing Federation, a past member of the National Olympic Canoe-Kayak Committee and the United States Olympic Committee, and he served as coach and Vice President of the Berkeley Rowing and Canoe Club; now, therefore, be it

RESOLVED BY THE SENATE RULES COMMITTEE, That the Members take pride in honoring Andras "Andy" Istvan Toro for his outstanding athletic achievements, as well as his illustrious record of personal and professional achievements, and convey best wishes for continued success in his future endeavors.

Senate Rules Committee Resolution No. 519 adopted April 7, 1989.

David Robert
CHAIRMAN
Senatoris Est Civitatis

SENATOR - 31ST DISTRICT
Libertatem Tueri

CHAPTER 11
Memories of my Olympic Tenure

There are many great stories and memories from my tenure in the Olympic movement. I had the pleasure of serving with many distinguished US sports figures, both amateur and professional. Perhaps the most well-known and loved or reviled was Mr. George Steinbrenner, principal owner of the New York Yankees, who was on the USOC Board for eight years at the same time that I served as a Vice President. He was recruited as a public sector member to help restructure the USOC Board, which had become too large and unmanageable.

With George Steinbrenner at a USOC meeting, 1988.

So, there I was at many meetings sitting next to Mr. Steinbrenner, one of the most controversial figures in US professional sports, the person the media loved to pick on. In comparison, I was a poor Hungarian canoe paddler whose net worth was minuscule compared to his, but on equal footing where amateur sports were concerned. George, as he asked us to call him, was a very fair player when it came to amateur athletes. He understood our problems and searched for solutions. I was always kidding him about his manager's (Billy Martin's) European heritage. There are too many stories to tell about our relationship, but a couple of them are worth repeating.

The USOC Board had a meeting in New York City, and during that meeting, George announced that he'd asked Mickey Mantle to visit us so we could meet him. I asked unwittingly, "Who is Mickey Mantle?" It was a genuine question but it made everyone laugh. George gave me a headlock and a hard knuckle rub on the head. "He is a famous soccer player, you dumb Hungarian," he exclaimed, which made the board laugh even harder. Two weeks later in the mail, I received a New York Yankee's signature gold watch!

The other interesting episode was in 1991, before the Pan American Games, which were awarded in Havana, Cuba. Four USOC Board members, including me, met in Tampa, Florida at George's place. We were supposed to go on to Havana to discuss preparation for team processing. We were scheduled on a midnight charter flight out of Miami—the so-called *Dead Trip* because the plane was pretty much filled with old Cuban folks flying home to visit their relatives for the last time. The plane was an old Soviet-made military charter. We had been on it before and didn't like it at all, but it was the only official way to fly to Cuba. When we told George that we had to head to the airport to catch this contraption to Havana, he said, "Hell, why don't you take my plane?" He picked up the phone and called his hangar. An hour later, we were in the air on George's private plane flying in luxury to Cuba. I will never forget the reception in Havana. A plane with the Yankee logo was landing on the runway! The ground crew thought that the Messiah had come. Baseball is huge in Cuba and everyone knows the Yankees. Over the years, many Cuban baseball players had defected to the US, and the Yankees had a fair share of them. The airport ground crew begged for souvenirs. We had only a few Yankee drink coasters and small Yankee flags to give, but they were eagerly snatched up. Then the plane turned around and left.

After our meeting with the Pan American Games organizers, we had a reception with *El Jefe* himself, Fidel Castro. I found him a very imposing figure. Although he speaks fluent English, he communicated with us through a translator. He was pleased that we confirmed the US Team participation in spite of the talk in the press of boycotting the 1991 Pan American Games and some opposition in Miami. His compound was typical of Caribbean architecture. He asked us not to take any pictures. He didn't give us any reasons, but we guessed that he did not want his people or the rest of the world to see his compound. The next day, we returned to Miami on another *Dead Trip* flight, a very different trip from the one we came on.

The 1991 Pan American Games were very unusual. Perhaps the most interesting episode happened during the Opening Ceremony. In the summer time, a rain shower occurs nearly every afternoon. As the athletes filed into the stadium, the sky became black with ominous clouds. The afternoon storm had arrived and everyone prepared to get soaked. Fidel Castro came to the microphone welcoming the athletes. As he delivered his speech, the black clouds began to move away from the stadium and the sky completely cleared. We all joked that he had power to part the sea, just like Moses.

I was on the competition jury as a member of the ICF Board of Management as an American continental representative and, as it was customary, I was supposed to present the medals at the podium. However, El Jefe beat me to it. President Castro showed up at the canoeing competition that morning anticipating a victory for Cuba, but Mike Herbert, the US kayak paddler won. He presented the medal as well as a souvenir to Mike. I decided not to argue with his decision.

I thoroughly enjoyed my stay in Havana. The friendship and hospitality of the Cuban people were warm and genuine. All the political differences between the US and Cuba were set aside for the duration of the Games, and sportsmanship overcame ideological differences. The best should be able to compete without any political interference, and I felt sorry for the common people of Cuba caught up in the US embargo and all the resulting economic suffering.

Cuban President Fidel Castro presenting the medal for winner Mike Herbert (USA) during the 1991 Pan American Games.

The late '80s and early '90s brought considerable change to Europe. The communist system cracked and the Soviet Union broke up into 11 separate countries. The hated Berlin Wall came down, and monumental changes happened without bloodshed. A very remarkable human accomplishment. The map of the world was redrawn again.

Hungary, leading the revolution again, had to switch to a non-communist ruling party. The first orders of business were to overhaul the Constitution, allow free parliamentary elections, disband the Soviet military occupation, and establish a free economic system. The transition was not easy. I monitored all the progress from abroad and was happy to see all the changes. I was happily surprised to experience the *new* Hungary when I first visited with my family in 1992.

Another Olympic year, 1992, had come around. The Games were held in Barcelona, Spain. I was scheduled again to be on the Competition Jury for Sprint Canoeing, so I decided to take my whole family to Europe and make a grand tour. My daughter, Katalin, was almost fourteen and my son, Tamás, was ten. I felt that they were a good age to enjoy and remember an Olympic Games and experience the Olympic movement that had occupied their father for so much of his life.

We departed San Francisco two-and-a-half weeks before the Opening Ceremony of the Barcelona Games. We landed in Munich and first took the train to our German friend's house. Tamás was so excited during the flight that he couldn't sleep, but as soon as we landed, he was out! I had to carry him to the railroad station. We spent a couple of days in Germany and then continued on to Budapest by train. I had been telling my family about the feared border crossing and my experience there. As we came to the border between Austria and Hungary, the border guard came, glanced at our US passports, smiled, and moved on. What a big difference, I thought, never imagining the border crossing could be such a relaxing experience.

My whole Hungarian family was waiting for us at the railroad station. My mother and my brothers were very happy to see us, and everyone began to ask all sorts of questions that I had to translate back and forth. My mother and my brothers only spoke Hungarian, so it was all on my shoulders to carry the conversation. By the end of two weeks, my English-speaking family knew a few Hungarian words and vice versa. Needless to say, everywhere we went we had to sit down and eat. All the women in the family are great cooks. We had several versions of *meggy leves* (cold, sour cherry soup served in the summer), *lecso* (a typical Hungarian fried vegetable dish), *lángos*, (fried bread with garlic), and, of course, *chicken paprikás* and *gulás*.

Our stay in Hungary was short, but very memorable. My children still talk about it at family gatherings, and we'd like to go back again. I was very happy that they experienced the place where I grew up and met my family, whom I had talked about so much. We visited all the usual tourist places in Budapest and the countryside where we enjoyed Lake Balaton, the Hungarian equivalent of Lake Tahoe. My mother secretly stashed some Hungarian money in my children's pockets (an old Hungarian habit). She wanted to show her appreciation for their visit and express her love and affection. As it turned out, this would be the only visit that my children had with their grandmother. She would pass away in 1998 before we could make another trip to Hungary.

However, we had to take leave from my family for the next leg of our trip, a train ride to Switzerland for a visit with other friends before heading to Barcelona. It was an overnight trip in a sleeping car, which was quite a novel experience for my wife and children. After three days in Switzerland, we were back on the train for Barcelona. Our first order of business was to get everyone Olympic ID accreditation to allow us to visit any event we wanted, a wonderful token of appreciation from the USOC for my volunteer services over the years. We were able to walk into any venue for any event and sit in the VIP section. One of Tamás' favorite experiences was getting an autograph from Jack Nicholson, the famous actor, who was sitting a couple of rows in front of us during the Track and Field finals. His biggest disappointment was when the Terminator (Arnold Schwarzenegger) did not show up as expected at a USOC reception.

With USOC President Helmick and IOC President Samaranch, 1992 Barcelona.

The 1992 Barcelona Olympic Games brought major changes to the Olympic movement. The President of the International Olympic Committee (IOC) and native of Barcelona, Mr. Juan Antonio Samaranch, promised that the city and NBC would deliver a spectacular show. Part of the spectacle was allowing professional basketball players to compete. The US and worldwide TV audiences loved *the Dream Team*. But in doing so, he opened the floodgate to professionalism in the Olympic movement. Until Barcelona, the IOC had strictly enforced amateur status for Olympic athletes. Mr. Avery Brundage, long-time President of the IOC, was a champion of amateurism, and enforced the Olympic Charter at all costs. With professional basketball on the program, the other International Sport Federations demanded relaxation of all amateur rules including rules against financial sponsorship for Olympic athletes. The IOC had to oblige, and amateurism, as we know it, disappeared from the eligibility requirements forever. Professionalism invaded the Olympic movement.

I have very mixed feelings about the direction of the Olympic Movement with its rapidly increasing commercialism. In my opinion, professionalism and sponsorship brought unwanted behavior to the Olympic competition, namely doping, cheating, disrespect for the racing rules, and a drive to win at all costs in order to please sponsors. The popular sports' athletes benefit from sponsorship opportunities, but the minor sports' athletes do not. Sponsors are not interested in having an association with non-marketable athletes or sports. Minor Olympic sports (such as canoeing) with good standing, tradition, and a long Olympic history are left behind. I really dislike seeing athletes show up at the Games with agents, lawyers, advertising reps, and a whole entourage of special and private handlers.

Looking at the ancient Olympic Games in Greece, the same pattern emerged, which led to the cancellation of the Games after some 300 years. In modern times, this process will be accelerated. The modern Games have a short 100 years of history. It is impossible to shut the floodgate on commercialism, but I think, with careful planning and understanding the needs of each sport, equilibrium can be reached. However, I have a feeling that with the corruptive influence of money, the future of the Olympic Games is bleak. I am glad that I participated while the Games were still comparatively pure.

Unfortunately, canoeing is one of the minor sports. Canoeing and kayaking are still very much amateur, despite of the relaxation of amateur rules. Canoeing is not a collegiate sport and not affiliated with the NCAA, therefore, it has very little recognition, popularity, or support in the USA The handful of clubs that exist here are struggling to survive, and the numbers of sprint races are few and far between, even though the American Canoe Association (ACA) is the oldest organized sport association in the USA and that North America is the birth place of Olympic-style canoeing. Unfortunately, competitive canoeing in the US has almost reached the level of extinction with little hope on the horizon, which makes me very sad. In contrast, in Europe and other parts of the world, there's considerable development of the sport.

After 1992, I continued my involvement in the Olympic movement mainly through my sport. I still served on some of the USOC committees as a National Governing Body representative, but my role was considerably less time-consuming.

Last picture with my mother, 1998.

In the spring of 1998, I got a call from my brother, Lajos, saying, "If you want to see your mother while she is still alive, you had better come. She is failing." I got on a plane right away. It was in the middle of March, but I arrived to very pleasant weather in Budapest. Mother and I were reunited at my home in the Motherland, where I had many wonderful memories and a childhood I would not have traded for anything. *What can I do for her?* I asked myself. I knew what mother would say, as she was very frugal and did not want me to spend any of my money on her. She refused all my suggestions, so I decided to dig up the garden for her, as I'd done many times in the past. She loved seeing her little American son preparing her garden for things to grow. It was the greatest gift I could have given her. Despite her failing health, she had already grown some seedlings for transplanting. I worked on the soil for two days, raking it and parsing it up the way she wanted. I had forgotten how nice and hopeful a new garden looks. The fresh smell of the dirt brought back many good memories—pulling carrots out of the ground, picking strawberries, and harvesting peas. Mother sat outside with me in her favorite chair, enjoying every shovel stroke I took, sometimes dozing off peacefully. When I was done, she gave me a big hug and a kiss, and I saw some tears in her eyes.

That evening, I wanted to take her out to a nice dinner, but she refused. Thinking back on it, my family had never had a formal dinner in a restaurant while I was growing up. It would have been considered by my parents as splurging or a waste of money. We barely had enough money to survive. My parents were very frugal, and my mother's cooking tasted best to us anyway.

That night, she had already prepared my favorite dinner for me—*chicken paprikas* with *spatzle*. Leaving her again was very hard for me. I was very much attached to my mother and felt sorry that I caused problems for her by my defection. I wished I could make it up to her, but I had to go back to my own family. I knew this would be the last time I saw her, so it was a sad trip back to California.

Two months later, I got another call from Lajos. "Mother passed away," he said. She was 89 years old and had lived a very hard life. She raised a family of four under very difficult circumstances, through WWII, its aftermath, and communism, never wavering from her duty as a provider. She was known and remembered as a gentle, loving soul. I flew back to my homeland for the funeral, and with teary eyes, my brothers and I returned my mother's remains to the earth. Her final request was to be buried next to my father in the same grave. She had forgiven him for leaving her after my defection.

During the past twenty years, the 1990s and the 2000s, I decided to continue to train and compete in my sport at the Master's level. The World Masters Games became organized in 1985 and canoeing, to my surprise, was a part of it held every four years. To date, I've participated in four World Master's Games, winning an abundance of medals in my age category. It's a serious competition, and I have met some of my former international competitors. Canoeing is a lifetime activity, either for sport or recreation. It is so much in my blood that there is no way I can stay away from practicing or racing.

During that time, I also was introduced to another discipline of canoeing

Decorated Masters Games Champion, Edmonton, Canada, 2006.

called outrigger. Originating with the indigenous people of the Pacific Islands, this new discipline brought me a new perspective on canoeing. Open ocean paddling is totally different from Olympic-style paddling; not only the boat itself but the whole environment. The competition is really against nature itself. I mainly paddle and race in San Francisco Bay, but frequently go to the Hawaiian Islands for vacation (my favorite place and childhood fantasy) and learn how to navigate the surf.

    I would be remiss if I did not mention an episode related to my involvement in outrigger racing. In early 1978, I got a call from the manager of a Southern California outrigger canoe club asking if my Olympic canoe team would be interested in competing under his club's name at the Molokai Channel race. This race is the granddaddy of all long-distance outrigger canoe races. It is like the Superbowl of outrigger. The first race was held in 1952 but in 26 years, it had never been won by a mainland crew.

MEMORIES OF MY OLYMPIC TENURE

Rafting on the Middle Fork of the Salmon River, 1975.

Of course, I was enthused and so were my athletes. The team flew to Oahu in September of 1978 after a summer of competing in Europe. Upon my suggestion, we took our own marathon paddles, which had "T" top handles and bent blades. At first, the traditional old-timer racing committee wanted to disqualify us with our paddles. However, with some research, the team found supporting documents in the Bishop Museum that showed similar handles on traditional paddles. The committee relented and one of the head race organizers said, "Let them use it. It won't make any difference. They are not going to win."

A couple of days later, my team *did* win, and the rest is history. The "T" top canoe paddle for outrigger became standard equipment. The heavy, old-style wooden paddle with a straight shaft and no handle can still be seen on the islands as restaurant décor or at ceremonial luau parties. I am proud that my team introduced improved equipment to this traditional sport. Some members of the team went on to repeat victories with the Offshore Canoe Club of Newport Beach, CA in 1981 and 1982.

During the 1990s, a call came from one of my Hawaiian friends, asking me to go to Tahiti with him to set up an International Federation for Outrigger. The new organization's vision was for outriggers to become an Olympic

My 1981 Molokai team with the legendary Waikiki beach boy, "Rabbit" Kekai, at center. He was our steersman during the race.

sport. Traveling to Tahiti was a dream come true. I knew this tropical paradise from the atlas that my father brought home. Dreaming about it is one thing, but seeing it is another! It was all I'd imagined and more. We established the Federation, but have not succeeded in getting outrigger into the Olympics yet. I have raced in four Outrigger World Championships and have medals to show for it.

During the 1980s, I decided to share my sports experience and knowledge, so I began to write a book about Olympic canoeing. I collected all the past results, analyzed the performances, drew conclusions, presented biomechanics of the canoe and kayak motion, and recommended workout schedules. It took me several years to complete, and my Magnificent Seven friend, Elbert Andor, offered to print it. He had established a thriving printing business (Olympian Graphics) in the Bay area. We have met many times during the years and the two families have grown close. During our gatherings, we always enjoyed reliving the Tokyo experience.

I self-published the book under the title *Canoeing: an Olympic Sport*.

My friend printed 2,000 copies and within half a year, I had sold all of them, keeping only a few to hand out to my friends. The book was also translated into Japanese, and many other countries and coaches have used it for teaching technique and designing workout schedules.

My canoeing book, self-published, 1986.

The new millennium brought new opportunities to expand my canoeing experiences. In 2003, I decided with some of my local friends to organize the US National Canoeing Championships at Lake Merritt in Oakland, California, just a few miles from my house. Lake Merritt is known for rowing activity, but there was also some canoeing on the lake in the late 60s and 70s. We formed an organizing committee and sent our proposal for the Championships to US Canoe and Kayak, the national governing body for US Olympic canoe sport. The proposal was accepted, and we went to work.

We had expenses so we had to find funding—a new area of expertise that I had never dealt with before. We managed and in the end, had a little surplus. In four days, we ran over 200 races in all age categories. The event was a success, and we received good media coverage. I was pleased to see all the volunteerism that was generated during the event. We followed proper international protocol for all the races and social activities. All the clubs and paddlers who participated expressed their desire to come back again. For me, race organization was an aspect of the sport that I had to try.

With Greg Barton at the 2003 Nationals.

Based on our 2003 success, the USOC asked us to organize the 2004 Olympic Trials with only 6 months prior notice. We accepted the challenge due to the fact that we had our team together from the year before and had some surplus money. However, the Olympic Trials were a more prestigious event, and the USOC kept a close eye on us. Due to prior IOC selection criteria, the US had qualified in only a handful of events, which made the schedule more compact and eliminated all of the age group races. The races provided some surprising results. Some of the paddlers who were heavily favored did not win, but the competition was fair, and there were no disputes over the results.

At the closing banquet, we announced the 2004 Athens Olympic Games participants for USA canoeing. When I saw the smiling faces of the selected Olympians, I knew how they felt. It brought back good memories from many years earlier. Perhaps they did not realize what was ahead of them, but it would be an experience they would never forget. Maybe even the possibility to medal and write their name into Olympic history. I gave an inspirational speech and wished them good luck.

After these two events, I decided to put more time into my profession and to enjoy my family as well as some masters racing and recreational canoeing.

Late in 2009, I received a letter of invitation from the Hungarian *Mező Ferenc Sports Foundation* to join the 50th anniversary celebration of the 1960 Olympic Games in Rome with the Hungarian Olympic team medalists from that Games. It was a complete surprise! I learned from my old partner, Farkas, that a similar reunion/celebration tour was carried out for the Hungarian Olympic team medalists from the 1956 Melbourne Olympic Games four years earlier. The *Mező Ferenc Sports Foundation* was established around 1995 for the sole purpose of taking the Hungarian Olympic team medalists back to Olympic sites for the 50th anniversary of their respective Games. The Foundation is supported by the government, the Hungarian Olympic Committee, and private sponsorship. Their budget covers all the expenses for the medalists from Budapest to the Olympic site and back with a 4-5 day cultural program at the site.

Needless to say, I accepted the invitation and flew to Budapest, where I joined my remaining 1960 Olympic team members. It was a wonderful reunion, seeing many of the faces I had not seen in fifty years. The Olympic bond was rekindled with many old stories retold with teary eyes. Rome was as fabulous as ever, and we strolled most of the Olympic sites and even visited Lago Albano, the site of rowing and canoeing. The Italian Olympic Committee had the official 50th anniversary celebration in the City Hall Square (*Campi-*

50th Anniversary Participation Diploma.

doglio) with over 25 countries participating. It was a very festive occasion. After the anniversary celebration, we had a reception at a country club with hors d'oeuvres and beverages. There was a spectacular memorabilia exhibit at the country club about the 1960 Rome Games. Our podium picture was even on the wall due to the exceptional performance of the Italian double canoe team.

The next day, we went to the Olympic Stadium and, arm in arm, sang the Hungarian National anthem, another moving experience. It was hard to leave Rome as the Olympic spirit was burning in each and every one of us, and we didn't want to let it go. The Hungarian organizers promised that in four years, they would offer a similar reunion in Tokyo.

In early 2014, I wrote to the Hungarian *Mező Ferenc Sports Foundation* requesting information on the 50th anniversary celebration of the 1964 Tokyo Games. I knew that I was not eligible for a free ride because I had placed fourth, and it might be awkward joining the Hungarian team from which I defected fifty years ago. However, they welcomed me and my wife to join them for their tour, and I arranged our transportation and for accommodations at the same hotel where the Hungarian team stayed.

When we arrived in Tokyo, the Hungarian team was already there and, although we were very tired, we joined them directly from the airport for a Tokyo Harbor tour with a dinner onboard the ship. One of the most amazing sights that evening was a display of windows in a high-rise office building along the waterfront. With a pattern of darkened and lit windows, *1964 Tokyo 50th* was spelled out in huge letters against the night sky.

Over the next two days, on October 10th and 11th, the Japanese Olympic

Committee (JOC) staged a memorable 50th Anniversary Celebration of the 1964 Tokyo Summer Olympic Games. On the first day, we visited a shrine and enjoyed a tea ceremony in a lovely, serene garden complete with a large koi pond, gazebos, and bonsai trees. The evening gala was held in the Palace Hotel ballroom. The Crown Prince of Japan, the Prime Minister, the JOC President, and the President of the 2020 Tokyo Summer Olympic Games Organizing Committee were present and addressed the athletes and delegations. A very elegant dinner followed, after which all of the participating athletes were called up to the podium by country, introduced, and applauded. Many photos were taken.

Marching with my teammates, 50 years later.

The next day, the Japanese organizers staged a mock Opening Ceremony in the old stadium. Each country's representatives marched around the oval track carrying their flag. After greetings and speeches, I got to see something I did not see fifty years ago—the old Olympic flame arriving in the stadium, receiving a big ovation from the crowd. The athletes had a second chance to reunite with their comrades after half a century. Later, all the delegations had a bus tour of other Olympic venues and a formal al fresco luncheon was served on the grounds of the Palace Hotel. In the afternoon, the former athletes were treated to a river boat tour, rickshaw ride, ninja fight, temple visit, and a dinner at the famous restaurant from *Kill Bill*. We all received a diploma from the JOC commemorating participation in the 1964 Tokyo Olympic Games 50th Anniversary Celebration.

My wife and I stayed another week in Japan after the Hungarian team left. I wanted to go back to Lake Sagami where my journey began. I was very excited as I stepped off the train onto the *Sagamiko* Station platform, and it looked just as I remembered it. Where had all those fifty years gone? We slowly walked down to the lake through the narrow streets of the town, past small shops, which also looked the same. When we reached the lake, I saw that the waterfront had changed. Along the water, there now stood a row of commercial operations—a boat rental, snack kiosks, souvenir stands, and little cafes. The old boathouse had been torn down and the finish tower was relocated. A new modern boathouse had been erected, but as we walked through its bays, we found that there were still some of the old-style Olympic kayaks and canoes up in the rafters. We were invited up to the club house to see the model of the 1964 Olympic facility on display there and look at some of the other memorabilia in cases and cabinets. There was a bronze plaque on the wall with the names of all the winners. I got very nostalgic about seeing the miniature version of the venue I remembered. I asked about the school, which had been our Olympic Village, and we were told it had been torn down and replaced by a small hotel. I wanted to get out on the water, so Jane and I rented a touring canoe and paddled out on the course. It was a beautiful, warm fall day, and the shoreline was still as wooded and mysterious as I remembered. We passed the lane buoys, the finish tower, and the pagodas, and

JAPANESE OLYMPIC COMMITTEE
1964 TOKYO OLYMPIC AND PARALYMPIC GAMES
50TH ANNIVERSARY WEEK

The Japanese Olympic Committee
certifies that

Mr. András TÖRŐ

has taken part in the memorial events
in October 2014

竹田恆和

Tsunekazu TAKEDA
President, Japanese Olympic Committee

Participation Diploma.

looked back at the docks and boathouse from a different perspective. This was a weekday, and we didn't see another visitor all morning, but looking across the water at the boathouse, I could picture the hustle and bustle and tense excitement of those racing days back in the fall of 1964.

Paddling on Lake Sagami, 50 years later.

With this 50th anniversary tour, I came full circle in my life. I wanted to see if *Sagamiko* had changed during the last fifty years but even more, I wanted to reflect on all that had happened to me over those same fifty years. It was sobering to be on the exact place on earth, Lake Sagami, where my life had taken a dramatic and irreversible turn a half-century years earlier. I wanted to remember as much as I could and write my story.

As we left, I realized that progress had changed many things, and some things would only exist in my memory now. We walked back to the railroad station, but this time my departure from *Sagamiko* was not life-changing.

Now that the 2020 Summer Olympic Games has been awarded to Tokyo, I feel like my *full circle* could be extended. I am anxiously waiting and counting the days until I can make this journey again. Although I will be eighty-years-*young*, I want to experience the Olympic magic again, perhaps for the last time, where it all began, that very special place—Tokyo. I promised my wife and myself that we will go back, even if I have to spend my four "lucky" one-dollar bills that I got on the plane coming to the US in October 1964.

Just recently, the World Olympian Association (WOA) in connection with the International Olympic Committee (IOC), established a project to recognize the achievement of past Olympians and grant the use of the post-nominal letters *OLY* to signifying their ongoing roles in society as Olympians living and promoting the Olympic values. I felt greatly honored for this recognition, especially because it took such a long time for the IOC to establish.

With 1964 memorabilia during the Hungarian Embassy reception, 2014.

Only a few of us, out of millions of people, can distinguish ourselves by using the *OLY* designation post-nominally. It is a symbol of accomplishment that one should be proud of. I have always felt that we Olympians are special and should be distinguished in some way for our sacrifice, discipline, and commitment.

As I sit back, having come to the end of my chronicle, I realize how fortunate my journey was through times and tribulations, overcoming many challenges on the way to freedom and beyond. A lucky sequence of events, particularly in the early stages after my arrival in the US, shaped my future. I learned how to trust people, and in turn, they trusted me. There are so many people to thank for their kindness and understanding of my situation. I'm proof that American people see the goodness in you and are willing to help. My English teacher at the U of M advised me, "Andy, don't ever lose your accent. People will remember you." My accent has stayed, whether I wanted it or not, and people do tend to remember me.

I often wonder how different my life would have been if I had not made the

1964 Olympic Team and had stayed in Hungary. I think the outcome would have been unbelievably different and perhaps unhappy. Would I have earned my Physical Education diploma and worked as a coach, or followed my father's footsteps and remained a factory worker? Would I have had a chance to visit those little islands on the map that I enjoy now yearly? I will never know. Regardless, I would always have been known as an Olympic medalist. I wrote (paddled) my name into the history books. I earned that respect.

The unknown was calling, the opportunities came, and I took a chance on change. My destiny began to find shape in the pages of *The Last of the Mohicans* and the centerfold of that *World Atlas* my father brought home. I found I thrived on the physical challenge of canoeing—this demanding, technical sport that is so close to nature and my heart. I have been able to steer my way through life on turbulent waters but never lost focus on *keeping the Olympic dream alive.*

AFTERWORD

This chronicle would not be complete without telling the reader more about my always-supportive family. They stood beside me, enduring my fascination with and commitment to the Olympic movement, and for that I will always be grateful.

My wife, Jane, retired in 2014 after 18 years of service as a kindergarten teacher in a multicultural and multilingual district. Jane gave 110% to her teaching duties, working with her students on many extra projects, such as raising chicks and butterflies in the classroom and putting on plays and holiday programs. There were lots of fieldtrips to museums, plays, and aquariums.

Before her public school career, she taught quiltmaking and had her own bakery to supplement the family's income. Babcock Bakery was a successful business, turning out hundreds of loaves of bread each week. It was strictly a family affair with our children helping to label, bag, and clean up. I laughingly called myself the *Vice President of Weights and Measures*. My job was to cut off just the right amount of dough for Jane to shape into loaves.

In retirement, Jane hopes to spend more time on quilt making. Many yards of colorful fabric have been cut up and stored in our small house. Personally, I cannot understand why you would cut up large pieces of fabric and then sew them together again. However, I must admit that when finished, the quilts look artistic and beautiful!

Jane at her sewing machine—quilting.

Jane has maintained friendships with her Cal crew teammates and still rows regularly, as well as paddles outrigger with me. She has recently been introduced to backpacking and plans trips to the high country of Yosemite as often as possible, where photographing the natural beauty is a passion. When she's home, she is working on the next quilt, editing her photographs, reading, hiking, or gardening. Jane has been a vegan since 2011 and has fun with new vegetable recipes. One of our great joys is to spend time on the Big Island and paddle in the gorgeous blue waters there. Every time we launch our boat, I know one of my life's dreams has come true.

We raised two wonderful kids in our small El Cerrito home. Our first child, Katalin Ellen (1978), was a swimmer and soccer goalie in high school, and went to the Academy of Art College in San Francisco. She majored in fashion design with an emphasis on knitted wear. At her graduation fashion show in 2003, she was awarded an internship with Natori and was off to the New York City fashion district a couple of weeks later. In 2004, she married Benjamin Jullien. They now live in the D.C. area with our grandchildren, Oliver Andras (2009) and Emily Jane (2011). Katie is currently a preschool teacher, costume creator for afterschool drama programs, and *Mommy Extraordinaire*.

Katie's graduation, 2003.

AFTERWORD

Tamás (7th seat) rowing with the Yale lightweight crew, 2002.

My son, Tamás Babcock (1982) was a soccer player and rower, graduated at the top of his high school class, and went to Yale in 2000 to study and row on the lightweight crew team. Highlights were a national championship in 2002, where they won the title and a trip to Henley, the famous annual Regatta in England. In 2004, he became the Yale Lightweight Crew Captain. After

Tamás graduating from Yale in 2004.

Yale, he went to the NYU Tisch School of the Arts in film for two years. In 2013, Tom married Marissa Wolf, and they are currently living in Portland, Oregon, where he enjoys cartooning as a contributor to the *New Yorker* and other prestigious publications since 2010, writing, and being *Daddy Extraordinaire*. In 2017, his first cartoon book, *Tiny Hands*, was published. It's available on his website. They have one son, Elijah Wallace Wolf, who was born in 2015.

Working in the engine room of a ship, 1973-2015.

My work through the years as an independent naval architect and marine consultant was challenging. I had many great professionally stimulating projects that required educated technical knowledge and time management to satisfy the customers. In the beginning, working with Miki Kossa, who was an accomplished naval architect, made my transition easier from a student to being a ship designer/architect. We never kept regular working hours. Our philosophy was to get the work done on time whatever it took and to give a bit more to the customers as professional courtesy.

AFTERWORD

Working in the office, 1973-2000.

We had an office in North Berkeley, very close to my home and walking distance from Miki's house. In this office, we did all the design work. For the first twenty years, it was all hand drafting and calculations, then computers changed the whole industry, almost overnight. We converted to electronic design and calculations. It was a sudden change that required adjustments on our part to stay with the industry. Besides the routine design work in the office, we often traveled to see the ships we worked on in other parts of the States and the world. This field work was very interesting and professionally challenging. We would take many measurements, sketches, and photos back to the office to develop the conceived design. Often it required several visits to finalize the design. This field work many times covered all parts and systems of the ship, depending on the repair or design project. We knew some of the local ships like the back of our hands from the keel to the top of the smokestack.

After Miki's unfortunate stroke, I continued the practice and moved operations to a home office. Since everything was done on the computer, this was easy and did not take up much space in our small house. It would have been much harder in the 1970s and 80s with the children growing up. Being an independent has many good and bad sides. The good side is the freedom that I always enjoyed. No boss to listen to and no day-to-day routine and commute. The bad part is you never know when the next project (dollar) will show up. I learned that income management is the key to being an independent consultant.

After forty years of work, I finally decided to enjoy my monthly Social Security and retired. There was no fanfare, party, or gold watch. I just faded away from the profession the way I wanted it. Now that I have more free time on my hands, I do a lot of recreational canoeing and occasional coaching at the local club, and spend more time with the growing family.

Visiting our children and grandchildren are joyful events throughout the year. I feel extremely fortunate and happy to see them grow and know that my lineage will continue. The future is for them.

A NOTE FROM THE AUTHOR

Chronicles of an Olympic Defector is a memoir about my passion for the sport of canoeing and how it shaped my life in profound ways. The sport turned a boy from Soviet Bloc Hungary into a young man competing in 1960s America and has continued to influence my life every day since. My experience has been unique because I competed at the highest levels of the sport under both communist and democratic systems, and I had the opportunity to represent both countries at two Olympic Games each. My decision to defect from Hungary to the United States at the Tokyo Olympics was fraught with anxiety, heartache, and danger. It was the ultimate turning point of my life.

The early chapters of the book describe my experiences leading up to my introduction to canoeing. My family lived on the outskirts of Budapest and my parents worked hard to put food on the table for their four growing boys. World War II made things much worse, but we managed to survive, and in the aftermath, I was sent to Denmark as part of a relief program. Seeing a different culture up-close and learning a new language broadened my perspective of the world around me. However, back in Hungary, conditions became increasingly restrictive as the Iron Curtain closed in on us.

Sports were heavily promoted to the youth of Hungary, and one of my brothers joined a club, taking up canoeing with some of his friends. I followed in his footsteps a year later and found that I had a talent for the sport. I quickly realized that being a top athlete came with perks that most people in Hungary could never hope to have–access to better food and clothing, paid time off from work and military duty, national recognition, and most importantly, access to the West. When I made the national junior and senior teams, getting to travel with them to races in non-communist countries was my primary incentive. In doing so, I began to realize that the way of life I glimpsed there was what I wanted most of all. But achieving it felt impossible.

CHRONICLES OF AN OLYMPIC DEFECTOR

As long as I remained a top athlete, my life was decent. However, my independent streak rubbed the coaches the wrong way, and they had me drafted into the Army just prior to the 1964 Olympics. This was devastating and probably the lowest point in my life. My chronicle, in part, describes that time in the military and the turmoil that filled me. It was probably what I needed to straighten up and be humbler and more dedicated. I write about how hard I trained in my limited free time and how badly I wanted to make the 1964 Olympic team despite everything.

My hard work paid off, but it also took its toll. I was burned out and not at my peak by the time the Olympics came around. Although I had managed to make the team, I was exhausted and I knew that there was a good possibility that I wouldn't medal. In turn, my status as an athlete would diminish and the perks would disappear soon after. Not being a Communist party member, I would have limited opportunities and probably end up coaching at a backwater club in rural Hungary. I knew that I would not be satisfied living like an ordinary citizen.

The bulk of the book describes my decision to defect, how it was accomplished, and the people who helped me restart my life in America. I came to the States without knowing English, having no money or possessions other than the clothes on my back (my Olympic parade uniform), and without an education beyond high school. But my sponsors helped me enroll at the University of Michigan. Ann Arbor became my adopted home for the next nine years where I earned bachelor's and master's degrees in naval architecture. In my late 20s, I was still in prime competitive form. Soon, I resolved to make the US team. I trained on the Huron River and coached a small group of paddlers there. During this time, I also studied to become a citizen–a prerequisite for representing the United States in the Olympic Games. I did not reach that goal in time for the 1968 Olympics in Mexico City but I managed to gain citizenship by the time the Games were held in Munich four years later. My book includes the stories of the adventures I had in Mexico City traveling with the team and my experience of the tragedy that marred the Munich Games. I was still competitive for the 1976 Games in Montreal, and this time my new wife, Jane, came to watch and cheer me on.

A NOTE FROM THE AUTHOR

The conclusion of the book details how I have remained involved with canoeing through paddling and competing, coaching, serving on governing bodies, and competition judging. My actions became political with the boycott of the 1980 Games when the team, including the canoeing team for which I was the Olympic coach, was not allowed to compete in a misguided effort to punish the Soviet Union. This led me to a twelve-year-long tenure on the United States Olympic Committee, during which I traveled the world representing our athletes' best interests and attending several more winter and summer Olympic Games. Meanwhile, my family grew to include two children, and I was working as an independent naval architect.

Canoeing has been my calling and my passion for as long as I can remember. I hope readers will see how it defined who I am and how it shaped my journey. Writing this book was a great joy, and I have endeavored to share intimate, entertaining stories about my sport, family, travels, and Olympic experiences. I hope you enjoy my chronicles of being an Olympic defector!

András Törő OLY

APPENDIX

Chronological Summary of Personal, Professional, and Sport Achievements of András "Andy" István Toro (Törő) OLY

1940	Born, July 10, 1940, XIXth District (*Kőbánya*), Budapest, Hungary.
1953	Participated in the Hungarian National Sport talent evaluation.
1954–1964	Joined the *Honvéd* (The Army Sport Club's canoeing division) in Budapest, Margaret Island.
1954–1959	Numerous times Hungarian National Canoeing Champion in the Juvenile and Junior category in the Canadian Ten-men (C10) and the Canadian Single (C1) events.
1958	Graduated high school, *Eötvös Loránd Gépipari Technikum*, Budapest.
1959	Invited by the Hungarian National Canoeing Team Coach to join the National Canoeing Senior Team.
1960	Teamed up with Farkas Imre for the Canadian Double (C2) 1,000-meter event and won several domestic and international races.
	After winning the Canoeing Olympic qualifying events, selected by the Hungarian Olympic Committee to be a member of the Hungarian Olympic Team for Canoeing for the XVII Summer Olympic Games in Rome, Italy in the Canadian Double (C2) 1,000-meter event with Farkas Imre.

1960	Third Place (Bronze Medal) finish at the XVII Summer Olympic Games in Rome, Italy in the Canadian Double (C2) 1,000-meter event.
	Received the *Szocialista Munkaért Érdemérem* decoration from the Hungarian Government for his Olympic performance.
1960–1964	Member of the Hungarian National Canoeing Team competing both in the Canadian Single (C1) and the Canadian Double (C2) event. Winner of numerous Hungarian National Championships and International Regattas in those events.
1962	First place finish in the (C1) 10,000-meter, and third place finish in the (C1) 1,000-meter event at the ICF Unofficial World Championship, Essen, West Germany.
1963	Enrolled in *Magyar Testnevelési Főiskola*, Budapest.
	(October) Drafted by the Hungarian Army and served 8 months. Honorably discharged as a private.
1964	After winning the Canoeing Olympic qualifying events, selected by the Hungarian Olympic Committee to be a member of the Hungarian Olympic Team for canoeing for the XVIII Summer Olympic Games in Tokyo, Japan in the Canadian Single (C1) 1,000-meter event.
	Fourth Place finish at the XVIII Summer Olympic Games in Tokyo, Japan in the Canadian Single (C1) 1,000-meter event.
	After completing the competition, defected from the Hungarian Olympic Team in Tokyo, Japan to the United States Embassy in Tokyo, Japan, asking for political asylum. Asylum was granted, arrived in United States on October 24th, 1964.
	In his absence, András was charged and sentenced by the Hungarian High Court for his defection. This sentence was commuted in 1982.

APPENDIX

1964	Fingerprinted and released by the US State Department after interrogation and the Presidential election. November 10th, 1964, stayed in Washington, D.C. until December and traveled with William "Bill" Smoke to Grosse Ile, Michigan.
1965	Studied English language at University of Michigan English Language Institute and after successful completion of the language requirement accepted as freshman for University of Michigan Engineering School of Naval Architecture and Marine Engineering Department in the fall of 1965. Received the Bachelor's of Science Degree (1970) and the Master's of Science Degree (1973) from University of Michigan Engineering School.
1965–1972	Member of the Michigan Marathon Canoe Racing Association competing in the Double Marathon Canoe (MC2) class and several times Michigan State Champion.
1965–1973	Worked in the University of Michigan Hydrodynamic Laboratory as a research assistant.
1965–1976	Member of the US National Canoeing Team, several times US National and North American Champion for Canoeing in the Canadian Single (C1), Canadian Double (C2), and the Canadian Four (C4) competition.
1965-Present	Member of the American Canoe Association (ACA) National Governing Body of the sport of Canoeing in the USA Later joined the United States Canoe Kayak Team organization.
1966–1974	Student member of the Society of Naval Architects and Marine Engineers (SNAME).
1967	Received permanent residency with a green card.
1969	Received the student paper award for *Shallow-Water Performance of a Planing Boat* from the Southeast Section of SNAME.
1970	Member of the US Canoeing Team for the International Canoe

	Federation's VIII World Championships in Copenhagen, Denmark finishing 7th in the Canadian Single (C1) 10,000 meter event.
1971	Member of the US Canoeing Team for the International Canoe Federation's IX World Championships in Belgrade, Yugoslavia finishing 5th in the Canadian Double (C2) 1,000-meter event.
	Competed and won the Murray River Marathon, sponsored by the Australian Red Cross in the Marathon Double (MC2) class with Douglas Soules, Murray River, New South Wales, Australia.
1972	Obtained the Certificate of Naturalization (Citizenship) from the District Court of United States, Eastern District of Michigan, Detroit, July 11, 1972.
	Selected to be a member of the United States Olympic Team for Canoeing for the XX Summer Olympic Games in Munich, Germany competing in the Canadian Single (C1) event advancing to the semi-final.
1973–1998	Moved to Berkeley, California to practice naval architecture and marine engineering with Miklos M. Kossa, naval architect.
1974	Married to Jane Marie Babcock, September 14, 1974, in Ohio, USA, and purchased a home in El Cerrito, California
1974–1977	Appointed to coach the US National Junior Canoeing Team and took them to the International Canoe Federation's World Championships in 1975 in Castel Gondalfo, Italy, as well as Vichy, France, in 1977. The Junior Team had the best results to date.
1976	US National Wild Water Champion, Double Canoe (WWC2) class with Chuck Lyda, American River, California, USA.
	After winning the Olympic Trials, selected to be a member

APPENDIX

	of the United States Olympic Team for Canoeing for the XXI Summer Olympic Games in Montreal, Canada, competing in the Canadian Double (C2) 1,000-meter event with Chuck Lyda advancing to the semi-final.
1977	Appointed to be the founding member of the newly formed Athletes Advisory Council (ACA) of the United States Olympic Committee (USOC) representing the sport of Canoeing and the US athletes in general.
1978	Daughter, Katalin Ellen Törő, was born, October 23, 1978.
	Elected as Vice President of the Pan American Canoe Council and Chairman of the Technical Committee, in Mexico City, Mexico.
1978–1982	Appointed to be the US National and Olympic Coach for the US Canoeing Team.
1978–1984	Elected to be a member of the United States Olympic Committee's Board of Directors as an Athletes Advisory representative.
1978–1995	Participated in eight out of the fourteen US Olympic Festivals as the canoeing representative or the USOC staff.
1980	Coach for the US Canoeing Olympic Team for the XXII Summer Olympic Games in Moscow, Soviet Union. The US Olympic Team, yielding the pressure of the government, boycotted the Games and the US Olympic Team did not participate.
	Was member of the athletes' negotiating team on behalf of the US athletes with the White House Councils to reverse the boycott decision.
1980–1992	Member of several constitutional and active USOC Committees including: Membership, Games Preparation, International Relations, Equipment and Technology, delegate to the International Olympic Academy.

1981	Proposed establishment of an *Athletes Board* for the International Olympic Committee (IOC) at their executive board meeting in Los Angeles, California. The Athletes Board was established at the 1992 Barcelona Olympic Games.
1982	Son, Tamás Babcock Törő, was born, May 22, 1982.
1982—1994	Elected to the International Canoe Federation Board of Directors as the Americas Continental Representative.
1983	Proposed *Operation Gold*, the athlete-support program to the US Olympic Committee Board of Directors.
1984	Member of the USOC's official delegation to the XIV Winter Olympic Games in Sarajevo, Yugoslavia, as an advance support team member for the athletes. XXIII Summer Olympic Games, Los Angeles, USA.
1984–1988	Elected by the United States Olympic Committee Congress at their quadrennial assembly to be the Secretary of the USOC and to be on the Executive Committee. While on the USOC's Executive Committee, served as delegate to several meetings of the Association of the Summer Olympic Sports and the Pan American Sport Organization.
1984–1996	Nominated and elected by the International Canoe Federation Board of Directors to be on the jury for the Olympic Games Canoeing competition.
1985–1990	Appointed to be member of the International Fair Play (IFP) Committee's Administrative Council, Association of Summer Olympic International Federations (ASOIF), and the Pan American Sports Organizations (PASO).
1986	Self-published *Canoeing: An Olympic Sport*, printed in the United States by Olympian Graphics in San Francisco, California. The book was translated to Japanese and published in Japan in 1990.

APPENDIX

	Instrumental in organizing the Pan American Canoeing Federation under the guidance of the International Canoe Federation.
1987	Assistant Chef de Mission of the US Pan American Team held in Indianapolis, USA and introduced the sport of canoeing to the Pan American competition.
	Elected by the International Canoe federation Board of Directors to serve on the Canoeing competition Jury for the: X Pan American Games in Indianapolis, Indiana, USA.
1988	XXIV Summer Olympic Games, Seoul, South Korea.
1989	Member of the Atlanta's Olympic Bid Team for the 1996 Centennial Olympic Games and the Salt Lake City's Olympic Bid Team for the 1998 and 2002 Winter Olympic Games.
	Awarded the first Master Coaching (level 1) Certificate by the United States Canoe and Kayak Team Organization.
	Established the US-Hungarian Olympic Sports Exchange Program.
1991	XI Pan American Games in Havana, Cuba.
	Member of the US Pan American delegation for the XI Pan American Games in Havana, Cuba.
1992	XXV Summer Olympic Games, Barcelona, Spain.
1994-2005	Competed in the World Masters Games (WMG) in both kayaking and canoeing, 3rd WMG, Brisbane, Australia (6 medals), 4th WMG, Portland, Oregon, USA (9 medals), 6th WMG, Edmonton, Canada (11 medals).
1995	XII Pan American Games in Mar del Plata, Argentina.
	Instrumental in establishing the Antigua Barbuda Canoe Kayak Federation and coached their team for the XII Pan American Team, Mar del Plata, Argentina and for the XXVI Summer Olympic Games, Atlanta, USA.

1996	XXVI Summer Olympic Games, Atlanta, USA.
1996–Present	Member of the Northern California Olympians and Paralympians (NCOP) chapter of the USOC.
1999	Competed in the California International Dragon Boat Championships, won 3 first places (gold medal), October 2 & 3, 1999, Foster City, California, USA.
2000	Member of the San Francisco Bay Area Organizing Committee for bidding on the 2008 Summer Olympic Games.
2002–Present	Competed in the Outrigger Sprint World Championships (Wa'a Championships) in the Single Canoe (V1), Double Canoe (V2), and Double Hull Canoe (V12) events in Bora Bora, French Polynesia, in 2002, Hamilton, New Zealand, in 2005, and Sacramento, California, in 2007.
2003	Organized the 2003 United States National Flatwater Canoeing Championships, Lake Merritt in Oakland, California.
2004	Organized the 2004 United Sates Olympic Trials for the US Olympic Flatwater Canoeing Team for the XXVIII Summer Olympic Games.
2018	The World Olympian Association (WOA) in connection with the International Olympic Committee (IOC) granted use of the post-nominal letters *OLY* after the names of designated Olympians.
Present	Member of the Northern California Olympian and Para-Olympian Association.
	Competing in the master's category for outrigger canoeing at both domestic and international levels and actively coaching both canoe and kayak disciplines.
	Retired naval architect, designing and building watercrafts mainly Olympic-style canoes and kayaks, outrigger canoes,

surf skis, and stand-up paddle boards (SUP). Still active in many disciplines of canoeing.

Awards

Awarded for *A Lifetime of Outstanding Service* presented by the National Paddling Committee of the American Canoe Association in Indianapolis, Indiana, 1986.

Outstanding Athletic Achievement Award given by the state of California's Senate Rules Committee on April 7, 1989.

Award in recognition of *Outstanding Services* by the United States Olympic Committee on February 18, 1989.

Award in *Appreciation for Outstanding Service* as co-chair on the International and Governmental Relations Committee for the United States Olympic Committee for the 1989-1992 quadrennial, Colorado Springs, Colorado, 1992.

American Canoe Association Commodore's Award, as a token of appreciation of your unrelenting efforts on behalf of Canoe Sport, 1992.

El Cerrito Olympian offers Moscow Games compromise

Political maneuvering reawakens Toro's bitterness

'Down deep, no one wanted to boycott'

Toro remains bullish about sport

- Four-time Olympian is 63 but is still heavily involved in canoeing

Andy Toro

Paddling a labor of love for Toro

- Olympic medalist from El Cerrito the expert when it comes to kayaks, canoes

Olympics: Kayak expert has winning advice

ANDRAS TORO competed four times in the Olympics from 1960 to '76.

Olympian coaches kayakers

El Cerrito's Andy Toro gets ready for Berkeley trials

He tries to match Olympic athletes with the right equipment

"We wanted a committee that would aid the technology transfer between the companies that develop it and the athletes who would use it."
— Andras Toro

Toro makes Olympic waves

EL CERRITO — Andy Toro, former United States canoeist...

A local kayak expert advises the Olympics

ABOUT THE AUTHOR

András Törő is an Olympic medalist and retired naval architect. He was inspired by his family and many friends to share the story of his unique odyssey from communist Hungary to the free world by way of the Olympic Games. In his spare time, András continues to enjoy his sport by coaching or practicing. Woodworking and spending time with his grandchildren are his other passions in life. He currently resides in El Cerrito, California, with his wife, Jane. *Chronicles of an Olympic Defector* is András Törő's second book.